Diversity, Equity, and Inclusion Efforts of Businesses in Rural Areas

Shashi Bala
V.V. Giri National Labour Institute, India

Puja Singhal
National Centre for School Leadership (NIEPA), India

A volume in the Advances in Human Resources Management and Organizational Development (AHRMOD) Book Series

IGI Global
PUBLISHER of TIMELY KNOWLEDGE

Published in the United States of America by
IGI Global
Business Science Reference (an imprint of IGI Global)
701 E. Chocolate Avenue
Hershey PA, USA 17033
Tel: 717-533-8845
Fax: 717-533-8661
E-mail: cust@igi-global.com
Web site: http://www.igi-global.com

Library of Congress Cataloging-in-Publication Data

Names: Shashi Bala, editor. | Singhal, Puja, DATE- editor.
Title: Diversity, equity, and inclusion efforts of businesses in rural areas / edited Shashi Bala, and Puja Singhal.
Description: Hershey, PA : Business Science Reference, [2023] | Includes bibliographical references and index. | Summary: "Diversity, Equity, and Inclusion Efforts of Businesses in Rural Areas evaluates growth trajectories and educational opportunities in rural areas. It further explores the inclusion efforts of marginalized groups in rural society. Covering topics such as the construction industry, rural populations, and workplace inclusivity, this premier reference source is a valuable resource for policymakers, investors, professionals, business leaders and managers, economists, sociologists, students and educators of higher education, librarians, researchers, and academicians"-- Provided by publisher.
Identifiers: LCCN 2022058415 (print) | LCCN 2022058416 (ebook) | ISBN 9781668468784 (hardcover) | ISBN 9781668468791 (paperback) | ISBN 9781668468807 (ebook)
Subjects: LCSH: Economic development--Social aspects. | Diversity in the workplace. | Cultural pluralism. | Rural development.
Classification: LCC HD75 .D58 2023 (print) | LCC HD75 (ebook) | DDC 338.9--dc23/eng/20230123
LC record available at https://lccn.loc.gov/2022058415
LC ebook record available at https://lccn.loc.gov/2022058416

This book is published in the IGI Global book series Advances in Human Resources Management and Organizational Development (AHRMOD) (ISSN: 2327-3372; eISSN: 2327-3380)

British Cataloguing in Publication Data
A Cataloguing in Publication record for this book is available from the British Library.

Advances in Human Resources Management and Organizational Development (AHRMOD) Book Series

Patricia Ordóñez de Pablos
Universidad de Oviedo, Spain

ISSN:2327-3372
EISSN:2327-3380

MISSION

A solid foundation is essential to the development and success of any organization and can be accomplished through the effective and careful management of an organization's human capital. Research in human resources management and organizational development is necessary in providing business leaders with the tools and methodologies which will assist in the development and maintenance of their organizational structure.

The **Advances in Human Resources Management and Organizational Development (AHRMOD) Book Series** aims to publish the latest research on all aspects of human resources as well as the latest methodologies, tools, and theories regarding organizational development and sustainability. The **AHRMOD Book Series** intends to provide business professionals, managers, researchers, and students with the necessary resources to effectively develop and implement organizational strategies.

COVERAGE

- Disputes Resolution
- Change Management
- Personnel Retention
- Skills Management
- Human Resources Development
- Employee Benefits
- Executive Education
- Employee Relations
- Executive Compensation
- Process Improvement

IGI Global is currently accepting manuscripts for publication within this series. To submit a proposal for a volume in this series, please contact our Acquisition Editors at Acquisitions@igi-global.com or visit: http://www.igi-global.com/publish/.

The Advances in Human Resources Management and Organizational Development (AHRMOD) Book Series (ISSN 2327-3372) is published by IGI Global, 701 E. Chocolate Avenue, Hershey, PA 17033-1240, USA, www.igi-global.com. This series is composed of titles available for purchase individually; each title is edited to be contextually exclusive from any other title within the series. For pricing and ordering information please visit http://www.igi-global.com/book-series/advances-human-resources-management-organizational/73670. Postmaster: Send all address changes to above address.

Titles in this Series

For a list of additional titles in this series, please visit: http://www.igi-global.com/book-series/

Developing Diversity, Equity, and Inclusion Policies for Promoting Employee Sustainability and Well-Being
Sónia P. Gonçalves (ISCSP, Universidade de Lisboa, Portugal) Paula Cristina Nunes Figueiredo (Universidade Lusófona, Portugal) Eduardo Luis Soares Tomé (ULHT, Universidade Lusófona, Portugal) and José Baptista (ISCSP, Universidade de Lisboa, Portugal)
Business Science Reference • © 2023 • 333pp • H/C (ISBN: 9781668441817) • US $240.00

Valuing People and Technology in the Workplace Ethical Implications and Imperatives for Success
Claretha Hughes (University of Arkansas, USA)
Business Science Reference • © 2023 • 367pp • H/C (ISBN: 9781668453216) • US $205.00

Talent Acquisition and Retention Strategies in Global Startups
Neetima Agarwal (Symbiosis International University, India) Leo Paul Dana (Kingston University, UK) and Sujata Khandai (Amity University, India)
Business Science Reference • © 2023 • 305pp • H/C (ISBN: 9781668475140) • US $250.00

Female Entrepreneurship as a Driving Force of Economic Growth and Social Change
Ana Dias Daniel (Universidade de Aveiro, Portugal) and Cristina Fernandes (Universidade da Beira Interior, Portugal)
Business Science Reference • © 2023 • 320pp • H/C (ISBN: 9781668476697) • US $250.00

Strategic Human Resource Management in the Hospitality Industry A Digitalized Economic Paradigm
Kannapat Kankaew (Suan Sunandha Rajabhat University, Thailand)
Business Science Reference • © 2023 • 309pp • H/C (ISBN: 9781668474945) • US $250.00

Corporate Sustainability as a Tool for Improving Economic, Social, and Environmental Performance
Bartolomé Marco-Lajara (University of Alicante, Spain) Javier Martínez-Falcó (University of Alicante, Spain & Stellenbosch University, South Africa) and Luis A. Millán-Tudela (University of Alicante, Spain)
Business Science Reference • © 2023 • 337pp • H/C (ISBN: 9781668474228) • US $250.00

IGI Global
PUBLISHER of TIMELY KNOWLEDGE

701 East Chocolate Avenue, Hershey, PA 17033, USA
Tel: 717-533-8845 x100 • Fax: 717-533-8661
E-Mail: cust@igi-global.com • www.igi-global.com

Editorial Advisory Board

List of Reviewers

Table of Contents

Detailed Table of Contents

and practices. In recent times, technology and its application have played an impactful role in entrepreneurship and there exists a strong relationship between the two. "Industry 5.0" refers to those who interact with robots and intelligent machines. It includes integrating cutting-edge technology, such as the internet of things (IoT) and big data, to allow robots to help people work more swiftly and efficiently. It adds a more personal touch to the efficiency and automation cornerstones of Industry 4.0.

The chapter looks into the unequal development parity which is excluding the equal participation of women in the labour market. Technical, vocational, education, and training are considered means to encourage women's participation. However, India continues to witness a declining labor force participation rate. In this context, this chapter throws light on the role TVET in empowering females. There is a wide gender gap in education and labour market. There are overwhelming distinctions in education between the sexes in some developing countries. In the economics of education literature, an important explanation of gender inequality in education is that the labour market rewards women's education less well than men's, especially in developing countries. Unequal access to education and training perpetuates gender inequalities in the labour market, restricting the choices and bargaining power of women in particular.

Gujarat is one of the most industrially advanced states in India and consequently accounts for a large pie of CSR investments. Rs.676 crores have been spent in the year 2020-21 and these projects have made a significant contribution to the development of rural communities. In the current study, Devadthal village is selected because several CSR projects are being implemented in the village; in addition, this village was selected for the 'Integrated Tribal Village Development Programme' by different corporates operating in the region. The study attempts to explore different CSR projects undertaken by corporates in Devadthal village and what is the socioeconomic impact of CSR projects on these rural communities. Primary data is collected through interviews and focus group discussions with different stakeholders like CSR officials, NGO implementing partners, Panchayat members, and the community. This study clearly indicates positive outcomes that

This chapter portrays the constraints faced by the farmers in Uttar Pradesh in terms of infrastructure, production, marketing, irrigation, and finance. Apart from this, a few natural constraints are also responsible for low productivity in agriculture. Hence, the present study was undertaken in the selected eastern districts of Uttar Pradesh to identify the institutional, social, and economic constraints hampering the growth of agriculture in the selected districts. It analyses the farmers' perception regarding constraints which is responsible for low agricultural productivity.

The construction industry has always been a major pillar in the overall development of any economy. The boons of this industry are not only restricted to the structural development of the nation, but it is a major role player in the economic development of any nation. The hidden benefits this industry has provided cannot be ignored. Generating maximum employment, which is not only for the educated section but also for the uneducated section of society, regardless of the skilled or unskilled people, is worth discussing. This industry is a perfect example of the amalgamation of diversity as well as equity within the workplace. This chapter tries to focus on the variables that play a major role when the issues and benefits of diversity and equity are discussed in the context of the construction industry. The data from 450 workers were collected and a questionnaire was prepared to know the exact situation of diversity and equity in the construction industry at prevailing times.

Climate change is universally a shift in the existing flora and fauna and those natural systems that make the atmosphere congenial for the existence of humans and biodiversity. In this context a lot of research work is going on sustainable development for example: SDG Goals 2030 are a step forward in this direction, IPCC reports, conferences, and workshops. If we look at a scenario of the world from the past up till today, it has various divisions on account of settlements such as rural, suburban, and urban. All these divisions are crucial as they are interdependent on each other. According to these divisions, the availability of resources to the population in these areas differ at all levels as per their economic stability. But the climate has the power to change and impact this economic stability, the cycle of availability of resources, production, manufacturing, preservation, and consumption of goods and services in the short as well as long term.

Foreword

For strengthening any nation, diversity, equity, and inclusion plays a significant role. This will take into consideration the needs of people from different walks of life. Countries that promote diversity, equity, and inclusiveness are better able to adjust to the challenges and also meet the needs of their people. This also promotes the employees, and this has been happening in various companies via incorporating HR practices. Incorporation of diversity, equity, and inclusion (DEI) principles in HR practices are happening only in the organization of urban areas. Yet, a majority of the population resides in rural areas, worldwide. Various policy initiatives have been taken to include and promote awareness in rural areas like self-help Groups, entrepreneurship, startup initiatives banking facilities, etc.. Internet connection plays a significant role in mainstreaming these initiatives. As we know diversity means the representation of your total workforce which includes rural as well as urban population thus HR policies such as gender diversity, age diversity, ethnic diversity, physical ability, and neurodiversity should be equally incorporated in both urban and rural organizations.

Equity will promote a level playing field that can be witnessed in the policies and is yet to be witnessed in the norms and practices to get desired outcomes. This will also promote the search for talent by the employer and job opportunities among the future workforce. All the countries have different ministries for rural and skill development which will promote human resource development and address the issues pertaining to development of start-up ideas in rural areas. The present book is written with the objective to promote diversity, equity, and inclusion, which will ultimately promote growth and sustainable development in rural areas.

V. N. Srivastava
OD Skill Development Academy Pvt. Ltd., Gurgaon, India

Preface

Equity acts as the catalyst to achieve diversity and inclusion for reducing injustice and promoting fair distribution of the benefits of an equitable environment to all stakeholders. In this direction, corporate culture has already started efforts for sustainable development through Corporate Social Responsibility (CSR) initiatives in rural areas. This is an initiative to explore the inclusion efforts of the marginalised section of society. Within this context, this book is an attempt to look into equity efforts in rural areas. The infrastructure needs to be strengthened wherein web accessibility of technology will play a pivotal role which will help the rural communities to be part of the changing world of work. This book attempts to provide valuable insights and support for policymakers, investors, professionals, and researchers working in the field of rural communities' economy research and management. In this context, the objective of the book is to provide relevant theoretical frameworks and the latest empirical research findings in the area of rural communities in the global economy and their impact on the sustainable development of competitive markets. The present book is divided into three sections as mentioned below-

SECTION 1: BUSINESS IN RURAL DEVELOPMENT THROUGH ENTREPRENEURSHIP AND TECHNOLOGY

1. Assessment of Start-Up Ecosystem for Tribal Women Entrepreneurs in India

India has made a notable transition toward laws that support new businesses and an atmosphere that is conducive to entrepreneurship known as a start-up ecosystem. The start-up ecosystem in India has seen significant growth in recent years, with increased government support and investment from venture capital firms. Despite facing various challenges such as lack of access to funding and networks, cultural biases, and work-life balance difficulties, women entrepreneurs have made significant contributions to the global economy. Women from Indigenous communities who are working to build successful businesses are referred to as tribal women entrepreneurs. Indian tribal women have historically been underrepresented and marginalised in many facets of society. Tribal women have, however, begun assuming more entrepreneurial roles recently and utilizing their traditional expertise to develop new businesses. In this chapter, the role of the start-up ecosystem for tribal women in India, opportunities, challenges, and perspective have been discussed.

2. Essential Factors for Entrepreneurship Development Among Engineering Undergraduates

Employment generation is the first priority of any nation in the world, which facilitates healthy nations' growth and development. Nations like India have been fighting unemployment issues for more than a decade, but recently it has become worsened. Entrepreneurship is the only solution to this great issue. The present study attempts to investigate the social and environmental factors affecting engineering undergraduates' entrepreneurial behavior. 1000 responses were recorded for analysis and found that social and environmental factors play prominent roles in creating entrepreneurial temperament among engineering undergraduates.

3. Current State and Prospects of Business Development in the Republic of Belarus

The article is devoted to the problems and priorities of the development of agricultural business in the Republic of Belarus. An analysis of the state of the country's agricultural industry and its economic significance is given in detail. This chapter also considers the demographic situation in rural areas: the main problems and prospects. The article was written in order to tell the reader about the Belarusian experience of supporting agricultural businesses and its role in the Belarusian economy. The article uses the materials of the legislation and official statistics of the Republic of Belarus. The author tried not to express his personal opinion, but to describe the actual processes.

4. Technopreneurship and Industry 5.0: Promoting Equity and Diversity in Rural Areas

A recent digital paradigm shift in all sectors has resulted in amalgamating with it. It is witnessed that the business environment is shifting towards self-employment. Worldwide efforts are made to promote entrepreneurship which is also driven by intensive technological advancements. Entrepreneurship, in general, can be defined as the creation of value apparently by deviating from pre-existing business patterns and practices. In recent times, technology and its application have played an impactful role in entrepreneurship and there exists a strong relationship between the two. "Industry 5.0" refers to those who interact with robots and intelligent machines. It includes integrating cutting-edge technology, such as the Internet of Things (IoT) and big data, to allow robots to help people work more swiftly and efficiently. It adds a more personal touch to the efficiency and automation cornerstones of Industry 4.0.

SECTION 2: EFFORTS IN PROMOTING DIVERSITY IN THE RURAL AREAS

5. Role of TVET in Reducing Gender Inequality: A Review of Literature

The chapter looks into the unequal development parity which is excluding the equal participation of women in the labour market. Technical, Vocational, Education, and Training are considered means to encourage women's participation. However, India continues to witness a declining labor force participation rate. In this context, this chapter throws light on the role TVET in empowering females. There is a wide gender gaps in education and labour market. There are overwhelming distinctions in education between the sexes in some developing countries. In the economics of education literature, an important explanation of gender inequality in education is that the labour market rewards women's education less well than men's, especially in developing countries (Kingdon, 1998). Unequal access to education and training perpetuates gender inequalities in the labour market, restricting the choices and bargaining power of women in particular.

6. Corporate Social Responsibility and Rural Development in Gujarat: A Case Study of Devadthal (Navapura) Village, Ahmedabad

Gujarat is one of the most industrially advanced states in India and consequently accounts for a large pie of CSR investments too. Rs.676 crores have been spent in the year 2020-21 and these projects have made a significant contribution to the development of rural communities. In the current study, Devadthal village is selected because several CSR projects are being implemented in the village, in addition, this village was selected for the 'Integrated Tribal Village Development Programme' by different corporates operating in the region. The study attempts to explore different CSR projects undertaken by corporates in Devadthal village and what is the socioeconomic impact of CSR projects on these rural communities.

Primary data is collected through interviews and focus group discussions with different stakeholders like CSR officials, NGO implementing partners, Panchayat members, and the community. This study clearly indicates positive outcomes that resulted due to CSR intervention in Devadthal Village by the NGOs, Government, and Community for the development of the village.

7. Feminization of Migration

The migration of women has emerged as an important field of research within the larger domain of migration studies and is being explored under various disciplines. Despite the growing proportion of women in the global migration pattern, the contribution of women to the migrant labour force has been largely overlooked. The paper highlights the fact that the feminization of migration has undoubtedly increased the visibility of women in the migration but much more needs to be done in terms of evolving policies for ensuring their protection and security and above all empowering them and increasing their participation in the labour market. The findings of the study also suggest that though females accompany their spouses, their economic role need not be undermined. The work participation rate of female migrants as compared to female non-migrants increases in rural-urban migration over a period of time as is evident from the data, In a nutshell, the significance of economic factors in determining female migration should be given greater importance in migration studies.

8. The Impacts of Lavender Gardens on Rural Tourism

In this study, the impacts of lavender gardens in terms of rural tourism were examined. For this purpose, data were collected by interview form in Gözler Neighborhood of Pamukkale district of Denizli province. When the data were analyzed, the economic, environmental and socio-cultural effects of lavender gardens were determined. It has been determined that lavender gardens support rural development by increasing number of products, entrepreneurship, job opportunities, investment, and quality of life. Social relations have increased in the region, leisure and tourism awareness has been created, and loyalty, participation, and solidarity have increased. The importance of natural resources has been understood, ecological awareness has been created, environmental protection and environmental awareness have increased, the importance of lavender in agricultural areas has increased and the importance of a sustainable environment has emerged.

SECTION 3: ENCOURAGING INCLUSIVITY THROUGH A LEVEL PLAYING FIELD IN RURAL BUSINESSES

9. Agriculture and Farmer Plight in the Backward Region of Uttar Pradesh After 75 Years of Independence

This chapter portrays the constraints faced by the farmers in Uttar Pradesh in terms of infrastructure, production, marketing, irrigation, and finance. Apart from this, a few natural constraints are also responsible for low productivity in agriculture. Hence, the present study was undertaken in the selected eastern districts of Uttar Pradesh to identify the institutional, social, and economic constraints hampering the growth of agriculture in the selected districts. It analyses the farmers' perception regarding constraints which is responsible for low agricultural productivity.

10. Construction Industry: A Case of Rural Inclusiveness at the Workplace in the Indian Perspective

The construction industry has always been a major pillar in the overall development of any economy. The boons of this industry are not only restricted to the structural development of the nation but it is a major role player in the economic development of any nation. The hidden benefits this industry has provided cannot be ignored. Generating maximum employment which is not only for the educated section but also for the uneducated section of society, regardless of the skilled or unskilled people is worth discussing. This industry is a perfect example of the amalgamation of diversity as well as equity within the workplace. This chapter tries to focus on the variables that play a major role when the issues and benefits of diversity and equity are discussed in the context of the construction industry. The data from 450 workers were collected and a questionnaire was prepared to know the exact situation of diversity and equity in the construction industry at prevailing times.

11. Climate Change: Its Impact on Equity, Diversity, and Livelihood of the Rural Population

Climate change is universally a shift in the existing flora and fauna and those natural systems that make the atmosphere congenial for the existence of humans and biodiversity. In this context a lot of research work is going on sustainable development for example: - SDG Goals 2030 are a step forward in this direction, IPCC reports, conferences, and workshops. If we see a scenario of the world from the past up till today, it has various divisions on account of settlements such as Rural, Sub-urban, and urban. All these divisions are crucial as they are interdependent on each other.

According to these divisions' the availability of resources to the population in these areas differ at all levels as per their economic stability. But the climate has the power to change and impact this economic stability, the cycle of availability of resources, production, manufacturing, preservation, and consumption of goods and services in the short as well as long term.

Considering the post-Covid transition phase wherein the majority of us were confined to our homes as an extended workplace. This phase witnessed the significance of diversity, equity, and inclusion in mainstreaming the world of work. This book is therefore timely and highly relevant and will make a significant contribution to a better understanding of diversity, equity, and inclusion in rural businesses. It is hoped that the present book would be useful to the researchers, the policymakers, and other academicians who can contribute towards mainstreaming the challenges pertaining to inclusivity in the world of work for sustainable inclusive development.

In summing up, we would like to heartily express our gratitude to the authors, EAB members, reviewers, and almighty for guiding and supporting us in this journey towards mainstreaming these significant issues.

DISCLAIMER

The views expressed by the authors in this book are personal and not necessarily those of the organisations they represent.

Shashi Bala
V. V. Giri National Labour Institute, India

Puja Singhal
National Centre for School Leadership (NIEPA), India

Acknowledgment

We would like to acknowledge the help of all the people involved in this project and more specifically, the authors and reviewers who took part in the review process. Without their contribution, this book would not have become a reality.

First, we would like to thank each one of the authors for their contributions. Our sincere gratitude goes to the chapter's authors who contributed their time and expertise to this book.

We as editors wish to acknowledge the valuable contributions of all the Editorial Advisory board members namely Paula E. Faulkner, Ph.D. (Penn State), Professor of Agricultural Education, European Scientific Journal Editorial Board, North Carolina Fulbright Association Board, Ralph K. Morris Foundation Board, Dr. K. Tara Shankar, Professor & Dean At Faculty of Commerce & Management SGT University, Haryana, Rashmi Mani, Assistant Professor, Human Resource Management, Organisational Behaviour and Industrial Relations, Jaipuria Institute of Management, Ghaziabad, Dr. Rashmi Chauhan, Associate Professor in B.S Anangpuria Institute of Technology & Management, Dr. Shikha Bhardwaj, Assistant Professor – OB & HR, Indian Institute of Management Sambalpur, Rajiv Kumar Hasija, Freelance Corporate & Behavioral Skills Trainer, Dr. Sachin Goyal, Central Research Institute, Noida regarding the improvement of quality, coherence, and content presentation of chapters. We are very grateful to Prof. V.N.Srivastava, Director, OD Skill Development Academy Pvt. Ltd., (ODSDAPL), Gurugram for his kind gesture to foreword this book. Most of the authors also served as referees; we highly appreciate their immeasurable tasks.

We also wish to acknowledge the valuable help we received from our Seniors, Colleagues, and friends who came forward to extend their support. We wish to place on record our deep appreciation and thanks to (Ms) Jan Travers, Director of Intellectual Property and Contracts, Book Development Editors, IGI Global for their support, cooperation, and attention to detail and the entire team of IGI for bringing out the publication of this book in time

Finally, we wish to thank our family members for their unconditional support in shaping this valuable output, especially in the post-transition phase of COVID-19 which was highly enabling for both of us.

Chapter 1
Assessment of Start-Up Ecosystems for Tribal Women Entrepreneurs in India

Sonam Prabhakar
Central University of Jharkhand, India

Ashok Nimesh
Central University of Jharkhand, India

Pawan Prabhakar
Indian Institute of Technology, Kharagpur, India

ABSTRACT

India has made a notable transition toward laws that support new businesses and an atmosphere that is conducive to entrepreneurship known as a start-up ecosystem. The start-up ecosystem in India has seen significant growth in recent years, with increased government support and investment from venture capital firms. Despite facing various challenges such as lack of access to funding and networks, cultural biases, and work-life balance difficulties, women entrepreneurs have made significant contributions to the global economy. Women from indigenous communities who are working to build successful businesses are referred to as tribal women entrepreneurs. Indian tribal women have historically been underrepresented and marginalised in many facets of society. Tribal women have, however, begun assuming more entrepreneurial roles recently and utilizing their traditional expertise to develop new businesses. In this chapter, the role of the start-up ecosystem for tribal women in India, opportunities, challenges, and future perspective has been discussed.

DOI: 10.4018/978-1-6684-6878-4.ch001

1. INTRODUCTION

In business parlance, a "startup" refers to a company that has recently launched and is still in its infancy. Startup refers to a business that is just getting started. Startups are created by one or more business owners who want to create a good or service they feel there is a market for their customers (Spender et al., 2017). These businesses typically have high startup costs and little income, which is why they seek funding from a variety of sources, including venture capitalists (Krishna et al., 2016; David et al., 2021). Therefore, companies or ventures that are focused on a single product or service that the founders want to bring to the market that can be either public or private. In most cases, these businesses do not have a fully formed business model, and more importantly, they do not have sufficient financial resources to advance to the next phase of business (Bocken and Snihur, 2020; Kamariotou and Kitsios, 2022). The majority of these businesses get their start with funding from their founders. Rapid expansion and scalability are hallmarks of startups, which frequently seek out outside investment, grants, and other forms of capital to get off the ground and expand. Startups can be risky businesses because they frequently aim to create new markets or disrupt existing ones (Todeschini et al., 2017; Bortolini et al., 2018). Seed capital allows startups to make investments in research and develop business plans, both of which are necessary steps in the startup process. In contrast to market research, which assists in determining the demand for a product or service, a comprehensive business plan details not only the mission statement, vision, and goals of the organisation, but also its management and marketing strategies (Jin et al., 2017; Prohorovs et al., 2019).

1.1. Startup Ecosystem: Framework and Role in Economic Development

A startup ecosystem is a collective of interconnected elements that are essential for the growth and development of a startup. It is made up of investors, entrepreneurs, mentors, employees, and customers, all of which interact and support each other. The startup ecosystem is an important part of the overall economy, as it is a place where new ideas and businesses can be nurtured and developed (Jain et al., 2016; Salamzadeh et al., 2017; Escalfoni et al., 2020). Startups are typically more laid back, creating a more social work environment with flexible hours, more employee interaction, and flexibility.

Additionally, startups frequently offer better workplace perks like child care centres, free meals, and compressed workweeks. This helps to create jobs and drive innovation, both of which are essential for economic growth. The startup ecosystem also helps to foster collaboration and cross-pollination of ideas, which are vital for any new venture (Berger and Kuckertz, 2016). It is a key tool for encouraging innovation and creating a culture of entrepreneurship. Startup ecosystems are networks of organizations, people, and activities that are focused on creating new businesses and products. They are made up of entrepreneurs, investors, mentors, government agencies, universities, incubators, accelerators, and other support organizations (Korreck, 2019). These ecosystems can be found in cities, states, countries, and regions, and each one is unique depending on the region's economy, culture, and resources. The significance of startup ecosystems is that they provide entrepreneurs with the resources, infrastructure, and support they need to launch and grow successful businesses. They not only provide funding, but also connect entrepreneurs with mentors and advisors, provide access to networks, and give them access to talent and markets. They foster collaboration and innovation, and help create an environment where new businesses can thrive (O'Connor et al., 2018; Kalaiselvi, 2021). With the help of startup ecosystems, entrepreneurs can create new jobs, scale their businesses, and generate new ideas. Some of the key features of startup ecosystems are:

1. **Access to Funding:** Start-ups need capital to develop their product, hire a team, and bring their idea to life. Raising funds through angel investors, venture capital, government grants, and crowd funding platforms can help make that happen.
2. **Networking Opportunities:** Start-ups need to make connections and build relationships with potential customers, industry experts, investors, and other entrepreneurs. Start-up ecosystems provide a platform for networking and collaboration.
3. **Mentorship:** Start-ups need experienced entrepreneurs, mentors, and advisors to help them navigate the complexities of the business world. Start-up ecosystems offer mentorship and guidance through workshops, boot camps, and seminars.
4. **Collaboration:** Start-ups need to collaborate with other entrepreneurs, investors, and industry veterans to make the best use of their resources and leverage their skills. Start-up ecosystems offer a platform for collaboration and knowledge sharing.

5. **Talent Acquisition:** Start-ups need to recruit talented individuals to help them bring their idea to life. Start-up ecosystems provide access to a wide range of professionals and experts who can help startups with their hiring needs, and
6. **Market Access:** Start-ups need access to the right markets. Therefore, startup ecosystem supports women to develop a network of mentors and advisors to create a network of experienced mentors and advisors who can provide guidance and advice to women entrepreneurs in their communities. These mentors and advisors can help women entrepreneurs in identifying and take advantage of opportunities, provide resources, and offer advice on how to navigate the startup ecosystem. They also help in running funding programs to provide capital to women entrepreneurs in their tribal communities. This funding can be used to help women entrepreneurs turn their ideas into businesses, cover operational costs, and create jobs in their communities (Mason and Brown, 2014; Audretsch and Belitski, 2017; Stam et al., 2021).

1.2. Startup Ecosystem in India

India is a South Asian nation that is developing and ranks seventh in terms of size and has the highest population. Large population increases demand for employment in India and suggests a sizable potential market. India is making a significant shift toward policies that support new businesses and a business-friendly environment in the current decade (Subrahmanya, 2017; Dinseh and Sushil, 2019). People in India who are interested in beginning their own businesses can now get revolutionary assistance through a new programme called Startup India. Because these individuals have capabilities as well as ideas, and the government will provide support for them so that they can put their ideas into action and continue to develop. If this plan is successful, India will eventually have a more robust economy and become a more powerful nation (Baporikar, 2015; Jacob,2017). As per the Ministry of Commerce and Industries (MCI), Government of India, India has the third-largest startup ecosystem in the world, and it is anticipated that it will grow by 12 to 15% annually year over year. In 2018, there were about 50,000 startups in India, with 8,900 to 9,300 of them being technology-focused. There were 1300 new tech startups founded in 2019 alone, which suggests that two to three startups are founded every day (Durda and Ključnikov, 2017; MCI, 2022). Even in developing nations, governments and investors are becoming more interested in the emergence of startup ecosystems. India, behind the

US and China, was ranked as having the third-largest startup ecosystem globally in the Economic Survey 2021-22. In 2021-2022, the government officially recognised over 14,000 new startups, bringing the total number of officially recognised startups in the nation to 61,400. A record 44 of these startups achieved unicorn status in 2021 (Chaudhari and Sinha, 2021; Economic Times, 2022; Tomar, 2023). All these figures present a positive picture of India as a startup nation; they also highlight the significance of an ecosystem that fosters creativity and aspiration. Startups do not exist in a vacuum; rather, they thrive when surrounded by a network of like-minded individuals and institutions committed to fostering innovation makes an ecosystem for nurturing the startup called 'startup ecosystem' (Krishna, 2018; Sheoran and Kumar, 2020). These startup ecosystems can assist the startup sector in maintaining its exponential growth and transforming into a long-lasting valuable industry by facilitating easier access to resources, shared knowledge, and investment (Singh, 2021). The term "ecosystem" itself implies a symbiotic relationship in which various entities mutually benefit. Startup owners learn from other business owners who have already made the journey because it is a long and arduous one and get insight into opposing viewpoints and find motivation through working with other entrepreneurs (Kasturi and Bala Subrahmanya, 2014; Tripathi et al., 2019; Nuthalapti et al., 2020). Since innovation is encouraged and managers trust talented employees to run with ideas unrestricted, working for startups can also be more rewarding. The political and economic landscape of developing nations must include entrepreneurship that is frequently seen as the driving force behind both economic and technological advancement (Soriano and Huarng, 2013; Dharni and Goyal, 2013; Agarwal et al., 2021). There are ongoing worries that entrepreneurs in general, and women entrepreneurs in particular, are disproportionately affected by a continuum of impediments, most of which are related to cultural, social, economic, political, and natural constraints. Therefore, supporting small businesses can conflict with efforts to address other issues, particularly those related to social, economic, cultural, and regulatory issues (Cesaroni et al., 2017; Patel et al., 2022).

1.3. Socio-Economic Status of Tribal Women in India

Tribal groups, or *Adivasis*, make up a sizable community with a population of over 100 million India (Bhattacharya et al., 2017). The tribal population, which is primarily restricted to the forests and villages of central, southern, and north-eastern India, has historically relied on the jungle and its produce for their subsistence (Dasgupta et al., 2018). Over 104 million tribal people, or 33.3% of the world's tribal and indigenous population, reside in India (8.6%) (Ashifa, 2021). They are dispersed among 705 communities and exhibit distinctive cultural diversity. About 2.6 million (2.5%) of the population of Schedule Tribes are "Particularly Vulnerable Tribal Groups" (PVTGs), also referred to as "Primitive Tribes" (Gorai et al., 2022). The Schedule Tribe communities that are the most underprivileged are given this designation. In India, there are 18 States and Union Territories, totaling 75 identified PVTGs. In 90 districts or 809 blocks have more than 50% tribal residents, making up 45% of the population of Schedule Tribes and 55% are outside of Scheduled areas (Narain, 2019; Kujur and Minz, 2021). Tribal groups have always had a special bond with nature and use sustainable living methods. The tribal way of life is distinctive because it incorporates rituals for worshipping nature and land laws that grant communities collective rights (Gluckman, 2017; Kumar et al., 2020; Sonam, 2022). However, the quality of life among tribal groups continues to be low due to a lack of accessibility, development, and long-term neglect. The tribal population of India is plagued by low literacy rates, high school dropout rates, malnutrition, and poverty (Islary, 2014; Brahmanandam and BosuBabu, 2016; Punnaiah, 2018).

Tribal women entrepreneurs are women who come from indigenous communities and are striving to become successful business owners of startups. The socio-economic status of tribal women in India is largely determined by their social and economic marginalization. Tribal women are among the most impoverished and disadvantaged sections of Indian society. They are often denied access to resources and services, lack adequate education and health care, and face discrimination in the employment sector (Sahoo and Pradhan, 2021; Choudhury and Kumar, 2022;). The tribal women of India face a number of challenges due to their social and economic marginalization. These include limited access to education, health care, and employment opportunities, as well as discrimination in terms of wages and access to land and resources (Paray, 2019). In addition, their traditional customs and practices, including their customary laws and practices, are often not respected and their rights are not adequately protected (Gangte, 2016). Therefore, in this chapter the problem and challenges faced by tribal women entrepreneurs with future perspective in reference to startup ecosystem has been discussed.

1.4. Women in Small Business

Although the number of women running businesses has increased in the last ten years or so, there is still much work to be done to remove the specific barriers that prevent them from starting or taking over small businesses (Loscocco and Bird, 2012). Even more crucially, we must foster an environment that enables women who do own small businesses to expand those businesses more easily. It is now urgently necessary to foster innovation among women in order to promote and fully utilise their skills in all fields. This is due to the changing role of women, their increasing involvement in business sectors, and the importance of science and technology in the modern economy (Dua et al., 2020). For a variety of reasons, not enough people find owning a small business to be sufficiently more appealing than working for a company, big or small, or for the government. These reasons hold true for both men and women, but there are some extra factors that make starting a business even less appealing or practical for women (Chaudhuri and Sasidharan, 2020). Family businesses primarily rely on the unpaid skills and effort of women to operate successfully. Both the families who take it for granted and academic studies underestimate the importance of this effort. On the other hand, many of the businesses that are classified as being run by women (i.e., businesses in which women hold the controlling share) are actually managed and made decisions for by men under their names (De Vita et al., 2014; Cesroni et al., 2017).

2. STARTUP ECOSYSTEM AND WOMEN ENTREPRENEURS

The process of economic empowerment for marginalised groups is a two-pronged one, involving both the state and civil society's creation of socio-political space for these groups and the groups' own efforts to increase their economic standing in the community. This achievement also symbolises the fulfillment of the aspirations of underrepresented communities for a society devoid of the political, social, and economic inequalities that have long plagued them (Lal, 2021). Equality, freedom, and fraternity are all connected to the problem of economic empowerment. Women are viewed as both weaker and fairer than men, and they are expected to rely on men their entire lives, both within and outside of the family. They were only allowed to serve as the executors of the decisions made by other male family members in the traditional Indian family structure (Habeeb et al., 2021). In the contemporary era, the conventional setup is changing. The social fabric of Indian society was changing as a result of women's increased educational status and varied aspirations for a better life, which forced Indian women in both urban and rural areas to alter their way of life. Women entrepreneurs are people who take on difficult roles in order to fulfill their own needs and achieve financial independence (Agarwal, 2021). Entrepreneurial women possess a strong desire to make a difference and are capable of adding values to both family and social life. However, some women in some regions of the nation are still unaware of their power. They are unaware that they can overcome men's dominance, continue living their lives, and fight for their freedom. There is still much to be done to close the innovation gap and end illiteracy, despite the significant progress made by women in innovation and new technology (Siddiqui, 2012; Thapar-Björkert et al., 2019; Bhrathi et al., 2021).

Women entrepreneurs have a significant impact on socio-economic outcomes. They often create jobs and generate income, and are often more likely to reinvest their profits in their communities. This can lead to higher wages, better educational opportunities, and improved healthcare and social services. Women entrepreneurs also help to reduce disparities in access to finance, technology, and other resources, which can lead to greater economic stability. In addition, women entrepreneurs are often more likely to be committed to sustainable and fair business practices, which can benefit communities at large (Sharma et al., 2020). Through their businesses, they provide economic opportunities and bring their culture and values to their products and services. The socio-economic status of women in India has seen significant improvement over the past few decades. Women are now accorded equal rights in many areas such as education, health care, employment, and political representation. Women have also achieved greater access to credit, and the number of female-owned businesses has increased. However, despite these improvements, there are still many challenges facing women in India. They face a high degree of discrimination and violence, and are disproportionately affected by poverty and malnutrition and this makes women the most vulnerable part of our society (Olarewaju and Fernando, 2020; Bullough et al., 2022). Women entrepreneurs in startup ecosystem are often under-represented in the formal economy, and have less access to finance and other resources than their male counterparts. In addition, they often face cultural and social pressures that limit their ability to succeed in business (Sharma, 2013). Social scientists, policy makers, and development activists have only recently given the term "Economic Empowerment" of women a new meaning and context. Startup ecosystem encourages collaboration among women entrepreneurs in their communities. This could be done through workshops, seminars, and other events that bring women entrepreneurs together to share ideas, resources, and knowledge. Startup ecosystem also provides resources and networks to women entrepreneurs in their tribal communities include mentorship programs, business incubators, and other resources that provide support to women entrepreneurs (Manshani and Dubey, 2017). They also increase access to technology and resources for women entrepreneurs in their communities like computers, internet, and other technology resources that can help women entrepreneurs become more productive and successful. They offer financial literacy training to women entrepreneurs who could include teaching them about budgeting, financial planning, and other important topics related to managing their finances. Startup ecosystems also promote role models within their communities who have achieved success as entrepreneurs. This could include featuring their stories in the media, hosting events, and creating other opportunities for women entrepreneurs to learn from their experiences (Ozkazanc-Pan and Clark Muntean, 2018; Suseno and Abbott, 2021).

3. STARTUP ECOSYSTEM FOR TRIBAL WOMEN ENTREPRENEURS: OPPORTUNITIES, CHALLENGES AND FUTURE PERSPECTIVES

Tribal women in India face additional challenges due to their marginalised status in society. They are often disadvantaged in terms of access to education, healthcare, economic opportunities, and political participation. Moreover, they are particularly vulnerable to gender-based violence, exploitation, and trafficking (Khanday and Akram, 2012; Bhagavatheeswaran, 2016). Tribal women continue to face widespread gender discrimination, with men often seen as the head of the household and the primary breadwinner. This has led to women being denied access to education, resources and decision-making processes, leaving them in a vulnerable position (Gupta, 2016). Tribal women in India often suffer from poor health due to limited access to healthcare and nutrition, as well as cultural stigmas around seeking medical help (Chisty and Singh, 2018). They are often denied access to economic opportunities due to lack of education and resources, making it difficult for them to support themselves and their families. Tribal women often face stigma and discrimination from the wider society, leading to social exclusion (Kannan, 2018). Because they do not have access to legal protection, tribal women are susceptible to being exploited and abused (Bain, 2021).

3.1. Change in Socio-economic Status of Tribal Women

Tribal women in India have long been marginalized and underrepresented in many aspects of society. Despite of all these hurdles, there has been an increasing interest in tribal women entrepreneurship in India in recent years. This is largely due to the realization of the role these women can play in driving economic growth and reducing poverty. In particular, tribal women are seen as having the potential to create jobs, increase access to markets and generate income for their communities (Manjunatha and Gangadhar, 2018). The Government of India has taken various measures to promote the empowerment of tribal women. These include setting up of dedicated schemes to support tribal women entrepreneurs, providing access to financial services and credit, and creating an enabling environment for their enterprise. In addition, several non-governmental organizations (NGOs) in India are working to strengthen the entrepreneurship skills of tribal women. These organizations are providing training on business skills, conducting market research, and helping to connect tribal women to markets (Tiwary, 2017; Prabhakar and Nimesh, 2022). The success of tribal women entrepreneurs in India will depend on the availability of resources and support from the government, civil society and other stakeholders. It is also important that tribal women have access to the right training and mentorship to ensure their success. A number of tribal entrepreneurs are transforming tribal India by using technology to connect agriculture and forest produce with markets, creating self-help groups, empowering women, and developing self-sustaining businesses. In recent years, tribal women have been increasingly taking on the role of entrepreneurs and using their traditional knowledge to create innovative businesses. These businesses range from handicrafts, traditional clothing, organic farming, apiary-related products, and natural products (Sharma, 2015; Sahu et al., 2021). Many of these businesses are helping to boost the local economy in tribal regions, while also providing tribal women with much-needed economic independence and empowerment. Additionally, these businesses are helping to preserve and promote tribal culture and traditions. Tribal women are increasingly becoming entrepreneurs in India, with many of them creating innovative organizations, building businesses, and creating jobs (Tripathy, 2017).

In India, tribal women are working to create sustainable livelihoods, improve their socio-economic status, and strengthen their communities. There are a number of tribal women entrepreneurs in India; they are working on a variety of projects, including organic farming, eco-tourism, small-scale manufacturing, and handicrafts (Kumar et al., 2021). These women entrepreneurs are not only contributing to economic growth and employment, but also helping to create social change and to promote gender equality. Organic farming has become an important endeavor for tribal women entrepreneurs in India. They are using traditional methods to grow and cultivate crops, as well as experimenting with crop rotation and introducing new varieties of crops. This is helping to increase the income of tribal women, while also providing healthy food to their communities. Eco-tourism is another avenue that tribal women in India are exploring. This type of tourism focuses on the environment, local culture, and the natural beauty of the area. Tribal women are establishing eco-tourism opportunities in remote areas, helping to bring much needed income to their communities. Small-scale manufacturing is another way that tribal women entrepreneurs can do in agriculture sector (Chakraborty, 2020; Sonam et al., 2021).

3.2. Government Initiatives and Schemes for Promotion Entrepreneurial Activities

Government policies and initiatives can play an important role in addressing these challenges for women entrepreneurs. These include providing access to finance, supporting small business development, and offering training and mentoring programs. In addition, creating a business-friendly environment, increasing access to technology and resources, and strengthening legal and regulatory frameworks can help to promote greater economic opportunities for women entrepreneurs (Kaneru, 2017). The government of India has launched a number of programmes to encourage entrepreneurship and strengthen the country's nascent startup ecosystem. The goals of programmes like Start-up India, Make-in-India, Digital India, Skill India, Bharat Mala, and Mudra Bank are to foster entrepreneurial growth, increase employment opportunities, and foster financial autonomy in India (Kumar, 2021). Government Bank schemes like Annapurna Scheme, Stree Shakti Package, Orient Mahila Vikas Yojana

Scheme, Dena Shakti Scheme, Cent Kalyani Scheme, Mahila Udyam Nidhi Scheme and others are notable scheme to promote entrepreneurial activity among women (Naik and Patel, 2022). Under this initiative, the government hopes to set up a framework that promotes entrepreneurship and innovation in the country, which will lead to sustainable economic growth and the creation of many new employments. So, the fundamental objective of this programme is to lay the groundwork for employment for all job seekers, regardless of their level of expertise. People in India are discouraged from starting their own businesses due to the extensive red tapism involved in doing things like getting land approval, environmental permits, and attracting foreign investments. Start-up India's overarching goal is to change the public's perception of the government from that of a stumbling block to development to that of a guiding light for budding enterprises, pointing them in the direction of success (Singh, 2021).

Therefore, Startup ecosystems for tribal women can be tailored to their specific needs, taking into account the challenges they face in their communities. Such ecosystems should include a range of resources, such as access to capital, mentorship, and support networks. Financial resources are essential for the success of any business, and tribal women need access to seed capital, venture capital, and other forms of financing. Mentorship can be provided by experienced entrepreneurs, business leaders, and other professionals who can provide guidance and advice. Support networks can be created to connect tribal women with other entrepreneurs and investors, and to provide access to resources such as legal and accounting services (Malpani and Ghosh, 2020; Tiwary et al., 2021).

In addition, educational opportunities need to exist for tribal women to gain the skills and knowledge necessary to launch and grow their businesses. Programs aimed at women entrepreneurs will only be successful if they consider both this paradox and the familial and social conditioning that limits women's confidence, independence, and mobility. This could include business courses, workshops, seminars, and networking events. Finally, access to technology is also essential for tribal women to be able to compete in the modern economy. This could include access to computers and the internet, as well as training on how to use these tools (Sarma, 2014; Hazarika and Goswami, 2018; Sahu et al., 2021). Despite some government initiatives to improve the status of tribal women, much work remains to be done to ensure that they are able to access their rights and enjoy a life of dignity.

4. CONCLUSION

India is become one of the largest startup oriented countries after America and China due to the transition in laws and regulations. Women entrepreneurs bring unique perspectives, creativity, and drive to starting and growing businesses. Despite facing numerous challenges, including gender bias and limited access to resources, women entrepreneurs continue to make significant strides and achieve great success. Tribal women entrepreneurship plays a crucial role in promoting economic growth, empowering women, and preserving cultural heritage. Even after facing numerous challenges like gender discrimination, poor health condition, no access to education, resources and no role in decision-making processes, tribal women have proven their resilience and determination in starting and running successful businesses. By providing access to resources, mentorship, and networking opportunities, a supportive startup ecosystem can help tribal women overcome the unique challenges they face and achieve their entrepreneurial goals. As these women succeed, they not only drive economic growth and create jobs, but also play a vital role in preserving their cultural heritage and empowering their communities. By investing in the development of a strong startup ecosystem for tribal women, we can create a brighter future for everyone.

ACKNOWLEDGMENT

Authors are thankful to Ministry of Education, Government of India for providing funding for the research work.

REFERENCES

Agrawal, A., Gandhi, P., & Khare, P. (2021). Women empowerment through entrepreneurship: case study of a social entrepreneurial intervention in rural India. *International Journal of Organizational Analysis.*

Ashifa, K. M. (2021). Analysis On The Determinants Of Health Status Among Tribal Communities. *Journal of Cardiovascular Disease Research, 12*(3), 531534.

Audretsch, D. B., & Belitski, M. (2017). Entrepreneurial ecosystems in cities: Establishing the framework conditions. *The Journal of Technology Transfer*, *42*(5), 1030–1051. doi:10.100710961-016-9473-8

Bain, P. M. (2021). The Inherent Rights of Tribal Women. *Jus Corpus LJ*, *2*, 773.

Baporikar, N. (2015). Framework for social change through startups in India. [IJCESC]. *International Journal of Civic Engagement and Social Change*, *2*(1), 30–42. doi:10.4018/IJCESC.2015010103

Berger, E. S., & Kuckertz, A. (2016). Female entrepreneurship in startup ecosystems worldwide. *Journal of Business Research*, *69*(11), 5163–5168. doi:10.1016/j.jbusres.2016.04.098

Bhagavatheeswaran, L., Nair, S., Stone, H., Isac, S., Hiremath, T., Raghavendra, T., & Beattie, T. S. (2016). The barriers and enablers to education among scheduled caste and scheduled tribe adolescent girls in northern Karnataka, South India: A qualitative study. *International Journal of Educational Development*, *49*, 262–270. doi:10.1016/j.ijedudev.2016.04.004

Bharathi, N. S., Balaji, V., Christina, D., & Akash, A. (2021). *Vital Analysis of Women Empowerment in Marginalised Communities*.

Bhattacharya, R., Bhattacharya, S., & Gill, K. (2017). The Adivasi land question in the neoliberal era. *The Land Question in India: State, Dispossession, and Capitalist Transition, 176*.

Bocken, N., & Snihur, Y. (2020). Lean Startup and the business model: Experimenting for novelty and impact. *Long Range Planning*, *53*(4), 101953. doi:10.1016/j.lrp.2019.101953

Bortolini, R. F., Nogueira Cortimiglia, M., Danilevicz, A. D. M. F., & Ghezzi, A. (2021). Lean Startup: A comprehensive historical review. *Management Decision*, *59*(8), 1765–1783. doi:10.1108/MD-07-2017-0663

Brahmanandam, T., & BosuBabu, T. (2016). Educational status among the scheduled tribes: Issues and challenges. *Journal of Politics and Governance*, *5*(3), 57–66.

Bullough, A., Guelich, U., Manolova, T. S., & Schjoedt, L. (2022). Women's entrepreneurship and culture: Gender role expectations and identities, societal culture, and the entrepreneurial environment. *Small Business Economics*, *58*(2), 985–996. doi:10.100711187-020-00429-6

Cesaroni, F. M., Demartini, P., & Paoloni, P. (2017). Women in business and social media: Implications for female entrepreneurship in emerging countries. *African Journal of Business Management*, *11*(14), 316–326. doi:10.5897/AJBM2017.8281

Chakraborty, U. K. (2020). Opportunities for tribal entrepreneurship development in Jharkhand to combat post Covid-19 challenges. *Parikalpana: KIIT Journal of Management*, *16*(1and2), 150-163.

Chaudhari, S. L., & Sinha, M. (2021). A study on emerging trends in Indian startup ecosystem: Big data, crowd funding, shared economy. *International Journal of Innovation Science*, *13*(1), 1–16. doi:10.1108/IJIS-09-2020-0156

Chaudhuri, K., Sasidharan, S., & Raj, R. S. N. (2020). Gender, small firm ownership, and credit access: Some insights from India. *Small Business Economics*, *54*(4), 1165–1181. doi:10.100711187-018-0124-3

Chishty, S., & Singh, N. (2018). Nutritional status of tribal women (Saharia and Meena), Baran district of Rajasthan, India. *Nutrition & Food Science*, *48*(6), 922–939. doi:10.1108/NFS-01-2018-0018

Choudhury, S., & Kumar, S. (2022). Gender discrimination and marginalization of women in North-East India. *Journal of Public Affairs*, *22*(4), e2625. doi:10.1002/pa.2625

Dasgupta, S. (2018). Adivasi studies: From a historian's perspective. *History Compass*, *16*(10), e12486. doi:10.1111/hic3.12486

David, D., Gopalan, S., & Ramachandran, S. (2021). The startup environment and funding activity in India. In Investment in Startups and Small Business Financing (pp. 193-232). doi:10.1142/9789811235825_0007

De Vita, L., Mari, M., & Poggesi, S. (2014). Women entrepreneurs in and from developing countries: Evidences from the literature. *European Management Journal*, *32*(3), 451–460. doi:10.1016/j.emj.2013.07.009

Dharni, K., & Goel, D. (2013). Startup operations and problems of honey bee entrepreneurs: Experience from India. *International Journal of Entrepreneurship and Small Business*, *18*(3), 332–348. doi:10.1504/IJESB.2013.052520

Dinesh, K. K., & Sushil, N. A. (2019). Strategic innovation factors in startups: Results of a cross-case analysis of Indian startups. *Journal for Global Business Advancement*, *12*(3), 449–470. doi:10.1504/JGBA.2019.10022956

Dua, A., Ellingrud, K., Mahajan, D., & Silberg, J. (2020). Which small businesses are most vulnerable to COVID-19—and when. McKinsey & Company, 18.

Durda, L., & Ključnikov, A. (2019). Social networks in entrepreneurial startups development. *Economia e Sociologia*, *12*(3), 192–208.

Economic Times. (2022). Economic Survey 2022: At least 14,000 new startups recognised in India, up 20 times in five years. *Economic Times*. https://economictimes.indiatimes.com/tech/startups/economic-survey-2022-at-least-14000-new-startups-recognised-in-india/articleshow/89243366.cms

Escalfoni, R., Silva, M. F. D., & Oliveira, J. (2020, November). Analyzing social relations in startup ecosystems. In *XVI Brazilian Symposium on Information Systems* (pp. 1-7).

Gangte, M. (2016). Gender and customary law: A case study of Mizo Tribe in North East India. *Indian Anthropologist*, 17-30.

Gluckman, M. (2017). *Politics, law and ritual in tribal society*. Routledge. doi:10.4324/9781315126913

Gorai, P., Dey, A., & Modak, B. K. (2022). Birhors of Purulia: marching toward mainstream of the society. In *Indigenous People and Nature* (pp. 29–60). Elsevier. doi:10.1016/B978-0-323-91603-5.00009-9

Gupta, P. (2016). Status of tribal women in India: some observations. *Anudhyan: an international journal of social science*, *1*(1), 181-188.

Habeeb, S., Arya, V., & Ahmad, N. (2021). Home-based entrepreneuring for empowerment and sustainability of Muslim women: A study in the Indian context. *World Review of Science, Technology and Sustainable Development*, *17*(4), 334–347. doi:10.1504/WRSTSD.2021.117840

Hazarika, B., & Goswami, K. (2018). Micro-entrepreneurship development in the handloom industry: An empirical analysis among the tribal women in Assam. *International Journal of Rural Management*, *14*(1), 22–38. doi:10.1177/0973005218754437

Islary, J. (2014). Health and health seeking behaviour among tribal communities in India: a socio-cultural perspective. *Journal of Tribal Intellectual Collective India*, 1-16.

Jacob, M. (2017). Entrepreneurships and Startup Programmes: Opportunities in Travel and Tourism. *Atna Journal of Tourism Studies*, *12*(2), 51–65. doi:10.12727/ajts.18.3

Jain, S. (2016). Growth of startup ecosystems in India. *International Journal of Applied Research*, *2*(12), 152–154.

Jin, F., Wu, A., & Hitt, L. (2017, February). Social is the new financial: How startup social media activity influences funding outcomes. In Academy of Management Proceedings (Vol. 1, p. 13329). Academy of Management.

Kalaiselvi, S. (2021). The Indian start up Ecosystem: Drivers, challenges and pillars of support. *GEDRAG & ORGANISATIE REVIEW*, *34*(4), 386–402.

Kamariotou, M., & Kitsios, F. (2022). Bringing Digital Innovation Strategies and Entrepreneurship: The Business Model Canvas in Open Data Ecosystem and Startups. *Future Internet*, *14*(5), 127. doi:10.3390/fi14050127

Kannan, S. (2018). Excluded among the excluded: Status of Tribal women in Telangana. *International Journal of Innovative Studies in Sociology and Humanities*, *3*(12), 30–39.

Kasturi, S. V., & Bala Subrahmanya, M. H. (2014). Start-ups and small scale industry growth in India: Do institutional credit and start-ups make a difference? *International Journal of Entrepreneurial Venturing*, *6*(3), 277–298. doi:10.1504/IJEV.2014.064692

Khanday, Z. A., & Akram, M. (2012). Health status of marginalized groups in India. *International journal of applied sociology*, *2*(6), 60-70.

KoneruK. (2017). Women entrepreneurship in India-problems and prospects. *Available at* SSRN 3110340.

Krishna, A., Agrawal, A., & Choudhary, A. (2016, December). Predicting the outcome of startups: less failure, more success. In 2016 *IEEE 16th International Conference on Data Mining Workshops* (ICDMW) (pp. 798-805). IEEE. 10.1109/ICDMW.2016.0118

Krishna, H. S. (2018). Entrepreneurial learning and Indian tech startup survival: An empirical investigation. *Asian Journal of Innovation and Policy*, *7*(1), 55–78.

Kujur, R., & Minz, S. K. (2021). Proliferation of Tribal Migrants and Repercussion: Case Study from the Tribal Areas of Sundargarh District, Odisha (India). *Current Res. J. Soc. Sci. & Human.*, *4*(1), 27–44. doi:10.12944/CRJSSH.4.1.04

Kumar, M. (2021). Startups, Barriers and its Opportunities in India. [TURCOMAT]. *Turkish Journal of Computer and Mathematics Education*, *12*(9), 2200–2205.

Kumar, M. M., Pathak, V. K., & Ruikar, M. (2020). Tribal population in India: A public health challenge and road to future. *Journal of Family Medicine and Primary Care*, *9*(2), 508. doi:10.4103/jfmpc.jfmpc_992_19 PMID:32318373

Kumar, R., Kanaujiya, R., & Mishra, K. (2019). Resurgent India: An Exploratory Study to comprehend the Interplay of Public Expenditure and Governance. *Think India Journal*, *22*(14), 1840–1883.

Kumar, R. R., Singh, K. P., & Ete, L. (2021). Social innovation and entrepreneurship in Arunachal Pradesh: Opportunities and challenges. *Space and Culture, India*, *8*(4), 48–59. doi:10.20896aci.v8i4.924

Lal, T. (2021). Impact of financial inclusion on economic development of marginalized communities through the mediation of social and economic empowerment. *International Journal of Social Economics*, *48*(12), 1768–1793. doi:10.1108/IJSE-12-2020-0830

Loscocco, K., & Bird, S. R. (2012). Gendered paths: Why women lag behind men in small business success. *Work and Occupations*, *39*(2), 183–219. doi:10.1177/0730888412444282

Malpani, R., & Ghosh, A. (2020). Business Sustainability Measures in Tribal Jharkhand. *Drishtikon: A Management Journal, 11*(1), 66.

Manjunatha, B. R., & Gangadhar, M. R. (2018). Socio-Economic Status of the Bettakuruba Tribal Women: a Case Study from the Chamarajanagara District, Karnataka. *Antrocom: Online Journal of Anthropology, 14*(1).

Manshani, S., & Dubey, A. (2017). Startup women in startup India: A study of women entrepreneurs in India. [IJBGM]. *International Journal of Business and Management*, *6*(4), 91–100.

Mason, C., & Brown, R. (2014). Entrepreneurial ecosystems and growth oriented entrepreneurship. *Final report to OECD, Paris, 30*(1), 77-102.

Naik, A., & Patel, P. (2022). Government Schemes for Entrepreneurship Programs. In *Agricultural Microbiology Based Entrepreneurship: Making Money from Microbes* (pp. 25–40). Springer Nature Singapore.

Narain, J. P. (2019). Health of tribal populations in India: How long can we afford to neglect? *The Indian Journal of Medical Research*, *149*(3), 313. doi:10.4103/ijmr.IJMR_2079_18 PMID:31249192

Nuthalapati, C. S., Srinivas, K., Pandey, N., & Sharma, R. (2020). Startups with open innovation: Accelerating technological change and food value chain flows in India. *Indian Journal of Agricultural Economics*, *75*(4), 415–437.

O'Connor, A., Stam, E., Sussan, F., & Audretsch, D. B. (2018). Entrepreneurial ecosystems: The foundations of place-based renewal. *Entrepreneurial ecosystems: Place-based transformations and transitions,* 1-21.

Olarewaju, T., & Fernando, J. (2020). Gender Inequality and Female Entrepreneurship in Developing Countries. In W. Leal Filho, A. Azul, L. Brandli, A. Lange Salvia, & T. Wall (Eds.), *Decent Work and Economic Growth. Encyclopedia of the UN Sustainable Development Goals*. Springer., doi:10.1007/978-3-319-71058-7_92-1

Ozkazanc-Pan, B., & Clark Muntean, S. (2018). Networking towards (in) equality: Women entrepreneurs in technology. *Gender, Work and Organization*, *25*(4), 379–400. doi:10.1111/gwao.12225

Paray, M. R. (2019). Status Of Tribal Women In India With Special Reference To The Socio-Economic And Educational Condition. *Ilkogretim Online*, *18*(4), 2284–2292.

Parmar, R. B. (2016*). A Study of the Problems of Girl Child Education in the Narmada District of Gujarat* [Doctoral dissertation, Maharaja Sayajirao University of Baroda (India)].

Patel, J., Matharu, S., Changle, R., & Pachori, C. D. S. (2022). Indofills Industries–A Venture seeking Turnaround. *Journal of Positive School Psychology*, 6590-6593.

Prabhakar, S., & Nimesh, A. (2022). Skill development programmes for women in India: Current status and future perspectives. *World Journal of Advanced Engineering Technology and Sciences*, *7*(1), 128–136. doi:10.30574/wjaets.2022.7.1.0105

Prohorovs, A., Bistrova, J., & Ten, D. (2019). Startup success factors in the capital attraction stage: Founders' perspective. *Journal of East-West Business*, *25*(1), 26–51. doi:10.1080/10669868.2018.1503211

Punnaiah, A. (2018). Issues and Challenges of Tribal Education: A Study of Telangana State. *International Education and Research Journal*, *4*(1), 49–51.

Sahoo, M., & Pradhan, J. (2021). Reproductive health care status of the displaced tribal women in India: An analysis using Nussbaum Central human capabilities. *Health Care for Women International*, *42*(4-6), 390–419. doi:10.1080/07399332.2020.1743994 PMID:32223700

Sahu, T. N., Agarwala, V., & Maity, S. (2021). Effectiveness of microcredit in employment generation and livelihood transformation of tribal women entrepreneurs: Evidence from PMMY. *Journal of Small Business and Entrepreneurship*, 1–22. doi:10.1080/08276331.2021.1928847

Sahu, T. N., Agarwala, V., & Maity, S. (2021). Effectiveness of microcredit in employment generation and livelihood transformation of tribal women entrepreneurs: Evidence from PMMY. *Journal of Small Business and Entrepreneurship*, 1–22. doi:10.1080/08276331.2021.1928847

Salamzadeh, A., & Kawamorita Kesim, H. (2017). The enterprising communities and startup ecosystem in Iran. *Journal of Enterprising Communities: People and Places in the Global Economy*, *11*(4), 456–479. doi:10.1108/JEC-07-2015-0036

Sarma, G. (2014). An analytical study on entrepreneurial activity as a tool for socio-economic development of tribal women in BTAD area of Assam. *IOSR Journal of Economics and Finance*, *3*(2), 49–52. doi:10.9790/5933-03214952

Sharma, D., Tiwari, B. K., Chaturvedi, S. S., & Diengdoh, E. (2015). Status, utilization and economic valuation of Non-timber Forest Products of Arunachal Pradesh, India. *Journal of Forest and Environmental Science*, *31*(1), 24–37. doi:10.7747/JFES.2015.31.1.24

Sharma, S., Mehra, D., Akhtar, F., & Mehra, S. (2020). Evaluation of a community-based intervention for health and economic empowerment of marginalized women in India. *BMC Public Health*, *20*(1), 1–16. doi:10.118612889-020-09884-y PMID:33228667

Sharma, Y. (2013). Women entrepreneur in India. *IOSR Journal of Business and Management*, *15*(3), 9–14. doi:10.9790/487X-1530914

Sheoran, M., & Kumar, D. (2020). Role of environmental concerns on the startups networking: A study of Indian startups. *International Journal of Mathematical. Engineering and Management Sciences*, *5*(6), 1300–1311.

Siddiqui, A. B. (2012). Problems encountered by women entrepreneurs in India. *International Journal of Applied Research & Studies, 1*(2), 01-11.

Singh, V. K. (2021). Policy and regulatory changes for a successful startup revolution: Experiences from the startup action plan in India. In Investment in Startups and Small Business Financing (pp. 33-67).

Singh, V. K. (2021). Policy and regulatory changes for a successful startup revolution: Experiences from the startup action plan in India. In Investment in Startups and Small Business Financing (pp. 33-67).

Sonam, Kala, S., Prabhakar, P., & Banerjee, M. (2021). Post-training Knowledge and Attitude Assessment of the Women Entrepreneurs towards Mushroom Cultivation. *International Journal of Agriculture Environment and Biotechnology*, *14*(2), 229–234.

Sonam (2022). Customary Laws: Cultural Identity of Indigenous People, *National Seminar on Tribal Culture and Philosophy in Oral Narratives*, *1*(1), 39.

Soriano, D. R., & Huarng, K. H. (2013). Innovation and entrepreneurship in knowledge industries. *Journal of Business Research*, *66*(10), 1964–1969. doi:10.1016/j.jbusres.2013.02.019

Spender, J. C., Corvello, V., Grimaldi, M., & Rippa, P. (2017). Startups and open innovation: A review of the literature. *European Journal of Innovation Management*, *20*(1), 4–30. doi:10.1108/EJIM-12-2015-0131

Stam, E., & Van de Ven, A. (2021). Entrepreneurial ecosystem elements. *Small Business Economics*, *56*(2), 809–832. doi:10.100711187-019-00270-6

Subrahmanya, M. B. (2017). Comparing the entrepreneurial ecosystems for technology startups in Bangalore and Hyderabad, India. *Technology Innovation Management Review*, *7*(7), 47–62. doi:10.22215/timreview/1090

Suseno, Y., & Abbott, L. (2021). Women entrepreneurs' digital social innovation: Linking gender, entrepreneurship, social innovation and information systems. *Information Systems Journal*, *31*(5), 717–744. doi:10.1111/isj.12327

Thapar-Björkert, S., Maiorano, D., & Blomkvist, H. (2019). Empowerment mechanisms-employment guarantee, women and Dalits in India. *Contemporary South Asia*, *27*(4), 486–501. doi:10.1080/09584935.2019.1686750

Tiwari, A., Hogan, T., & O'Gorman, C. (2021). The good, the bad, and the ugly of 'Startup India'-a review of India's entrepreneurship policy. [EPW]. *Economic and Political Weekly*, *56*(50), 45–52.

Tiwari, N. (2017). Women entrepreneurship in India: A literature review. *American Journal of Entrepreneurship*, *2*(1), 47–60.

Todeschini, B. V., Boelter, A. S., de Souza, J. S., & Cortimiglia, M. N. (2017). Risk management from the perspective of startups. *European Journal of Applied Business and Management*, *3*(3).

Tomar, S. (2023). Unicorn Start-ups in India: A Brief Study. *IJFMR-International Journal For Multidisciplinary Research*, *5*(1), 1–17.

Tripathi, N., Seppänen, P., Boominathan, G., Oivo, M., & Liukkunen, K. (2019). Insights into startup ecosystems through exploration of multi-vocal literature. *Information and Software Technology*, *105*, 56–77. doi:10.1016/j.infsof.2018.08.005

Tripathy, S. N. (2017). Microfinance in empowering tribal women: Evidence from the villages of KBK Districts (Odisha). *Journal of Land and Rural Studies*, *5*(2), 97–109. doi:10.1177/2321024917700938

Chapter 2
Essential Factors for Entrepreneurship Development Among Engineering Undergraduates

Pushkar Dubey
Pandit Sundarlal Sharma (Open) University, India

Parul Dubey
G.H. Raisoni College of Engineering, India

Kailash Kumar Sahu
Pandit Sundarlal Sharma (Open) University, India

ABSTRACT

Employment creation is the first priority of any nation in the world, which facilitates healthy nations' growth and development. Nations like India have been fighting unemployment issues for more than a decade, but recently it has worsened. Entrepreneurship is the only solution to this great issue. The present study attempts to investigate the social and environmental factors affecting engineering undergraduates' entrepreneurial behavior. 1000 responses were recorded for analysis and found that social and environmental factors play prominent roles in creating entrepreneurial temperament among engineering undergraduates.

DOI: 10.4018/978-1-6684-6878-4.ch002

INTRODUCTION

Unemployment is a major concern in emerging nations like India, which generates more graduates than jobs. Pandey (2019) stated that India's jobless rate jumped 1.9 times to 7.6% in April 2019, the highest in the preceding two years. The rural unemployment rate is 7.61%. According to State of India's Environment (SoE) 2017, one of the major reasons for rising unemployment rates is a lack of skills among young people. This is significant because, although India expected to be the youngest nation in the world by 2020, accounting for 20% of global youths, the majority would be classified as uneducated and unskilled. This is supported by the union ministry of skill development and entrepreneurship's official figure, which states that 4.69 percent of India's total workforce is formally skilled, compared to 52 percent in the United States of America (USA), 68 percent in the United Kingdom (UK), 75 percent in Germany, 80 percent in Japan, and 96 percent in South Korea (Pandey, 2019). Keeping these factors in mind, the World Bank forecasted that India would need to produce 8.1 million jobs each year to sustain its decreasing employment rate.

Talented and competent youngsters and graduates are an increasing concern, according to Bhagchandani (2017), since they are always looking for work instead of beginning a business venture. New and mature entrepreneurs lack direction and mentoring, and self-financing is fragmented, limited to a few locations, and low nationally. A lack of creative, inventive, and entrepreneurial culture prevents India from being the leading start-up ecosystem center. India's top priorities include fostering entrepreneurship and increasing employment. Entrepreneurship should be a career option for engineering graduates. According to Chaudhary (2018), science and technology have the potential to make major contributions to India's continued economic growth and development. Dr. A. P. J. Abdul Kalam, India's former president, also believes in science and technology. He also encouraged India's young minds to attain the objectives.

Even though India has the youngest population among the top ten economies in the world, job creation has been critical to the country's success in attaining equitable growth. The difficulty is that there are not enough jobs available, and graduates who are just entering the workforce do not have enough skills to make them employable. Under these circumstances, one must concentrate on student entrepreneurship, which accomplishes dual outcomes, namely, the upskilling of students as well as the creation of jobs (Rao, 2017).

Entrepreneurs in the 21st century need to recognise that we live in a "technology era" in which knowledge-based competition has emerged as the primary challenge. The success and expansion of businesses in the twenty-first century have largely depended on technical progress and innovation. The 21st-century entrepreneur must be well-versed in both technology and innovation. Thus, entrepreneurs should adopt new business practices rather than sticking to the old paradigm. Presently, technology-enabled firms effectively use more specialized resources and strategies (Alnafrah et al., 2019; Höflinger et al., 2018; Lin & Lai 2021). According to Seth (2021), an entrepreneur is an individual who is inspired to start a business by entrepreneurship training and its elements (role model, feedback, business plan efforts, and entrepreneurial network).

Entrepreneurship helps society flourish by producing employment and wealth (Dabo 2018). As a fact, entrepreneurship creates employment. Entrepreneurship is becoming more important as technological progress reduces the need for human labour. People may be inspired to lift themselves out of poverty if they have access to the education that will equip them with the skills and information they need to do so (Bakar et al., 2015). Social and environmental factors play vital role in creating entrepreneurial temperament among students. Thus, the present study attempts to investigate the role of social factors (includes parental role model, cultural role, and family support), and environmental factors (includes institutional environment, and economic resource) in developing entrepreneurial nature among engineering students enrolled in various private and public technical institutions of Chhattisgarh state.

THEORETICAL GROUNDING AND HYPOTHESES DEVELOPMENT

Social Factors (Including Parental Role Model, Cultural Role, and Family Support)

There are societal elements that impact entrepreneurial activity. These are considered to be social variables. Social and cultural perspective says that entrepreneur's conduct is determined by their social surroundings (Light & Siegel, 2008). Humans are social animals who are influenced by events in his/her community or society. The surrounding circumstances are crucial influences on the cognitive process. Individual elements, such as parental role models, cultural role models, family support, community support, etc., influence entrepreneurship (Birley, 1985; Aldrich & Zimmer, 1986; Dubini & Aldrich, 1991; Greve & Salaff, 2003).

Parental role model refers to the effect that entrepreneurs have on their children. Culture is the dominating set of beliefs and behaviours of a particular community. Entrepreneurship is affected by a community's entrepreneurial culture. Numerous more characteristics, such as family business experience, also contribute to an entrepreneurial temperament (Harris, Gibson & Taylor, 2007; Zampetakis et al., 2009; Roberts & Robinson, 2010). The cultural values of a person are also crucial to the formation of a new venture's purpose (Autio et al., 2001; Urban, 2006; Linan & Chen, 2009; Engle et al., 2010; Moriano et al., 2012).

The impact of immediate family and close friends is critical in moulding entrepreneurship since they provide venture capital for start-ups (Nanda & Sorensen, 2009). Entrepreneurship is guided by role models who serve as mentors and give advice (Postigo et al., 2006). Peer group in the form of friends also plays an important part in moulding entrepreneurship by encouraging individuals to pursue it (Nanda & Sorenson, 2009; Sergeant & Crawford, 2001). A network of people or the ties between individuals in social networks have a significant influence in developing entrepreneurship and the ambition to pursue it (Altinay et al., 2012; Yurtkoru et al., 2014).

The family history affects entrepreneurial intent (Zapkau et al., 2015). Additionally, it is clear that the majority of entrepreneurs come from entrepreneurial families (Nabi et al., 2008). Even if there is no direct family impact on entrepreneurial goals, Franco et al. (2010) suggest that individual family effects on the tendency for self-employment cannot be ignored. Evidently, entrepreneurs have a predisposition to persuade their children to start or establish new businesses (Devonish et al., 2010). However, according to the findings of Do Paco et al. (2011), social norm is not a major predictor of entrepreneurial intention and has traditionally only played a minor part in the process of forecasting entrepreneurial intention (Fini et al., 2009; Shook & Bratianu, 2010; Sommer & Haug, 2011). The outcomes of previous studies related to social factors in creating entrepreneurial temperament are fragmented and unclear, thus, the authors propose the following hypotheses to investigate:

H1. Parental role model dimension of social factor does not vary significantly between boys' and girls' mean scores.

H2. Cultural role dimension of social factor does not vary significantly between boys' and girls' mean scores.

H3. Family support dimension of social factor does not vary significantly between boys' and girls' mean scores.

H4. Overall social factor does not vary significantly between boys' and girls' mean scores.

Environmental Factors (Including Institutional Support, and Economic Resource)

Entrepreneurial environment refers to the immediate surrounding variables which encompass all the activities and tends to effect entrepreneurs. The surrounding variables of the environmental concern are likely to have an effect on the mind's inclination to choose entrepreneurship as a career choice. Because of the growing importance of one's environment or surrounding, the recognition of the function that environment plays in the formation of an entrepreneurial career has significantly expanded (Vondracek, 1990; Higgins, 2001; Savickas, 2002; Young et al., 2002). The sociological theories of career have traditionally given significant weight to the role performed by environmental circumstances (Maranda & Comeau, 2000). The interplay of persons and the environment has played a part in developing the career as an entrepreneur (Savickas, 2002). Intentions may be affected by an individual's personality qualities as well as external influences. It is common practice to see environmental influences as "gap fillers" in the link between personality qualities and the propensity to engage in entrepreneurial activity (Luthje & Franke, 2003).

Students' intentions to start their own businesses are significantly impacted both by the students' own personal characteristics (such as their locus of control and entrepreneurial self-efficacy) and by the environment in which they find themselves (such as their social networks and access to capital). Students' aspirations to start their own businesses can be influenced by a number of other aspects of their lives, including the proactive personalities of the students and the supportive environments that exist within universities (including support for the development of concepts and businesses, as well as educational support) (Mustafa et al., 2016). On the other hand, Sesen (2012) found that the atmosphere of the institution does not have a major impact on intention.

Access to capital (Luthje & Franke, 2003; Ozen Kutanis et al., 2006; Schwarz et al., 2009), knowledge of the potential business sector (Kristiansen & Indarti, 2004), social networks (Sequeira et al., 2007), and the educational system accessed by students are all environmental antecedents of entrepreneurial intentions (Souitaris et al., 2007; Cheng et al., 2009; Matlay et al., 2010). The findings of the previous studies were a few and results were fragmented and unclear. Thus, the present study proposes the following hypotheses:

H5. Institutional environment dimension of environmental factor does not vary significantly between boys' and girls' mean scores.
H6. Economic resource dimension of environmental factor does not vary significantly between boys' and girls mean scores.
H7. Overall environmental factor does not vary significantly between boys' and girls' mean scores.

METHODOLOGY

Sampling and Data Collection

Engineering undergraduates were selected as respondents in the present study. Those students who are enrolled in 3rd or 4th year of their technical programme in different technical institutes of Chhattisgarh state were only included in the study. Stratified random sampling were chosen to collect primary responses. About 1245 questionnaires were sent to participants, in which 1000 responses were found usable (approximately 80.32% response rate) as shown in the Table 1. The data was collected between November 2019 to March 2020.

Table 1. Description of primary data

Gender		Locality		Institutional Type		Total
Male	Female	Rural	Urban	Private Institution	Govt. Institution	
571	429	434	566	764	236	1000

Research Instrument

Authors adopted the scientific way of developing questionnaire for the study. Firstly, authors adopted/ modified the five-construct taken from the previous studies as per the present research objectives, and then, translated into regional official language (i.e., Hindi) to improve understanding about the subject matter. Secondly, it was sent to four subject experts to get valuable insights. The subject experts suggested few minor corrections in the items. Finally, to check the content validity and comprehensiveness, pilot study was administered using 50 respondents, which resulted no modification after responses. Thus, the final 17-item questionnaire were finalised to collect primary responses. It contains parental role model (2 items self-structured), cultural role (5 items from Diaz-Casero et al. (2012)), family support (2 items from Gelaidan & Abdullateef (2017)), institutional environment (5 items from Schwarz et al. (2009)), and economic resource (3 items from Kickul & D'Intino (2005)).

Reliability and Validity Measures

Confirmatory factor analysis was run to test the reliability and validity of the primary data. Factors' Reliability are measured through Cronbach's alpha and Rho A, whose value must be greater than 0.7 for all the variables. Table 1 explains that all the variables possess higher than the required value in Cronbach's alpha and Rho A. Similarly, Factors' validity is measured via composite reliability (must be CR>0.7), average variance extracted (must be AVE> 0.5) and discriminant validity (must be >0.5). Table 2 and 3 indicates the results of all the variables where each variable possesses higher value than the required.

Table 2. Measurement results

	Cronbach's Alpha	Rho A	Composite Reliability (CR)	Average Variance Extracted (AVE)
Cultural Factor	0.833	0.864	0.880	0.596
Economic Resource	0.800	0.864	0.878	0.706
Family Support	0.771	0.773	0.859	0.753
Institutional Environment	0.823	0.843	0.875	0.583
Parental Role Model	0.758	0.723	0.728	0.588

Table 3. Discriminant validity (Fornell-Larcker Criterion)

	Cultural Factor	Economic Resource	Family Support	Institutional Environment	Parental Role Model
Cultural Factor	0.772				
Economic Resource	0.554	0.840			
Family Support	0.663	0.551	0.867		
Institutional Environment	0.633	0.694	0.672	0.763	
Parental Role Model	0.564	0.419	0.411	0.480	0.767

ANALYSIS AND OBSERVATION

The present study applied independent t-test to examine the impact of social and environmental factor among engineering undergraduates.

Parental Role Model (Testing of H1)

Table 4. t-test of parental role model as per gender of undergraduates

Variable	Group	N	Mean	T	df	p-value	Significance
Parental Role Model	Girls	571	10.171	1.485	998	$p > 0.05$	Not Significant
	Boys	429	10.412				

It is observed from the Table 4 that girls (N= 571) and boys (N= 429) have a difference in the mean score for the parental role model construct of the social factor dimension. The mean score of boys (M = 10.412) was higher than that of girls (M = 10.171). The mean score of boys' and girls' differences is statistically insignificant, t (998) = 1.485, $p > 0.05$. Therefore, it can be inferred that the mean score on parental role model dimension of the social factor is not significantly different for boys and girls.

Cultural Role (Testing of H2)

Table 5. t-test of cultural role as per gender of undergraduate students

Variable	Group	N	Mean	t	df	p-value	Significance
Cultural Role	Girls	571	24.047	6.582	998	$p < 0.01$	Significant
	Boys	429	26.540				

It is observed from the Table 5 that girls (N= 571) and boys (N= 429) have a difference in the mean score for cultural role construct of social factor dimension. The mean score of boys (M =26.540) was higher than that of girls (M = 24.047). The mean score of boys' and girls' differences is statistically significant, t (998) = 6.582, $p < 0.01$. Therefore, it can be inferred that the mean score on cultural role dimension of social factor differs significantly for boys and girls.

Family Support (Testing of H3)

Table 6. t-test of family support as per gender of undergraduate students

Variable	Group	N	Mean	t	Df	p-value	Significance
Family Support	Girls	571	9.998	4.172	998	$p < 0.01$	Significant
	Boys	429	10.743				

It is observed from the Table 6 that girls (N= 571) and boys (N= 429) have a difference in the mean score for the family support construct of the social factor dimension. The mean score of boys (M =10.743) was higher than that of girls (M = 9.998). The mean score of boys' and girls' differences is statistically significant, t (998) = 4.172, $p < 0.01$. Therefore, it can be inferred that the mean score on family support dimension of social factor differs significantly for boys and girls.

Social Factor (Testing of H4)

Table 7. t-test of social factor as per gender of undergraduate students

Variable	Group	N	Mean	t	df	p-value	Significance
Social Factors	Girls	571	44.217	5.587	998	p < 0.01	Significant
	Boys	429	47.697				

It is observed from the Table 7 that girls (N= 571) and boys (N= 429) have a difference in the mean score for the social factor dimension. The mean score of boys (M =47.697) was higher than that of girls (M = 44.217). The mean score of boys' and girls' differences is statistically significant, t (998) = 5.587, $p < 0.01$. Therefore, it can be inferred that the mean score on social factors differs significantly for boys and girls.

Institutional Environment (Testing of H5)

Table 8. t-test of institutional environment as per gender of undergraduates

Variable	Group	N	Mean	t	df	p-value	Significance
Institutional Environment	Girls	571	24.262	4.323	998	p < 0.01	Significant
	Boys	429	25.934				

It is observed from the Table 8 that girls (N= 571) and boys (N= 429) have a difference in the mean score for institutional environment construct of environmental factor dimension. The mean score of boys (M = 25.934) was higher than that of girls (M = 24.262). The mean score of boys' and girls' differences is statistically significant, t (998) = 4.323, $p < 0.01$. Therefore, it can be inferred that the mean score on institutional environment dimension of environmental factor differs significantly for boys and girls.

Economic Resource (Testing of H6)

Table 9. t-test of economic resource as per gender of undergraduate students

Variable	Group	N	Mean	t	Df	p-value	Significance
Economic Resource	Girls	571	15.292	5.761	998	p < 0.01	Significant
	Boys	429	16.722				

It is observed from the Table 9 that girls (N= 571) and boys (N= 429) have a difference in the mean score for the economic resource construct of the environmental factor dimension. The mean score of boys (M = 16.722) was higher than that of girls (M = 15.292). The difference in boys' and girls' mean scores is statistically significant, $t(998) = 5.761$, $p < 0.01$. Therefore, it can be inferred that the mean score on economic resource dimension of environmental factor differs significantly for boys and girls.

Environmental Factor (Testing of H7)

Table 10. t-test of environmental factor as per gender of undergraduate students

Variable	Group	N	Mean	t	df	p-value	Significance
Environmental Factors	Girls	571	39.555	5.305	998	p < 0.01	Significant
	Boys	429	42.657				

It is observed from the Table 10 that girls (N= 571) and boys (N= 429) have differences in the mean score for the overall environmental factor dimension. The mean score of boys (M = 42.657) was higher than that of girls (M = 39.555). The difference in boys' and girls' mean scores is statistically significant, $t(998) = 5.305$, $p < 0.01$. Therefore, it can be inferred that the mean score on environmental factors differs significantly for boys and girls.

DISCUSSION

Entrepreneurs grow by solving society's challenges. Entrepreneurs can play economic, social, job creation, sports development, ecotourism, city resilience, and agricultural roles in the 21st century (Sampene et al., 2021). Entrepreneurship developments are highly required in the times where all the people are searching for jobs, and no one are even thinking of starting of new businesses. Job crisis has erupted in all the developing nations, especially in India where entrepreneurial culture could not have been developed in decades. The present study attempted to find out some root causes for the entrepreneurship development. Parental role model (H1) was found insignificant in the results which explains that parental role model is mostly unavailable in most of the families which deprives students to get essential and primary support in terms of advice, intellectual and financial support for starting up new businesses. The entrepreneurial ideas, at first, developed, accepted and run at home, and then, after a while, it gets a real shape.

Cultural role (H2) was also found statistically significant which indicates in India, national culture for entrepreneurial development is available which encourages to be more active in starting up new businesses among engineering undergraduates. Similar results were noted for family support (H3) as well, which predicts that engineering undergraduates will not hesitate to start new venture as he/she has friends and family support fully. The results of overall social factor also explain the same as significant (H4). Engineering students has positive social environment which encouraging them to be more entrepreneurial in nature and start-up new businesses.

Other than the social environment, institutional environment is also very important to discuss. In results, it was found significant (H5). Positive institutional environment encourages engineering undergraduates to be more entrepreneurial in nature and provide conducive environment to discuss different entrepreneurial aspects which offers overall knowledge about entrepreneurship among engineering undergraduates. Economic resource (H6) was also explained statistically significant which indicates that engineering undergraduates are confident in identifying new financial sources for their entrepreneurial venture. At last, overall environmental factor (H7) was also predicted statistically significant which indicates engineering undergraduates are well aware of their environment to exploit for their entrepreneurial venture.

The mean score of boys and girls for each variables indicate the significance in students' entrepreneurial behaviour. Male students were predicted to be more inclined or affected than females with the variables studied. When it comes to entrepreneurial venture, male students are more affected with societal rules and prejudices. They have more freedom with responsibilities to do something meaningful with their competencies. They always seek advices and support from their role model/ teacher/ parent at different times. These variable makes them more affected. Hence, it becomes highly imperative to address these variables separately by educational institutions and government for providing better nurturing and conducive entrepreneurial environment.

CONTRIBUTION OF THE STUDY

Engineering undergraduates has the capability to become successful entrepreneurs as the former president of India Dr. A. P. J. Abdul Kalam has stated that science and technology can pave India's way to success. The capacity to think creatively and act independently is a must for success in today's economy, and it is also essential for fighting poverty, boosting output, and fostering long-term sustainability (Aggarwal et al., 2016). It is widely known that engineering undergraduates have the better know-how of the different processes of entrepreneurial ventures which makes them the most prominent and aspiring students than the other discipline students. Thus, it became important to investigate the primary factors such as social and environmental factors influencing them to become entrepreneurs.

Since the rising unemployment has been the key issues in India. It becomes significant to discuss and promote entrepreneurship among the nascent entrepreneurs, specifically engineering undergraduates. The present study thoroughly discusses how social and environmental factors play vital role in creating entrepreneurial desire among engineering students. The study's results explain that social and environmental factors are favourable, and creating entrepreneurial nature among students, but still improved nurturing is still requiring to build better entrepreneurial culture. For instance, to encourage entrepreneurship, the All India Council of Technical Education (AICTE) has ordered all engineering colleges and technical institutions to allow the students to appear in the examination too whose attendance is short. The institutions are advised to provide on-campus accommodation to student entrepreneurs and allow students to take a semester break to work on their start-ups. The AICTE has emphasised students' work related to research and innovation and convert them into an entrepreneurial venture. This culture must be built in the institutions by transforming young students from job seekers into job givers. The institutions are also advised to award student entrepreneurs by giving academic credits to create an enterprise (Press Trust of India, 2019).

CONCLUSION

Entrepreneurs are the key to defeating unemployment. In India, millions of people are searching for jobs, and every year millions more add up. It will become worsen in the upcoming years if not addressed effectively. The present study attempts to test the social and environmental factors in creating entrepreneurial temperament among engineering undergraduates. Engineering undergraduates enrolled in 3rd and 4th year of their engineering programme were included as participants in the present study. About 1000 responses were collected and analysed. The authors found that social and environmental factors are very essential in creating positive entrepreneurial behaviour among students. Parental role model was not found significant which explain that mostly parents have not persuaded entrepreneurial activity, thus they could not guide or advice anything to their children. Hence, the educational institutions and government should engage in creating more conducive and positive environment for entrepreneurship.

ACKNOWLEDGMENT

This research is a part of a Minor ICSSR project (File No. IMPRESS/ P42/ 85/ 18-19/ ICSSR dated 20.03.2019), financed by the Indian Council for Social Science Research (ICSSR), New Delhi. The authors would like to express their gratitude to ICSSR, New Delhi for their assistance in funding and other aspects of the study.

REFERENCES

Alnafrah, I., Bogdanova, E., & Maximova, T. (2019). Text Mining as a Facilitating Tool for Deploying Blockchain Technology in the Intellectual Property Rights System. *International Journal of Intellectual Property Management*, *9*(2), 120–135. doi:10.1504/IJIPM.2019.100207

Altinay, L., Madanoglu, M., Daniele, R., & Lashley, C. (2012). The influence of family tradition and psychological traits on entrepreneurial intention. *International Journal of Hospitality Management*, *31*(2), 489–499. doi:10.1016/j.ijhm.2011.07.007

Autio, E. H., Keeley, R., Klofsten, M. G. C., Parker, G., & Hay, M. (2001). Entrepreneurial intent among students in Scandinavia and in the USA. *Enterprise and Innovation Management Studies*, *2*(2), 145–160. doi:10.1080/14632440110094632

Bakar, R., Islam, M. A., & Lee, J. (2015). Entrepreneurship Education: Experiences in Selected Countries. *International Education Studies*, *8*(1), 88–99. doi:10.5539/ies.v8n1p88

Bhagchandani, R. (2017). *How India can up its startup game by bolstering student entrepreneurship*. Your Story. https://yourstory.com/2017/01/india-startup-game-bolstering-student-entrepreneurship

Birley, S. (1985). The role of networks in the entrepreneurial process. *Journal of Business Venturing*, *1*(1), 107–117. doi:10.1016/0883-9026(85)90010-2

Chaudhary, A. (2018). *Why it is important to create and foster entrepreneurial mindset in India's high school students*. Your Story. https://yourstory.com/2018/02/entrepreneurship-mindset-high-school-students? utm _ pageloadtype = scroll

Cheng, M. Y., Chan, W. S., & Mahmood, A. (2009). The effectiveness of entrepreneurship education in Malaysia. *Education + Training*, *51*(7), 555–566. doi:10.1108/00400910910992754

Dabo, S. A. (2018). Critical Thinking in Entrepreneurship and Youth Attitudes towards Entrepreneurial Skill Acquisition in Plateau State, Nigeria. *International Journal of Scientific Research*. doi:10.21275/ART20203836

Devonish, D., Alleyne, P., Soverall, W. C., Marshall, A. Y., & Pounder, P. (2010). Explaining Entrepreneurial Intentions in the Caribbean. *International Journal of Entrepreneurial Behaviour & Research*, *16*(2), 149–171. doi:10.1108/13552551011027020

Do Paco, A., Ferreira, J., Raposo, M., Rodrigues, R., & Dinis, A. (2011). Entrepreneurial intention among secondary students: Findings from Portugal. *International Journal of Entrepreneurship and Small Business*, *13*(1), 92–106. doi:10.1504/IJESB.2011.040418

Dubini, P., & Aldrich, H. (1991). Personal and extended networks are central to the entrepreneurial process. *Journal of Business Venturing*, *6*(5), 305–313. doi:10.1016/0883-9026(91)90021-5

Engle, R. L., Dimitriadi, N., Gavidia, J. V., Schlaegel, C., Delanoe, S., Alvarado, I., He, X., Buame, S., & Wolff, B. (2010). Entrepreneurial intent. *International Journal of Entrepreneurial Behaviour & Research*, *16*(1), 35–37. doi:10.1108/13552551011020063

Fini, R., Grimaldi, R., Marzocchi, G. L., & Sobrero, M. (2009). The Foundation of Entrepreneurial Intention. *Conference proceedings in Summer Conference, 6,* 17-19.

Franco, M., Haase, H., & Lautenschläger, A. (2010). Students' Entrepreneurial Intentions: An Inter-Regional Comparison. *Education + Training*, *52*(4), 260–275. doi:10.1108/00400911011050945

Gelaidan, H. M., & Abdullateef, A. O. (2017). Entrepreneurial intentions of business students in Malaysia: The role of self-confidence, educational and relation support. *Journal of Small Business and Enterprise Development*, *24*(1), 54–67. doi:10.1108/JSBED-06-2016-0078

Greve, A., & Salaff, J. W. (2003). Social networks and entrepreneurship. *Entrepreneurship Theory and Practice*, *28*(1), 1–22. doi:10.1111/1540-8520.00029

Harris, M. L., Gibson, S. G., & Taylor, S. R. (2007). Examining the impact of small business institute participation on entrepreneurial attitudes. *Journal of Small Business Strategy*, *18*(2), 57–76.

Higgins, M. C. (2001). Changing careers: The effects of social context. *Journal of Organizational Behavior: The International Journal of Industrial. Occupational and Organizational Psychology and Behavior*, *22*(6), 595–618. doi:10.1002/job.104

Höflinger, P. J., Nagel, C., & Sandner, P. (2018). Reputation for Technological Innovation: Does It Actually Cohere with Innovative Activity? *Suma de Negocios*, *3*(1), 26–39. doi:10.1016/j.jik.2017.08.002

Kickul, J., & D'Intino, R. S. (2005). *Measure for measure: modeling entrepreneurial self-efficacy onto instrumental tasks within the new venture creation process*. New England Journal of Entrepreneurship.

Kristiansen, S., & Indarti, N. (2004). Entrepreneurial intention among Indonesian and Norwegian students. *Journal of Enterprising Culture*, *12*(01), 55–78. doi:10.1142/S021849580400004X

Light, A. N., & Siegel, J. I. (2008). The social dimensions of entrepreneurship. In M. Casson, B. Yeing, A. Basu, & N. Wadeson (Eds.), *The Oxford Handbook of Entrepreneurship*. Oxford University Press.

Lin, F.-J., & Lai, C. (2021). Key Factors Affecting Technological Capabilities in Small and Medium-Sized Enterprises in Taiwan. *The International Entrepreneurship and Management Journal*, *17*(1), 131–143. doi:10.100711365-019-00632-2

Linan, F., & Chen, Y. W. (2009). Development and cross–cultural application of a specific instrument to measure entrepreneurial intentions. *Entrepreneurship Theory and Practice*, *33*(3), 593–617. doi:10.1111/j.1540-6520.2009.00318.x

Luthje, C., & Franke, N. (2003). The 'making'of an entrepreneur: Testing a model of entrepreneurial intent among engineering students at MIT. *Research Management*, *33*(2), 135–147.

Maranda, M.F., & Comeau, Y. (2000). Some contributions of sociology to the understanding of career. *The future of career*, 37-52.

Matlay, H., Packham, G., Jones, P., Miller, C., Pickernell, D., & Thomas, B. (2010). Attitudes towards entrepreneurship education: A comparative analysis. *Education + Training*, *52*(8/9), 568–586. doi:10.1108/00400911011088926

Moriano, J. A., Gorgievski, M., Laguna, M., Stephan, U., & Zarafshani, K. (2012). A cross-cultural approach to understanding entrepreneurial intention. *Journal of Career Development*, *39*(2), 162–185. doi:10.1177/0894845310384481

Mustafa, M. J., Hernandez, E., Mahon, C., & Chee, L. K. (2016). Entrepreneurial intentions of university students in an emerging economy: The influence of university support and proactive personality on students' entrepreneurial intention. *Journal of Entrepreneurship in Emerging Economies*.

Nabi, G., Holden, R., & Birdthistle, N. (2008). An examination of tertiary students' desire to found an enterprise. *Education + Training*, *50*(7), 552–567. doi:10.1108/00400910810909027

Nanda, R., & Sorensen, J. (2009). Workplace Peers and Entrepreneurship. *Harvard Business School Entrepreneurial Management* (08-051).

Ozen Kutanis, R., Bayraktaroglu, S., & Bozkurt, O. (2006). Is the personality features important in entrepreneurial orientation and experience? In *14th National Management and Organization Congress Proceedings.* Ataturk University.

Pandey, K. (2019). India's Unemployment Rate Doubled in Two Years: SoE in Figures. *Down to Earth.* https://www.downtoearth.org.in/news/economy/india-s-unemployment-ratedoubled-in -two-years-soe-in-figures-64953

Postigo, S., Iacobucci, D., & Tamborini, M. F. (2006). Undergraduate students as a source of potential entrepreneurs: a comparative study between Italy and Argentina. *International entrepreneurship education: Issues and Newness,* 218-240.

Rao, V. (2017). *Can Student Entrepreneurship be the answer to India's Jobless-growth problem?* Your Story. https://yourstory.com/2017/07/student-entrepreneurship-sv-co

Roberts, L. P., & Robinson, P. B. (2010). Home-based entrepreneurs, commercial entrepreneurs and white-collar workers: A comparative study of attitudes toward self-esteem, personal control and business growth. *Journal of Small Business and Entrepreneurship, 23*(3), 333–353. doi:10.1080/08276331.2010.10593489

Sampene, A. K., Li, C., Agyeman, F. O., Robert, B., Nicholas, L., Moses, S., & Salomon, A. A. (2021). A Critical Assessment of The Role of Entrepreneurship Development in the 21st Century. *European Journal of Business and Innovation Research, 9*(5), 1–26.

Savickas, M. (2002). Career construction. A developmental theory of vocational behaviour. In *Career choice and development* (pp. 149–285). Jossey-Bass.

Savickas, M. (2002). Career construction. A developmental theory of vocational behaviour. In *Career choice and development* (pp. 149–285). Jossey-Bass.

Schwarz, E. J., Wdowiak, M. A., Almer-Jarz, D. A., & Breitenecker, R. J. (2009). The effects of attitudes and perceived environment conditions on students' entrepreneurial intent An Austrian perspective. *Education + Training, 51*(4), 272–291. doi:10.1108/00400910910964566

Schwarz, E. J., Wdowiak, M. A., Almer-Jarz, D. A., & Breitenecker, R. J. (2009). The effects of attitudes and perceived environment conditions on students' entrepreneurial intent An Austrian perspective. *Education + Training*, *51*(4), 272–291. doi:10.1108/00400910910964566

Sequeira, J., Mueller, S. L., & McGee, J. E. (2007). The influence of social ties and self-efficacy in forming entrepreneurial intentions and motivating nascent behavior. *Journal of Developmental Entrepreneurship*, *12*(03), 275–293. doi:10.1142/S108494670700068X

Sergeant, J., & Crawford, J. (2001). *National youth entrepreneurship attitude survey*. Department of Industry, Science and Resources.

Sesen, H. (2013). Personality or environment? A comprehensive study on the entrepreneurial intentions of university students. *Education + Training*, *55*(7), 624–640. doi:10.1108/ET-05-2012-0059

Seth, S. (2021). *Why Entrepreneurship Is Important to the Economy.* Investiopedia. (https://www.investopedia.com/articles/personal-finance/101414/why-entrepreneursare-important-economy.asp)

Shook, C. L., & Bratianu, C. (2010). Entrepreneurial intent in a transitional economy: An application of the theory of planned behavior to Romanian students. *The International Entrepreneurship and Management Journal*, *6*(3), 231–247. doi:10.100711365-008-0091-2

Sommer, L., & Haug, M. (2011). Intention as a Cognitive Antecedent to International Entrepreneurship: Understanding the Moderating Roles of Knowledge and Experience. *The International Entrepreneurship and Management Journal*, *7*(1), 111–142. doi:10.100711365-010-0162-z

Souitaris, V., Zerbinati, S., & Al-Laham, A. (2007). Do entrepreneurship programmes raise entrepreneurial intention of science and engineering students? The effect of learning, inspiration and resources. *Journal of Business Venturing*, *22*(4), 566–591. doi:10.1016/j.jbusvent.2006.05.002

Urban, B. (2006). Entrepreneurship in the rainbow nation: Effect of cultural values and ESE on intentions. *Journal of Developmental Entrepreneurship*, *11*(03), 171–186. doi:10.1142/S1084946706000386

Vondracek, F.W. (1990). A developmental-contextual approach to career development research. *Methodological approaches to the study of career*, 37-56.

Young, R.A., Valach, L., & Collin, A. (2002). A contextualist explanation of career. *Career choice and development, 4*, 206-252.

Yurtkoru, E. S., Kuşcu, Z. K., & Doğanay, A. (2014). Exploring the antecedents of entrepreneurial intention on Turkish university students. *Procedia: Social and Behavioral Sciences, 150*, 841–850. doi:10.1016/j.sbspro.2014.09.093

Zampetakis, L. A., Kafetsios, K., Bouranta, N., Dewett, T., & Moustakis, V. S. (2009). On the relationship between emotional intelligence and entrepreneurial attitudes and intentions. *International Journal of Entrepreneurial Behaviour & Research, 15*(6), 595–618. doi:10.1108/13552550910995452

Zapkau, F. B., Schwens, C., Steinmetz, H., & Kabst, R. (2015). Disentangling the effect of prior entrepreneurial exposure on entrepreneurial intention. *Journal of Business Research, 68*(3), 639–653. doi:10.1016/j.jbusres.2014.08.007

Chapter 3
Current State and Prospects of Business Development in the Republic of Belarus

Albina Sibirskaya
The Institute of Economics of the National Academy of Sciences of Belarus, Belarus

ABSTRACT

The article is devoted to the problems and priorities of the development of agricultural business in the Republic of Belarus. An analysis of the state of the country's agricultural industry and its economic significance is given in detail. This chapter also considers the demographic situation in rural areas: the main problems and prospects. The article was written in order to tell the reader about the Belarusian experience of supporting agricultural businesses and its role in the Belarusian economy. The article uses the materials of the legislation and official statistics of the Republic of Belarus. The author tried not to express his personal opinion, but to describe the actual processes.

INTRODUCTION

The article is devoted to the problems and priorities of the development of agricultural business in the Republic of Belarus. An analysis of the state of the country's agricultural industry and its economic significance is given in detail. We also consider the demographic situation in rural areas: the main problems and prospects. The article was written in order to tell the

DOI: 10.4018/978-1-6684-6878-4.ch003

reader about the Belarusian experience of supporting agricultural business and its role in the Belarusian economy. The article uses the materials of the legislation and official statistics of the Republic of Belarus. The author tried not to express his personal opinion, but to describe the actual processes. The chapter is arranged in four parts – first section deals with main indicators characterizing the agricultural sector of the Republic of Belarus such as volume of agricultural production, structure of the proceeds of agricultural products, Crop area, Foreign trade in agricultural products, Index of food security etc. Second section reflects the Gender Issues in the Agro-industrial complex. Third section of the chapter discuss the problems and prospects for the development of rural business in the Republic of Belarus and lastly chapter ends with some concluding remarks.

GENERAL CHARACTERISTICS OF AGRICULTURE

One of the most significant industries in the Republic of Belarus is agriculture. Agricultural products account for about 7% of GDP, about 5% of the country's population is employed in this industry. Occupying 0.15% of the world's territory and having 0.17% of the population, it produces 6% of flax fiber, 2.8% of potatoes, 0.9% of milk, 0.6% of sugar beet, 0.3% of meat in slaughter weight and 0.24% grain and ensures food independence.

In the structure of crop production, a high proportion is occupied by grain and leguminous crops, as well as fodder crops, which is due to the specialization of agriculture in the republic, mainly in dairy and meat animal husbandry. The main grain crops are barley, rye, triticale. A special place is occupied by potatoes and flax. The main vegetable crops are carrots, beets, cabbage.

There is a high share of the cost of agricultural products in total revenue (Figure 2).

Reducing the cost of the industry is possible through the modernization of production processes, the introduction of digital technologies and production automation. This will increase the yield of crop production and the efficiency of livestock production.

There is an increase in acreage in agriculture (Figure 3).

Their expansion is noted for sugar, rapeseed, and for potatoes, cereals and legumes and vegetables - a reduction.

Figure 1. The volume of agricultural production, million rubles
Source: National Statistical Committee of the Republic of Belarus (2021).

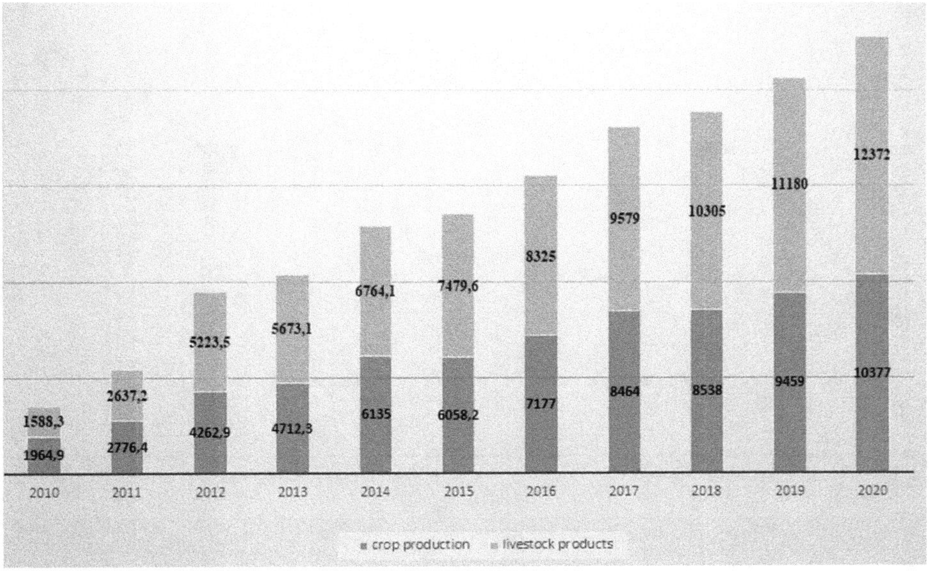

Figure 2. The structure of the proceeds of agricultural products, million rubles
Source: National Statistical Committee of the Republic of Belarus (2021).

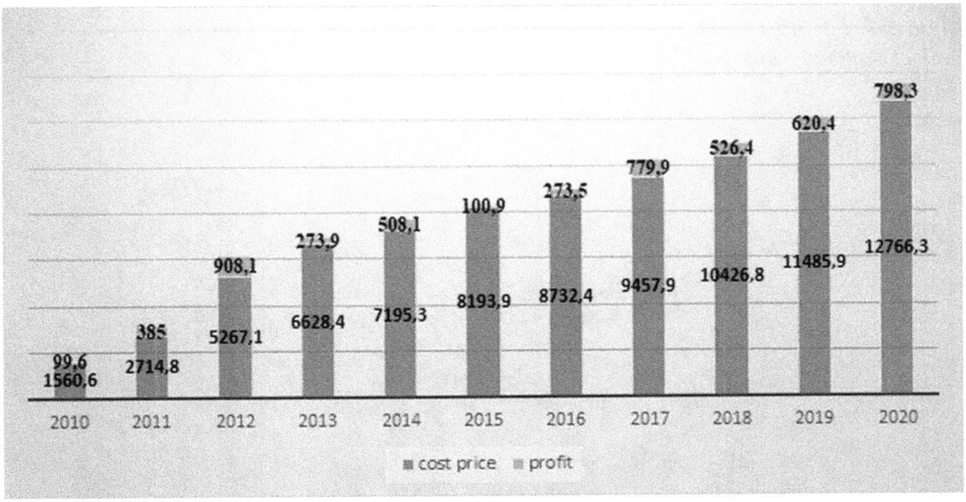

Figure 3. Crop area, thousand hectares
Source: National Statistical Committee of the Republic of Belarus (2021).

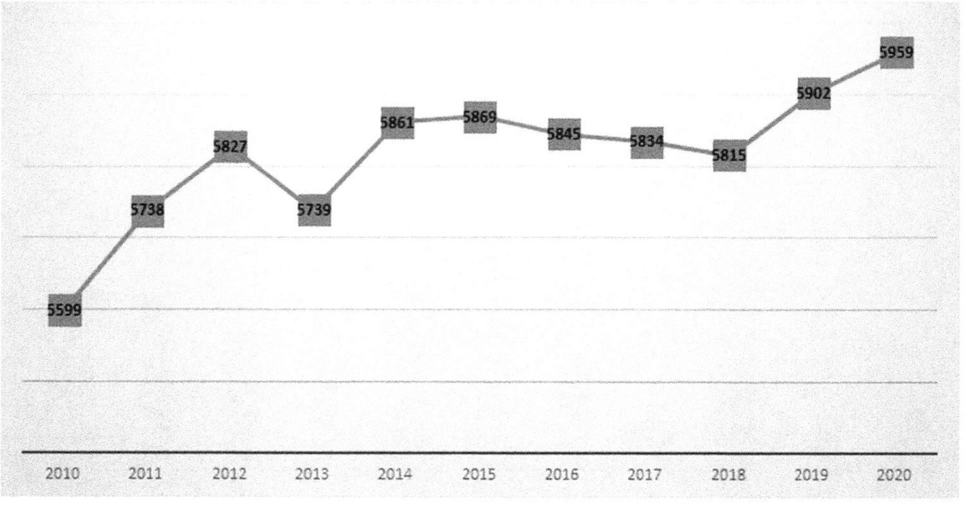

In foreign trade in agricultural products, there is a positive balance of trade with the CIS countries and a negative balance of trade with countries outside the CIS.

Figure 4. Foreign trade in agricultural products, million US dollars
Source: National Statistical Committee of the Republic of Belarus (2021).

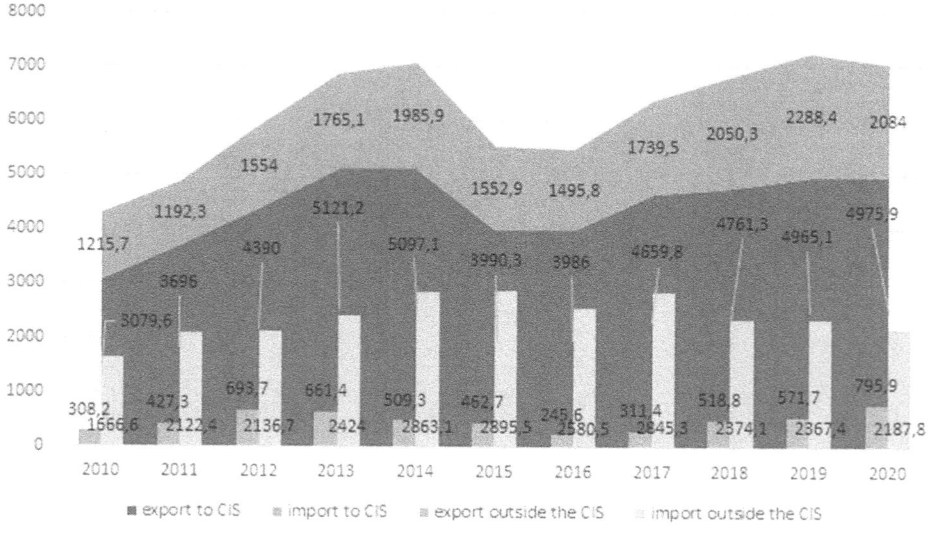

In 2020, the export of agricultural products and food products amounted to $5.8 billion, and the share of these products in the total exports of Belarus amounted to 19.9%.

The negative balance with non-CIS countries is explained by large import volumes of such imported products as frozen fish and fish products, apples and pears, apricots and peaches, cherries, bananas, tomatoes, citrus fruits, vegetable fats and oils, sunflower oil, pasta, chocolate, juices etc.

In the Republic of Belarus, food security is both a condition for the independence of the state and a factor in maintaining a favorable conjuncture of the national and regional food markets and the export orientation of the agro-industrial complex. The solution of the food problem presupposes the sustainable development of efficient agricultural production, which, in turn, requires the adoption of measures of agrarian protectionism that meets the conditions of a market economy and ensures food security.

Figure 5. Index of food security of the countries of the world
Source: National Statistical Committee of the Republic of Belarus (2021).

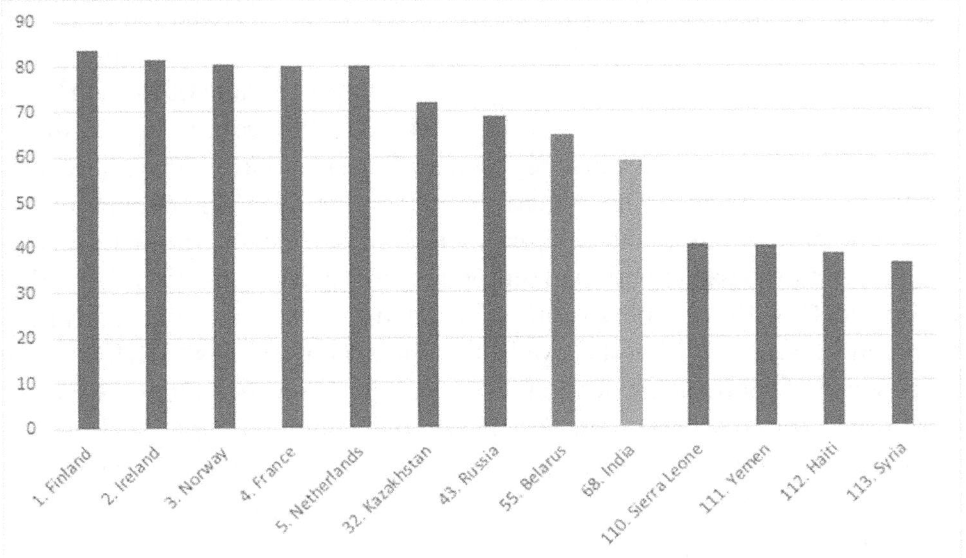

In the world ranking, the Republic of Belarus is at a fairly high level. At the same time, the republic, like all countries with economies in transition, is characterized by a number of negative trends, the overcoming of which is associated with the implementation of policies aimed at improving the quality of life.

Belarus belongs to the states with a high level of consumption (3000 - 3100 kilocalories per day), the availability of food to the population among the countries with economies in transition is the highest. The volume of food production exceeds the demand of the domestic market. Given the specialization of agriculture, as well as the sufficiency of processing organizations, the potential of the complex retains an export orientation, the implementation of which is determined by market conditions.

GENDER ISSUES IN THE AGRO-INDUSTRIAL COMPLEX

According to UN Women's Country Gender Equality Brief [CGEB] (2019) Belarus ranks 29th out of 153 nations in the 2020 World Economic Forum (WEF) Global Gender Gap Report. Belarus also outperforms the average globally in terms of women's overall economic participation and security, and it ranks first globally in terms of girls' secondary and tertiary enrollment rates as well as healthy life expectancy. All pertinent international legal instruments relating to gender equality and the empowerment of women have been signed and ratified by Belarus, and several legal structures bear witness to this dedication to equality and the absence of discrimination. The issues that remain are interconnected and primarily revolve around: the lack of stand-alone, legislative protections against all forms of gender-based discrimination; low levels of women's participation in senior decision-making positions in public and political life; the absence of consistently and completely available primary health and sexual and reproductive health rights and services (SRHRs); and the absence of robust legislative and service provisions to support women.

For the rural population, approximately the same number of living men and women of working age can be noted. At the same time, the proportion of men of working age is slightly greater. Such a proportion is optimal for agriculture, since despite the fact that in agriculture a significant share of work requires strong physical strength, while a significant share of work is performed by women. In total, 21.9% of the entire population of the country live in rural areas. Of the total number of residents in rural areas, 16.4% younger than working age, 54.2% of working age, 29.4% older than working age (men of 16–59 years old, women 16–54 years old) is considered working age in the Republic of Belarus).

Figure 6. The ratio of men and women living in rural areas, %
Source: National Statistical Committee of the Republic of Belarus (2021).

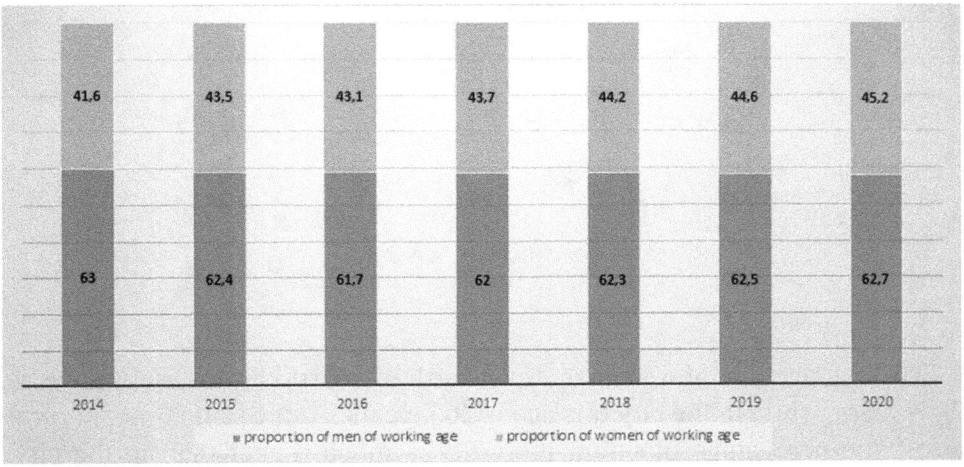

The fertility in the rural area relative to the urban population is high. The reason is a complete other rhythm of life, the lack of housing problems (all families in rural areas have their own house or a rental house provided by the state), the availability of their own economy, which eliminates the shortage of food and accessibility to environmentally friendly and healthy foods from agricultural collective farms.

However, in rural areas, as in the city, there is a problem of the birth of children outside the marriage. So for mothers of age up to 20 years, 30.1%of children are born in marriage, at the age of 20-24 years-16.5%, at the age of 25-29 years-14.1%, at the age of 30-34 years-19% . Dahla with an increase in the age of the woman in labor increases the share of registered marriages. So, at the age of 35-39, 23.5% of women give birth in a marriage, at the age of 40-44-29.4% of women, aged 45-49 years-56.3%.

This trend is explained by the fact that a woman after 35 years old gives birth to a child consciously and planned. Most often, this is not the first child, and both parents take part in his planning.

Figure 7. The number of children born in rural areas to a mother aged
Source: National Statistical Committee of the Republic of Belarus (2021).

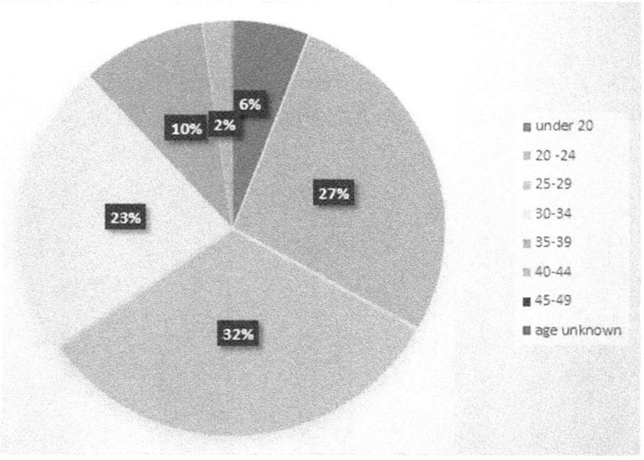

The average age of a woman at the birth of a first child in rural areas is 24.8 years, while in the city this age is 26.9 years. At the same time, in rural areas, the percentage of infant mortality is much higher than in the city. So, per 1000 people born in rural areas account for 3.6 girls who died in infancy (in the city the indicator is 2.8) and 5.2 dead in infancy (in the city - 2.8). These statistics indicate that the level of health and the protection of motherhood and childhood in rural areas is much lower than in the city. Not every village has a hospital or clinic. There is a paramedic office with one general practitioner on duty. In severe cases, patients are taken to another village or to the city. The lower level of healthcare is also reflected in the average life expectancy of a woman in rural areas - 77.0 years, while in the city this indicator reaches 79.9 years.

It is worth noting positive trends in rural areas. For 1000 people in the village there are 5.2 marriage and 1.9 divorces are recorded (in the city these indicators are 7.5 and 3.8, respectively). In rural areas, life is more stable, measured and without a sharp innovative development, therefore, divorces occur only in extreme cases when life together is impossible. At the same time, the average age for the first-time marriage in rural areas and in the city is the same (25.1 years and 25.9 years, respectively). In repeated marriage in the village, on average (39.6 years) enters the village than in the city (37.7 years).

It is also worth noting the lower coverage of the Internet of residents of rural areas (Figure 8).

Figure 8. Internet users, percent of total population of corresponding group
Source: National Statistical Committee of the Republic of Belarus (2021).

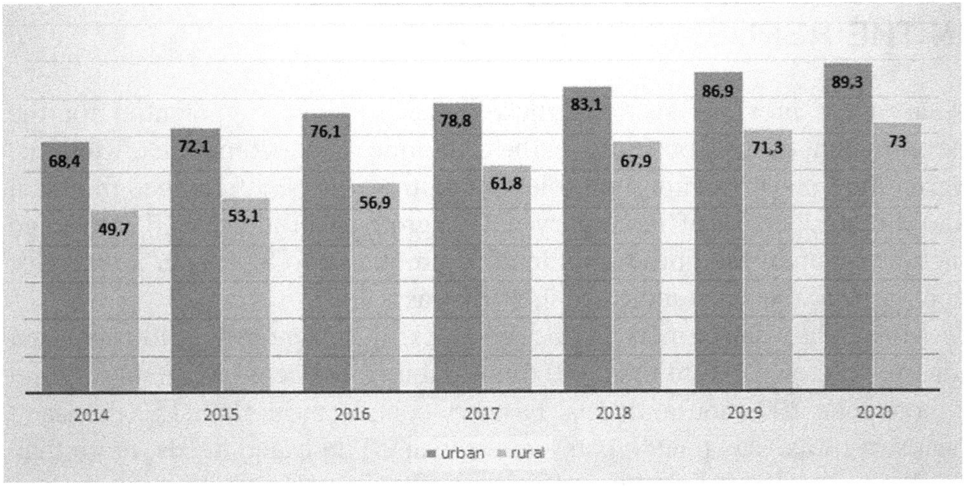

In 2020, 73% of rural residents and 89.3% of the urban population were covered by Internet technologies. For 7 years, the indicator has a stable growth trend. In rural schools, as well as in urban, computer classes are equipped with modern equipment.

Despite the existing problems in rural areas, it is worth noting that in general, the standard of living of the rural population is worthy, albeit slightly lower than the standard of living of the urban population.

Working women rural areas have their own social protection in the form of a trade union association and other public organizations. The largest public association of women is the Belarusian Union of Women, whose members are more than 141 thousand women (more than 4,200 organizations). Under the Union, the Selchanka organization operates, uniting rural women from the regions of Belarus.

The main objectives of the Selchanka organization are to protect the rights and legitimate interests of women, to ensure a worthy position of a woman in society, to increase her role in society, the promotion of women at the level of decision -making, the introduction and implementation of the principles of gender equality in society.

PROBLEMS AND PROSPECTS FOR THE DEVELOPMENT OF RURAL BUSINESS IN THE REPUBLIC OF BELARUS

Analysis of previous sections showed the presence of potential for the development of rural business. In the economies of the Republic of Belarus, agriculture plays an important role. In addition, the beneficial geographical and climatic location of the country makes agrotourism attractive. The average income of small food producers in 2021 amounted to $ 901 per month (for comparison: the same indicator in 2018 was $ 733).

Most Belarusian farmers produce potatoes: in 2021 more than 400 thousand tons were grown. More than 350 thousand tons collected vegetables, grain - more than 200 thousand tons. Farmers contain more than 150 thousand heads of birds, sheep and goats - more than 20 thousand heads, more than 25 thousand heads of cattle.

The country has developed a state program "Development of agricultural business in the Republic of Belarus for 2021–2025". This program is aimed at increasing the efficiency of agricultural production and sales, as well as the competitiveness of agricultural products and food, providing the domestic market for domestic agricultural products and food in the necessary volumes and appropriate quality based on the formation of market mechanisms for managing and developing the agricultural business.

Over five years, it is planned to increase production efficiency, strengthen the raw material base of the agricultural sector, carry out digitalization of industries, etc. According to the Ministry of Agriculture, in January-November 2020, the sales was 5.7%.

Independent subprograms, such as the development of industries of crop production and animal husbandry, processing and implementing various types of products of these industries, the creation and development of industries for the processing of local types of raw materials and secondary food industry products, are also relevant in resolving the further development of the food system. Important from the point of view of the modernization of the agro -industrial complex and its sustainable development are subprograms of further technical re -equipment and improvement of informatization of agro -industrial production, engineering antipartign measures, preservation and use of lemon balm.

For entrepreneurs in rural areas, favorable preferential conditions were created (*Rural Communities*, n.d.). In accordance with Belarus President Decree No. 9 "Regulation of business operations in rural areas" of December 20, 2007, businesses who operate in rural communities are given preferences. Organizations (including their branches, representative offices, and other independent corporate entities) and self-employed business people who operate in rural areas are entitled to unique taxation procedures, as well as the issuing of special permissions and the ability to modify them. Also, investments in particular sectors of the economy as well as investments in the growth of small and medium-sized firms are given preference under Belarusian legislation. Government guarantees are frequently utilised to obtain overseas loan lines (*Government of the Republic of Belarus*, 2005). For instance, Belarus implements investment projects using loans from banks in Germany, Italy, China, as well as the International Bank for Reconstruction and Development.

So, for example, an agricultural business has a number of tax benefits:

1. Exemption from VAT in terms of revolutions from the sale of goods (works, services) arising from the prefunded activity;
2. Income tax at a rate of 6% in terms of profit from the sale of goods (works, services) received from preferential activities instead of the general public rate of 18%;
3. Income tax for individual entrepreneurs is paid at a rate of 6% of income received from the beneficial activity and reduced by the amount of tax deductions instead of 13%.

The revenue from the implementation received in the implementation of this activity is exempt from the surcharge of a single tax.

Since 09/27/2017, in rural areas, the trade in alcoholic beverages was simplified - subject to other restrictions in the field of turnover of alcoholic beverages established by law. Organizations can carry out retail trade in alcoholic beverages:

- in stores and (or) pavilions located on the territory of rural areas with a trading area of less than 50 sq.m;
- using the auto -territory of car carpets, regardless of the presence of a store and (or) a pavilion in this legal entity, in which the retail trade in alcoholic beverages is carried out.

It should be noted that in general, the retail trade in alcoholic beverages in stores and pavilions with a trading hall with an area of less than 50 square meters, as well as trading in alcoholic beverages using a car shop without a stationary trading facility with such trade.

It is noted that the implementation of state programs will allow by 2026 to ensure the profitability of sales in agriculture at at least 10%. Submitted to the target volumes of agricultural production and favorable price conditions, the growth in food export and agricultural raw materials in 2025 is predicted to $ 7 billion (21.3% by 2020).

The proposed complex of organizational and economic measures, implemented both at the level of the producers themselves and at the macroeconomic level, will contribute to the stabilization and increase in the efficiency of the agricultural sector. We are talking about financial improvement, price and credit policy, investing and building new production facilities, optimizing the costs of agricultural products in order to reduce its cost.

At the same time, effective measures have been developed to optimize the institutional structure of the Republican Agro-Food market, create a favorable environment for the development of entrepreneurship, increase the investment attractiveness of agribusiness, and the development of public-private partnerships.

CONCLUSION

Belarusian agricultural producers to achieve marketing goals, first of all, need to develop marketing strategies using the following tools: determining the targeted market segment, positioning of the company and goods on the market, and in accordance with this - the formation of three interconnected elements: development of an adequate marketing complex, strategic planning and resolving investment issues. The only criterion for evaluating the effectiveness of marketing strategies is a satisfied consumer, which will be indicated by sales and growth of market share.

From the point of view of tactics, first of all, it is advisable to focus on the formation of a unique corporate identity of the producer and actively work on the creation of a strong corporate brand. Here, the fame, recognition and popularity of the product is of particular importance.

REFERENCES

Government of the Republic of Belarus. (2005). *State Program for the Revitalization and Development of Rural Areas, 2005-2010*. Government of the Republic of Belarus.

Ministry of Agriculture and Food of the Republic of Belarus. (2008): Agropromyshlenny complex (Agro-Industrial sector). Minsk.

Minsk. (2021). *National Statistical Committee of the Republic of Belarus*. Statistical book, Agriculture of the Republic of Belarus, Minsk

Rural Communities. (n.d.). Ministry of Economy of Belarus.https://economy.gov.by/en/selo-en/

UN. (2019). *Women's Country Gender Equality Brief (CGEB)*. UN.

ADDITIONAL READING

Nivievskyi, O., Cramon-Taubadel, S., Grueninger, M., & Prikhodko, D. (2009). *Belarus: Boosting agricultural productivity and competitiveness*. Options and Impact of State Support.

World Bank. (2005). *Belarus: Window of Opportunity to Enhance Competitiveness and Sustain Economic Growth – A Country Economic Memorandum for the Republic of Belarus. Report No. 32346-BY*. World Bank.

Chapter 4
Technopreneurship and Industry 5.0:
Promoting Equity and Diversity in Rural Areas

Shashi Bala
V.V. Giri National Labour Institute, India

Rinki Arora
V.V. Giri National Labour Institute, India

ABSTRACT

A recent digital paradigm shift in all sectors has resulted in amalgamating with it. It is witnessed that the business environment is shifting towards self-employment. Worldwide efforts are made to promote entrepreneurship which is also driven by intensive technological advancements. Entrepreneurship, in general, can be defined as the creation of value apparently by deviating from pre-existing business patterns and practices. In recent times, technology and its application have played an impactful role in entrepreneurship and there exists a strong relationship between the two. "Industry 5.0" refers to those who interact with robots and intelligent machines. It includes integrating cutting-edge technology, such as the internet of things (IoT) and big data, to allow robots to help people work more swiftly and efficiently. It adds a more personal touch to the efficiency and automation cornerstones of Industry 4.0.

DOI: 10.4018/978-1-6684-6878-4.ch004

INTRODUCTION

The virtual world continues to grow increasingly real. It is conventional to say we live in a "digital age," but there is no denying that the internet and social media have changed the way we communicate. This reliance on digital tools pervades the commercial world as well. The pandemic has intensified online purchasing habits, and many firms rely on Software as a Service (SaaS)[1] and Platform as a Service (PaaS)[2] to keep their operations running smoothly. This reliance on technology opens new options for entrepreneurs. As a result of this shift, a new kind of entrepreneur has emerged: the Techpreneur or Technopreneur. A new breed of entrepreneurship is technopreneurship. It entails bringing together people who are knowledgeable, motivated, inventive, tech-savvy, passionate, and willing to take measured risks. Technopreneurship is the confluence of technological advances and entrepreneurial abilities. From Facebook to Google, Skype to Snapchat, tech entrepreneurs have nurtured new methods of creating value and doing business while also launching totally new industries.

This research seeks to shed light on the conceptual framework of Technopreneurship. It will bring out to the fore a connection between technology, innovation, and entrepreneurship in rural areas. A noteworthy aspect about a prosperous nation is to have an enthusiastic entrepreneurial base brimming with ideas, creativity and business acumen which is likely to promote the activities of Self-Help Groups (SHGs). This study focuses on the need for adopting Technopreneurship to contribute towards societal development, thereby building inter-relationships between the different business sectors. It will also help in understanding the interdependence of technopreneurship and innovation thus resulting in equity and need for adopting to diversity. This chapter tries to identify the numerous issues and difficulties that rural entrepreneurship may face. It focuses on the main issues that rural business owners encounter.

LITERATURE REVIEW

Post liberalization, India has witnessed a rise in the number of innovative and entrepreneurial companies, notably in the technology sector. The improvement of India's economy's sustainable competitiveness depends on technology-focused developments. India is currently experiencing a boom in inclusive innovation through social entrepreneurs. However, because neither the banking system nor the microfinance industry are willing or able to finance them, these entrepreneurs suffer from a shortage of funding. To close this gap, nevertheless, innovative financial initiatives have recently emerged. The increasing alternative finance initiatives that are establishing an ecosystem of support for inclusive innovation and social entrepreneurship are discussed in this study. The study specifically addresses the usage of two instruments business incubation and venture capital in traditional innovation assistance (Sonne, 2012).

Entrepreneurship is a key goal of education and lifelong learning policy in the European community. For vocational graduates, the entrepreneurship educations in higher and vocational education promote entrepreneurial competences, enterprising conduct, and employability. Graduates with an entrepreneurship major are more likely to launch new enterprises and have stronger entrepreneurial goals than other graduates since entrepreneurship is now a subject that is frequently taught in universities and business schools. In vocational schools, a variety of factors have an impact on students' entrepreneurial thinking and attitudes. A critical analysis of the entrepreneurship education literature revealed some underlying definitional, conceptual, and contextual problems with this field of study. A new study would provide a reasonable and pertinent standard to assess and guide the advancement of entrepreneurship (Harlanu & Nugroho, 2015).

When applied to the learning process at Vocational Education and Training (VET), the design of the learning entrepreneurship model creates syntax or phases that are analogous to those used in other public higher education institutions. Discovering Issues, Needs Analysis, and Learning Analysis are the first three stages of the syntactic or production-based learning phases that were incorporated into the Technopreneurship Scientific Learning paradigm. The paradigm further comprises of using a collaborative approach to scientific entrepreneurship; creating a business plan; creating the product (a prototype of a good or service); and assessing the work. To meet the needs of Vocational Education and Training (VET) and other public higher education, a different model of learning entrepreneurship has been developed called the Technopreneurship Scientific Learning model. Also, the student can study entrepreneurship and identify the entrepreneurial character thanks to the Technopreneurship Scientific Learning Model. The Technopreneurship Scientific Learning model is also suggested as a means of fostering higher order thinking abilities. Entrepreneurship programmes can assist students in becoming ready for life beyond college and developing a strong work ethic (Hidayat et al., 2018).

The first industrial revolution made use of water and steam to mechanize manufacturing, the second made use of electricity to develop mass production, and the third made use of electronic and informational technologies to automate production. The third industrial revolution and the enormous amount of computer information it produced, which led to a digital revolution, provide the foundation for the fourth industrial revolution (4IR), also known as Industry 4.0. The technological possibilities have grown exponentially throughout this fourth revolution. Digital technologies are causing a significant change in the way we conduct business by obfuscating the distinctions between the physical, chemical, and biological spheres and utterly uprooting entire businesses around the world. These modifications have had remarkable effects on the production, management, and governance systems (Iqbal, Arti, Badar & Yadav, 2021).

Masenya (2021) in her paper titled Technopreneurship Development: Digital Strategy for Youth Self-Employment in the Digital Economy discusses Theory U which focuses on taking actions based on the future. The actions are implemented using creative and agile methodologies that result in organizational changes that too at a global level. The study has also highlighted few reasons such as inadequate funding to support young technopreneurs, weak ties between stakeholders, a lack of awareness of available opportunities, a lack of infrastructure, and a lack of suitable mentors and role models which curtail the technopreneurship development. Focusing on the theoretical framework where the study has emphasized on growth of successful technopreneurship.

In the study titled "Factors Influencing Intention towards Technopreneurship," focused on university students which found that individual Entrepreneurial Orientation (EO) and self-efficacy, such as computer and internet skills, had a favorable and significant impact on intentions towards technopreneurship. The report added that government and Higher Learning Institutions (HLIs) will need to put up further effort in the future to foster competitive technopreneurship. For example, HLIs and the government might implement non-traditional technopreneurship curricula, upgrade technological infrastructure, create a friendly business environment, and subsidize technopreneurship. There are two things that this study contributes, firstly it tested the effects of self-efficacy and individual EO on intentions towards technopreneurship by literally combining the two ideas. Practically speaking, it clarified university students' intentions towards technopreneurship and offered recommendations to HLIs and the government for the growth of technopreneurship, particularly in the post-COVID-19 age (Koe,2021).

Research Methodology

This study on *Technopreneurship and Industry 5.0 – Promoting Equity and Diversity in rural areas* is descriptive in nature and the primary focus is on description with lesser emphasis on examining correlations or associations. A comprehensive literature review is used in this study to determine the complete breadth, range, and nature of the available literature on this issue. It aims to explain a scenario, problem, phenomena in a systematic manner, disseminating information and describing views pertaining to Technopreneurship. By reviewing secondary data sources, the study would employ qualitative methodologies *viz.* case study method.

Research Questions

The following questions are the focus of the research study:

1. To gain a comprehensive view of the technopreneurship prospects in rural India
2. What elements influence the commercialization of recently created goods or technologies in Small and Medium Scale Enterprises?
3. To understand the relationship between skill, youth, technology, and entrepreneurship

These research questions have been discussed in detail in the coming sub sections in a sequential manner.

Technopreneurship: Meaning and Definition

The seed era of Technopreneurship dates to the 1970s, however it was initially used in 1987 but gained popularity during the second millennium owing to the widespread use of the internet (Kollmann, et al., 2022). Technopreneurship as the name suggests is a combination of two words technology and entrepreneur. Further, to simply put it refers to entrepreneurs in the technology sector. Technopreneurship business concepts are essential for advancing the integration of technology and human growth. It falls within the category of technological entrepreneurship. It requires an individual to be tech-savvy, imaginative and risk tolerant. A technopreneur needs to concentrate on a few key areas. It might include the information and technology (IT) industry, electronics, biotechnology, high-tech items, the use of technology to provide important services, and service businesses whose main goal is technology. The technopreneur of today is more inclined towards launching their company with little more than a brainstorming idea. They take into consideration the present scenario and explore certain novel suggestions that enable in doing things differently. Consequently, it can be said that technopreneurship is all about developing a product or solution that incorporates technological advancements to help change the way people are currently doing things in a conventional manner.

A technopreneur, as opposed to merely networking and selecting market demographic, will leverage technology as a key component of successful product development. They referred to the technopreneur as a technology-based "Modern Entrepreneur." They heavily rely on innovation and creativity to create superior products, which serves as the foundation for the country's knowledge-based economic development (Joshua, Swastika, & Primakara, 2016). Since the global epidemic began, people have developed an interest in technology and its uses. This is motivating aspiring entrepreneurs to launch innovative tech enterprises when the market demands them. As a result, investors are more likely to support tech-based businesses since they provide a higher rate of return.

Technology, innovation, and entrepreneurship are all topics that are now of interest to both theorists (as members of the academic and research community) and practitioners (as businesspeople and decision-makers at all levels), each of which has a reasonably clearly defined field of study. This essay explored the idea of technopreneurship as a point of intersection and multidisciplinary field of study for innovation, technology, and entrepreneurship. The idea naturally develops because of the development trends. The author, however, favors entrepreneurship (technology-based entrepreneurship). Entrepreneurial networks, intellectual entrepreneurship, social entrepreneurship, and entrepreneurship infrastructure are some of the more recent fields of study in this field. The article also stimulated conversation around the recently coined word "Technopreneurship," as well as even more recent ideas like "Technowledge," or "technology knowledge," and "Technowledgepreneurship" (technology knowledge entrepreneurship). The study analysed the themes surrounding entrepreneurship and is primarily conceptual in nature. It is based on a comprehensive literature review, and the conversation it sparks may be crucial for both academics and businesspeople (Scarlat, 2014).

In the simplest terms, Technopreneurship can be defined as a type of entrepreneurship that emphasises on technology. Technopreneurship is an amalgamation of technical competence with entrepreneurial talent and skills.

Comparative Analysis Between Entrepreneurs and Technopreneurs

Table 1. Comparative analysis between entrepreneurs and technopreneurs

Extracted from	Entrepreneurs	Technopreneurs
Barot (2015)	Entrepreneurship is derived from the French word Entreprendre and the German word entrenchment. An entrepreneur is imaginative and has a vision and goals.	A technopreneur is creative and has a larger vision.
Abbas (2018)	Entrepreneurs focus their attention on the possibility of success rather than the possibility of failure. The focus is majorly on the profits.	Technopreneurs tend to align more towards a visionary approach.
Diandra & Azmy (2020)	Finds a business idea, develops it into a product or service, estimates earnings and profits, and uses it to start a profitable operation.	Face difficulties and norms with courage to develop systems. Creative thinking and doing things differently, with nothing more than a "thought" as a starting point.

Role of Technopreneurs in Rural India

This section aims at answering the first two research question related to attaining a comprehensive view of the technopreneurship prospects in rural India and what elements influence the commercialization of recently created goods or technologies in Small and Medium Scale Enterprises?

Most people in India live in rural areas, where they depend on agriculture and other secondary services for their living. Except for the landowners and large zamindars, these individuals have extremely poor salaries. On the other side, the urban population makes more money because of its entrepreneurial drive. In case of the rural population, there is a dearth of entrepreneurship development.

In "Entrepreneurship as a strategic development intervention to accelerate rural development: the case of Drishtee. Asia Pacific Business Review," discusses case details for the rise of Drishtee, a for-profit business with the goal of bringing ICT benefits to rural India, where they can provide long-needed solutions for rural development. Drishtee, which is revolutionary in both concept and execution, has been effective in facilitating the invention of a rural networking infrastructure through a tiered franchising and partnership model, which has resulted in the formation of entrepreneurs dispersed across numerous villages in rural India. It currently has a network of more than 4100 franchisee entrepreneurs and 700 Rural Retail Points (RRPs) spread throughout 10 Indian states. A unique last mile distribution network built on information and communication technology (ICT) application and "ground level entrepreneurship" is another advantage it has over competitors because it was first to market (Lather, Gargs, & Vikas, 2009).

Answering the fundamental concerns of what can be done to assist grassroots innovations and entrepreneurships in India is an important field of research. Grassroots innovation is defined as a new product or method developed at the base of the pyramid, typically because of necessity, hardship, or difficulty. Grassroots innovators are those people who frequently develop just to address their own concerns, without any thought of commercialization. Most grassroots innovators lack entrepreneurial skills, have unstable finances, and have weak educational backgrounds. Business incubators are an essential part of the entrepreneurial ecosystem and have gained recognition as dynamic tools for incubating new businesses that assist technology commercialization, knowledge transfer, innovation acceleration, economic development, and job creation. Technological Business Incubators (TBIs) like the National Innovation Council (NIC) have acted as a facilitator in providing initial support to these grassroots innovators' budding businesses by offering mentorship, technological support, financial help, and even market connections. Despite these efforts by incubators, the commercialization success rate of these innovations has been only moderately successful, indicating a need to evaluate the technological role of business incubators in the ecosystem supporting grassroots innovations and provide recommendations to increase the success rate. (Sahoo,2015).

Another study examines that one of the most significant developments in the global economy is the interest in the globalization of commercial and economic activities. These are dependent on information technology and the spread of new organizations with advanced skills and continuous innovation, as well as research centers that constantly publish new technologies and move to technopreneurship by integrating entrepreneurship with technology so that they maintain its global competitive position. Many countries have begun to stimulate their communities and pool their resources to keep up with industrialized countries and create places like Silicon Valley in America, which is the wellspring of modern technologies (Abbas, 2018).

Technopreneurship is the convergence between entrepreneurship and technology. SME utilises technologies from higher education to develop innovative concepts. Innovations in products and services are the result of creative thinking. Product innovation takes into account taste, quality, shape, and colour. Moreover, advances in packaging are made to make products more appealing to potential buyers. By approaches like training and mentorship, higher education contributes to the transfer of knowledge and technology. Government agencies are responsible for creating policies that make life easier for SMEs and promote marketing. An increase in the quantity and quality of products is one sign that technopreneurship has an impact on SMEs' performance (Wibawa et al., 2020).

Technopreneurship creates opportunities and some businesses are transitioning from traditional to digital modes. To address unemployment and other social issues, increasing technopreneurial potential among young people is an effective solution. Small and Medium Enterprises (SME) development and technopreneurship are pathways to economic growth and self-employment in developing countries, generating income, self-sufficiency, and the cultivation of human capital. Technology has clearly changed our lives, enabling businesses to rethink their traditional methods of operation. It can be further stated that primary reason for SME below par performance is their continued adherence to conventional business models rather than embracing a technology-based approach (Qasim & Mahmood, 2022).

Technopreneurship: Focusing on Digital Divide and Gender Divide

The distance between people who have access to contemporary information and communication technology and those who do not is known as the digital divide, sometimes known as the digital split. In terms of the use of the Internet and communication technologies, it illustrates the differences between demographics and geographic areas at various social, economic, or other levels. The digital divide can exist between people who live in rural and urban areas, between educated and uneducated people, between different socioeconomic levels, and globally between more and less industrialized countries (Singh, 2010).

In the study titled "ICT Imperatives to bridge the Digital Divide- Gender Perspective," the author highlights there is a significant difference in education between male and female entrepreneurs in six selected areas (GautamBuddh Nagar, Ghaziabad, Sitapur, Gorakhpur, Rae Bareli and Sultanpur) in Uttar Pradesh. Most males have graduated, whereas most females have only completed high school. This obviously suggests that more education should be supplied to females not only for their performance in business and careers, but also for the nation's economic prosperity. Statistics demonstrate that IT access is the best solution for mainstreaming female business. According to the study, most of the entrepreneurs in these districts have small businesses (1-9 employees), yet they are using ITC to improve the performance of their businesses. Yet, females continue to lag in adopting ITC for their enterprises and are involved in their traditional business techniques. IT entrepreneurship has reduced stress and allowed entrepreneurs to devote more time to exercise, meditation, yoga, and hobbies. As a result, we may claim that Technology is modifying traditions while also transforming corporate procedures (Bala, 2017).

The study titled "Exploring challenges faced by Female Technopreneurs in Sri Lanka" examines the issues and difficulties high-tech female entrepreneurs in Sri Lanka. Data were gathered and analyzed using the qualitative research approach, notably a narrative design, and feminist theory. Purposefully approaching and interviewing three female technopreneurs. The research reveals that women, prioritized issues such a lack of technologically novel company ideas, a lack of digital resources, a lack of business networks, and concerns about online safety. Moreover, sociocultural perspectives dissuade women from entering the tech industry. It will have an influence to give lower-income ladies linked devices and to expand their digital knowledge and access. Rules and regulations should be put in place to force businesses to hire at least a certain percentage of women. The results should help generate benchmark data for reducing gender gaps. The study guarantees SDG 05, which is to achieve gender equality and give all women and girls the power (Sahira, & Surangi, 2022).

Technopreneurship and Economic Development

This section emphasizes on the third research question which seeks to comprehend the relationship between skill, youth, technology, and entrepreneurship. Starting a business is a fundamental act of someone seeking to create something new. Technopreneurs are the offspring of technology-based entrepreneurs, but they also take risks in their business ventures and explore into potentially dangerous territory by coming up with novel products and services that benefit society.

Paramasivan and Muthusamy (2016, 2017) had explained of the many economic sectors, the IT and ITeS (IT enabled Services) industry is one that is crucial to the economy's rapid expansion. Information technology and IT enabling services to have mostly been used to fund the internal development of a country's infrastructure. Most of the official and unofficial information is often handled by IT and ITeS. Throughout the last two decades, the Indian software industry has experienced rapid expansion owing to the involvement of powerful international corporations. The manufacturing and distribution of software-based applications throughout the world has been primarily facilitated by the Indian IT sector. This essay studied the development and contribution of IT and ITeS in Indian industry as well as their growth and performance. It has been determined that the most desired and profitable sector for the economy is IT and ITeS.

The former Wipro employee Shashi Kumar and veterinarian GNS Reddy cofounded Akshayakalpa Farms and Foods, a cooperative dairy farming company. Nearly 37 farmers in rural Karnataka are involved in the three-year-old business. To monitor the quantity and quality of milk as well as the cow's body temperature, Kumar has created milking equipment incorporating sensors. (Economictimes, 2013).

Key Findings

The development of technology, innovations, and entrepreneurship are closely related. It is interesting to note that entrepreneurship serves as the foundation upon which science and technology are formed. As far as we can tell, technopreneurship is still largely entrepreneurship. The distinction is that in technopreneurship, a company either creates an innovative high-tech product (like Microsoft) or uses high technology in an inventive method to reach consumers (like eBay), or both (e.g., most pharmaceutical companies).

Technopreneurship is a process of synthesis used to design the future of an individual, a company, a country, and the entire planet. Decision-making procedures or strategic directions are growing increasingly complex and demanding. It can be said that one need not invent anything to be a successful technopreneur; rather one must emphasize on innovation. An individual must consider using the existing tools to solve an existing problem, but in a novel and improved manner. Educated Youths should therefore inspire and encourage others to participate in technopreneurship activities. Although technopreneurs' performance is noticeably good, they still have several issues, including operational, financial, and marketing issues. Technopreneurs will be a key driver of regional and national economic growth if the governing body effectively oversees and controls them.

CONCLUSION AND RECOMMENDATIONS

It can be said that as nothing is permanent in this world one must alter what is currently present to create new things for the people or new things that contribute to the growth or betterment of our society. Accordingly, technopreneurship will be necessary for every entrepreneur looking for flexibility and a range of other essential aspects for their business to be interesting. Given that India has recently prioritized the expansion of the start-up ecosystem and deserves it, this is indeed fruitful to promote the tech start-up that will serve as a significant pillar in forthcoming trends. Since 2010, the scream of our country's technopreneurs has drawn attention from the whole developed world. In the current environment, the Indian government is delivering exceptional prospects to a great extent, which could establish a new benchmark for the startup environment.

Further the government should support entrepreneurial education system for the nation's youth which can be beneficial in increasing jobs. Universities can play an important role in the sphere of technopreneurship by forming relationships with universities and sophisticated technology firms and introducing them to the country. Academic leadership is also crucial to achieving technopreneurship. With the help of research and educational training institutions the government is encouraging both employed and unemployed youth to participate more for the entrepreneurial environment. By giving so many instances of successful people who have achieved success in real life and by showcasing awareness campaigns on technopreneurship, it is possible to easily inculcate and nurture the spirit of entrepreneurship in people. This will further motivate people to enroll themselves in and receive appropriate education for technical-based entrepreneurship initiatives by visiting research training institutes and incubation centers. Although universities and other higher education institutions may increase the productivity and efficiency of their technopreneurship education programmes.

An important role could be played by the Atmanirbhar Abhiyan's support of the development of indigenous information and communication technologies. Promoting low-cost smartphones and switching to new technologies like 5G can help augment the technology ecosystem in the rural areas. Some of the bandwidth issues would be resolved. Services may become more affordable because of increased market competition amongst service suppliers. In addition to this, the government needs to make certain changes to the accelerate the ease of doing business and focusing more on encouraging young people to start their own businesses. If the technological plans are carried out and well implemented, India might improve the lives of many people and establish an active place in the world.

REFERENCES

Abbas, A. A. (2018). The bright future of Technopreneurship. *International Journal of Scientific and Engineering Research*, *9*(12), 563–566.

Bala, S. (2017). *ICT Imperatives to Bridge the Digital Divide: Gender Perspective*. VVGNLI. https://vvgnli.gov.in/en/nliresearchstudiesseries/nli-research-studies-series-no-1292017

Barot, H. (2015). *Entrepreneurship - A Key to Success.*

Bhardwaj, B. R. (2021). Adoption, diffusion and consumer behaviour in technopreneurship. *International Journal of Emerging Markets*, *16*(2), 179–220. doi:10.1108/IJOEM-11-2018-0577

Diandra, D., & Azmy, A. (2020). Understanding Definition of Entrepreneurship. *Journal of Management Accounting and Economics.*, *7*, 2020–2383.

Economic Times. (2013) 'Technopreneurs' take agriculture-related ventures to reap farm gain. *Economic Times.* https://economictimes.indiatimes.com/small-biz/startups/technopreneurs-take-agriculture-related-ventures-to-reap-farm-gain/articleshow/22620386.cms

Fowosire, R. A. (2017). Technopreneurship: A view of technology, innovations and entrepreneurship. *Global Journals of Research in Engineering*, *17*(F7), 41–46.

Harlanu, M., & Nugroho, A. (2015, February). The importance of technopreneurship management model for vocational school. In *3rd UPI International Conference on Technical and Vocational Education and Training* (pp. 147-150). Atlantis Press. 10.2991/ictvet-14.2015.33

Hidayat, H., Herawati, S., Syahmaidi, E., Hidayati, A., & Ardi, Z. (2018). Designing of technopreneurship scientific learning framework in vocational-based higher education in Indonesia. [UAE]. *IACSIT International Journal of Engineering and Technology*, *7*(4), 123–127. doi:10.14419/ijet.v7i4.9.20632

Iqbal, B., & Yadav, A. (2021). Fourth Industrial Revolution. *Its Role and Contribution in Employment Generation and Skills Development.*, *1*, 85–96. doi:10.47509/JGETIB.1.1.2021.85-96

Joshua, J. N., Swastika, I. P. A., & Primakara, S. T. M. I. K. (2020). *Competency Development of Computer and IT to Enhance the Innovative Human Resources through Technopreneurship Curriculum Implementation in Higher Education.*

Kaur, P. (2011). Rural Technopreneurship: An Innovative Key To Development. [IJBMR]. *International Journal of Business Management & Research*, *1*, 8–16.

Koe, W. L., Mahphoth, M. H., Alias, N. E., Krishnan, R., & Arham, A. F. (2021). Factors influencing intention towards technopreneurship among university students. *Journal of Educational and Social Research*, *11*(1), 162–169. doi:10.36941/jesr-2021-0016

Kollmann, T., Kleine-Stegemann, L., de Cruppe, K., & Strauss, C. (2022). Eras of digital entrepreneurship: connecting the past, present, and future. In *Handbook of Digital Entrepreneurship* (pp. 49–73). Edward Elgar Publishing. doi:10.1007/978-3-658-37260-6

Lather, A. S., Garg, S., & Vikas, S. (2009). Entrepreneurship as a strategic development intervention to accelerate rural development: The case of Drishtee. *Asia Pacific Business Review*, *5*(1), 126–137. doi:10.1177/097324700900500115

Masenya, T. M. (2021). Technopreneurship development: digital strategy for youth self-employment in the digital economy. In *Handbook of Research on Management and Strategies for Digital Enterprise Transformation* (pp. 196–218). IGI Global. doi:10.4018/978-1-7998-5015-1.ch010

Paramasivan, C., & Muthusamy, S. (2016). Emerging trends in new start-up technopreneurs. *Journal of Business and Management*, *2*(7).

Paramasivan, C., & Muthusamy, S. (2017). Technopreneurship and development of IT and ITeS industry in India. *Imperial Journal of Interdisciplinary Research, 3*(11).

Qasim, Y., & Mahmood, Z. (2022). Technopreneurship Education: The Way to Rebuild COVID-19 Affected Economy. *Journal of Management Research, 9*(1).

Sahira, S., & Surangi, H. A. K. N. S. (2022). *Is there any Digital Gender Divide? Exploring challenges faced by Female Technopreneurs in Sri Lanka.*

Sahoo, S. R. (2015). Technopreneurship: A Synthesis Based on Case Studies of Rural Innovators in India. In *Eleventh Biennial Conference on Entrepreneurship* (pp. 410-417).

Scarlat, C. (2014). Technopreneurship-An emerging concept. *FAIMA Business & Management Journal*, *2*(3), 5.

Singh, S. (2010). Digital divide in India: Measurement, determinants and policy for addressing the challenges in bridging the digital divide. [IJIDE]. *International Journal of Innovation in the Digital Economy*, *1*(2), 1–24. doi:10.4018/jide.2010040101

Sonne, L. (2012). Innovative initiatives supporting inclusive innovation in India: Social business incubation and micro venture capital. *Technological Forecasting and Social Change*, *79*(4), 638–647. doi:10.1016/j.techfore.2011.06.008

Wibawa, T., Widjanarko, H., Utomo, H. S., Suratna, S., & Wahyurini, E. (2020, October). Technopreneurship Based Product Innovation: a Case Study on Small Entrepreneur. In *Proceeding of LPPM UPN "Veteran" Yogyakarta Conference Series 2020–Engineering and Science Series* (*Vol. 1,* pp. 439-444).

ENDNOTES

1. **SaaS** Software as a service (or SaaS) is a method of delivering software as a service through the Internet. Web-based software, on-demand software, and hosted software are other terms for SaaS applications.
2. **PaaS** Platform as a service (PaaS) is a complete cloud development and deployment environment with resources to create everything from simple cloud-based apps to sophisticated, cloud-enabled business systems.

Chapter 5
Role of TVET in Reducing Gender Inequality:
A Review of the Literature

Shashi Bala
V.V. Giri National Labour Institute, India

Meghna Khurania
Jawaharlal Nehru University, India

ABSTRACT

The chapter looks into the unequal development parity which is excluding the equal participation of women in the labour market. Technical, vocational, education, and training are considered means to encourage women's participation. However, India continues to witness a declining labor force participation rate. In this context, this chapter throws light on the role TVET in empowering females. There is a wide gender gap in education and labour market. There are overwhelming distinctions in education between the sexes in some developing countries. In the economics of education literature, an important explanation of gender inequality in education is that the labour market rewards women's education less well than men's, especially in developing countries. Unequal access to education and training perpetuates gender inequalities in the labour market, restricting the choices and bargaining power of women in particular.

DOI: 10.4018/978-1-6684-6878-4.ch005

INTRODUCTION

Global Inequality

The global economy has seen an impressive growth since the 20th century with integration of economies around the world, primarily through expansion of trade, technological progress and increased financial flows (International Monetary Fund [IMF], 2007). While this has been the key to economic growth and development, it has also been found to increase inequalities within and between countries, adversely affecting employment, living standards and social progress. In 2021, the global economy grew by 5.5. percent, which has been the highest growth rate since the mid-1970s (United Nations [UN], 2022). Despite this progress, the implications of a globalised economy on the economic wellbeing of citizens and inequalities have been an area of debate and policy discussion. This discussion is relevant in the context of India. With economic liberalization that began from the start of the 1990s, the Indian economy has witnessed increasing economic growth. The evidence also indicates that while growth was accompanied by a rise in per capital GDP, it also led to an increase in inequalities (World Bank, 2011). Pointing towards this inequality, Dreze and Sen (2013) claimed that though liberalisation in India have been successful in promoting economic growth, it has failed in improving living conditions and social indicators One of the central aspects in this debate concerns the gendered dimension (Spilerman, 2009; Eichhorst et al., 2012). According to the World Inequality Report (2022), income inequality in India is at a historical high with the top one percent largely benefiting from economic reforms by holding 22 percent share of the total national income and very less growth for low- and middle-income groups. In addition to overall inequalities in wealth and income, gender inequalities in India are very high as well (Chancel et al., 2022). The report quotes that the share of income accruing to women through labour market participation in India is only 18 percent in 2020 as compared to 21 percent in Asia (excluding China where the share is 33%). Despite women playing an important role in the evolution of economies for years (Freeman, 2000), prevailing gender inequalities have raised important questions for social scientists as economies grow.

Forms of Inequalities

Inequalities based on gender can take many forms. Gender inequality, as defined by Sen (2001) is not a homogeneous phenomenon, rather a combination of interlinked problems. These, according to him, could be related to inequalities in mortality and natality rates; inequalities in access to schooling, higher education, or professional trainings; or inequalities in ownership of assets, division of labour within the household or professional inequality in certain occupations. A substantial body of work documents gender inequality in access to opportunities creating disparities between men and women in outcomes related to education, health, employment as well as earning (Bertay et al., 2022). The intersection between these areas is rather complex and are overlapping, which has generated considerable attention especially on women's labour market participation. The policy and literature focus on gender inequality because women comprise half of the global population, and yet, form less than one third of the world's labour force (Lagarde, 2013). UNICEF (2022) study finds that one in four women who are 15-19 years old to be neither employed nor in any education or training, as compared to one in ten boys. The current global rate for women's labour market participation is under 47 percent, as against 72 percent for men and the gap is even higher in some regions such as in Southeast Asian countries (International Labour Organisation [ILO], 2022).

Inequality in Education and Labour Market

There are a range of gender gaps in education and labour market. There are overwhelming distinctions in education between the sexes in some developing countries. In the economics of education literature, an important explanation of the gender inequality in education is that the labour market rewards women's education less well than men's, especially in developing countries (Kingdon, 1998). Education is seen as an investment in human capital and as its amount increases, individual's skills and competencies also increase (Becker, 1964). Employment opportunities and earnings differ greatly by gender in most developing nations (World Bank, 2001). A primary determinant of labour market participation in developed as well as developing countries is levels of education attainment (Cazes and Verick, 2013). Female education has a great impact on the well-being of the families and societies. It is an important issue for number of reasons. Firstly, education of females increases females' productivity by rising output in economic activities. Secondly, it increases children's education profile which results in better educated people. The first step in education is literacy which gives a fundamental skill to empower women to take control of their own lives. With an increasing literacy rate, they will have more access for getting a better position in the labour market. This will then enhance women's position in the society. However, even when the educational level of young women is equal to or exceeds that of men, they are unlikely to receive equal opportunities in the labour market, particularly in developing countries (ILO, 2014). Women trailed behind men in the employment-to-population ratio in all regions in 2011, with the largest difference in North Africa, the Middle East and South Asia (ILO, 2014). Occupational segregation by gender is often associated with lower status and pay for women, implying under-valuation of women's skills and work. For instance, 'feminized' professions, including clerical, service and domestic labour, are amongst the lowest paid in the world (Gaidzanwa, 2008). There is some indication that women have less security in the labour market than men, partly as a result of their concentration in certain sectors. There are few reliable estimates, although women are generally considered to make up a majority of 'informal' workers in developing countries (UNGEI, 2012). For instance, in Sub-Saharan Africa, many women are subsistence farmers, unpaid family workers or own-account workers (with few social protections, etc.) (Arnot, 2010). There are also some signs that the financial crisis has pushed more women into vulnerable employment, particularly in countries with low female enrolment in education (UNGEI, 2012).

Unequal access to education and training perpetuates gender inequalities in the labour market, restricting the choices and bargaining power of women. For instance, many multinational corporations exploit women's willingness to accept any employment, offering work in the textile and clothing sectors characterised by long hours, little security, and low pay (UNGEI, 2012). Poverty, illiteracy, and domestic responsibilities can force many young women to enter the informal sector, due to a lack of alternative prospects (Ibid.). Labour force statistics suggest that educational gains have not translated into labor market gains for women, in general. It is in this light, Technical, Vocational, Education and Training (TVET) is touted against the current mainstream educational model. TVET is widely believed to align well with labor market needs and help in better transition to world of work (Powell, 2019). However, traditional expectations of the roles and responsibilities of women and men can impact upon the educational pathways of girls and boys (World Inequality Report, 2022). TVET plays a pivotal role in achieving gender equality in skill development (McGrath, 2020) and it impacts the participation of women in labour market in a positive way (Lagarde, 2013). However, gender inequality in education gives way to gender inequality in labour force participation of women. It is important to study gender inequality in TVET and how it translates into gender inequalities in the labour market.

Declining Female Labour Force Participation Rate

As defined by ILO (2022), the labour force participation rate is "a measure of the proportion of a country's working age population that is either working or looking for work". It is an indicator of the size of the labour force available for economic activities as a share of the working age population (ILOSTAT, 2022). A low and unequal participation rate of women in the labour force is a lost opportunity for economies. The 'Global Gender Gap Report' published by the World Economic Forum (2014) has cited positive relationship between gender equality with a country's GDP and with indicators of human development. Having more women work expands the available pool of skills in the labour force and ensures its better utilization (Norberto, 2016). Improvements in female labour force participation bring in positive effect in household and individual behaviour in financial decisions (Luke and Munshi, 2011) as well as decisions related to marriage (Van Der Klaauw, 1996) and fertility (Goldin and Katz, 2002). Female labour force participation is a driver of growth and therefore, participation rates indicate the potential for a country to grow more rapidly. However, the relationship between women's engagement in the labour market and broader development outcomes is complex (Fersterer,2003). A wide variety of economic and social factors including economic growth, increasing educational attainment, falling fertility rates and social norms affect female labour force participation. Labour market gender gaps are more pronounced in developing countries. Most notable is the falling engagement of women in the Indian labour force, which occurred despite strong economic growth and rising wages and incomes (Afridi, et.al., 2018). Longer term trends suggest that female labour force participation rates in India have been puzzling. From 30.7% in 2006, the proportion of working age women taking part in paid work dropped to 19.2% in 2021, according to the World Bank. While the pandemic could be partly responsible for severe job losses among women, the percentage of employed women has been quite low, averaging 21% between 2012 and 2021. Status of other countries- 46% of the women were part of the workforce on an average globally in 2020. China had 61% of its women in workforce while the US had 55% (World Bank, 2022). Overall, the female participation rates declined In India and wide gender differences in participation rate also persists. Also, there are considerable variations between urban and rural areas (PLFS, 2018). Data from the Periodic Labour Force Survey (PLFS) (2019-20) shows female labour force participation at 22.8 percent, compared to a far higher 56.8 percent for men.

The decline in women's economic activity is a cause for concern as women are valuable resources and as it implies a decline in their well-being (Mammen and Paxson 2008). Literature states that there are many reasons for a decline in the female labour force participation- factors include both supply side and demand side factors (Rangarajan et al., 2011; Kannan and Raveendran, 2012; Hirway, 2012; Neff et al., 2012; Mehrotra et al., 2013). Factors like reduced farm jobs and lack of women-friendly non-farm jobs reduce demand for women labour (Chand and Srivastava, 2014). On the other hand, supply side factors like a greater number of women enrolling in higher education (Kannan and Raveendran, 2012), rising income of spouses (Mehrotra and Parida, 2017), inadequate infrastructure like lack of roads, banking facilities (Sorsa et al., 2015) among others, have been found to be the primary reasons for a declining trend in their labour market participation. India posits an interesting case, where cultural and social factors have an equally important role in women's employment outcomes (Dev, 2005; Rao, 2014).

TVET as a Solution

It is widely believed that being equipped with relevant skills for decent work, especially through technical and vocational education and training (TVET) via formal and non-formal learning, is key to the economic empowerment of women and girls, including those who face multiple sources of discrimination (e.g., women and girls with disabilities), and to improving their employment and entrepreneurship opportunities (ILO, 2022; Zancajo and Valiente, 2019; McGrath et. Al., 2020; Winch, 2013). Technical, vocational education and training (TVET) is often considered as an effective strategy to empower marginalized groups in a society by increasing their employability, especially for females (Tikly, 2020; McGrath et.al. 2020). However, gender inequality in education may have contrary impacts on economic growth. It may decrease some human capital determinants such as total fertility and unemployment of female. Thus, TVET is seen as an alternative pathway to work, which helps improve the transition to the workforce. Studies suggest that transition rates to the workforce are higher for those with TVET qualifications than those without. TVET could help connect students to specific industries and provide skills demanded by specific occupations, thus improving real-world employability. But available training opportunities are often confined to 'feminine' areas, which may not necessarily lead to profitable work (Hirway, 2012). Unequal access to education and training perpetuates gender inequalities in the labour market, restricting the choices and bargaining power of women. Even when enrolled in training courses in more male dominated areas, girls and women can face barriers, for example, when the learning environments are de-motivating and do not consider their specific needs (UNESCO, 2021). Within male dominated TVET centres, women may face additional obstacles to attendance. For instance, prescriptive gender stereotypes may lead women to doubt their technical abilities and undermine their confidence within particular fields (Richardson, 2012). In some developing countries, it is not socially acceptable for men and women to work together in technical/engineering roles, and TVET courses targeted at women focus on specific 'female' tasks, such as the clothing, food, and health sectors (UNESCO and UNEVOC, 2011). In an international online discussion, some women in TVET reported experiencing exclusive masculinity, such as discouraging language from peers/teachers and few role models in the form of female teachers, trainers, and leaders (ibid.). In addition, a lack of basic schooling can prevent many young women from meeting the entry criteria for TVET institutions, as occurs in Sub-Saharan Africa (Gaidzanwa, 2008). Many TVET bodies lack counselling/assistance to support students to get job placements, which may hit women particularly hard if they have fewer contacts and less awareness of a particular sector (UNESCO and UNEVOC, 2011). It is worth noting that the extra costs of TVET (equipment, work placements, etc.) mean that it accounts for a relatively small proportion of education in many African countries (Gaidzanwa, 2008).

TVET in India

In India, a renewed focus is seen on TVET through the recent National Education Policy (NEP) (2020). The NEP (2020) underlines the urgency of hastening the spread of vocational education in India and impart vocational education and training to at least 50% of learners by 2025. Similarly, National Policy for Skill Development and Entrepreneurship (2015) aims to train about 104.62 million people afresh, and an additional 460 million are to be reskilled, up-skilled and skilled by 2022 (NSDC, 2018; EY-FICCI, 2013). For an emerging economy like India, providing vocational education is seen to enhance the productivity of youth in India and help in the nation's development by becoming an engine of growth (Allais, 2012; Pradalier et al., 2012; Mehrotra et al., 2014; Kumar, et al., 2019). To this effect, a dedicated Ministry of Skill Development and Entrepreneurship (MSDE) was created in 2015. And several departments which worked separately in different ministries were brought together under one ministry to fulfil the agenda of "Skilling India". However, harnessing a young demographic dividend that is prevailing in India, currently, through "skilling" needs to be seen in the context of gender inequality in TVET and labour market.

Gender Inequality in TVET

Equipping women with employable skills is a far greater challenge than skilling men, as most women in India work low-skill and low-paying jobs in the informal economy. It is a gap that needs to be addressed urgently, as skilling can expand work opportunities for women and increase their participation in the workforce (Cages et.al., 2013). Equipping women with employable skills is a far greater challenge than skilling men, as most women in India work low-skill and low-paying jobs in the informal economy. 'It is a gap that needs to be addressed urgently, as skilling can expand work opportunities for women and increase their participation in the workforce' (Hirway, 2012). Her paper analyses the participation of women in skills training programmes, underlining the biases that lead to women being trained for jobs close to their traditional gender roles and thereby getting left out of better-paying jobs. It finds that skills training for women has failed to achieve expected outcomes as programmes struggle to recruit and retain women in training courses and in employment. To be effective, these programmes need to be gender-sensitive in design and cognisant of social norms (Kumar, 2022).

There is no single policy measure that can address the complex issue of women's participation in the workforce. However, skilling can provide women with occupational choices and expand their work opportunities. Studies have shown that skilling has a proven impact on workforce participation. Women in India who have attended skills training programmes, whether formal or informal, are more likely to be in the workforce, regardless of educational levels. For this, Skilling needs to keep pace with the transformations of the digital age and the future of work— factors which have only deepened the gendered digital divide (Hirway, 2012; Kumar, 2022; WDR, 2019).

Persisting skill gaps in the Indian labur market have been a serious concern for both policy makers and industrialists in India. Various studies have highlighted skill gaps in different sectors in India (Nasscom, 2011; Mehrotra and Ghosh, 2012; Das, 2013). At an aggregate level, hardly 2 per cent of the Indian workforce has skill training in vocational education and only another 2.4 per cent workers have some technical education. The graduates who are trained in vocational education also lack the skills required in the labor market. Thus, the employability of graduates continues to be a major concern and there is no formal link between general education and vocational training in the country. In addition to this, the labor market in India is undergoing a dynamic change. According to National Policy on Skill Development 2009, it is expected that over the next 15 years, 365 million people will be eligible to join the workforce and about 11–13 million people are expected to look for employment opportunities each year. Sensing this urgency, 12th five-year plan positions the skill development in different sectors as an important task (Mehrotra, 2014).

The inescapable gender gap shows up in skills training. According to Labour Bureau data from 2013-14, only 3.8 percent of India's adult women had ever received vocational training at that time, compared to 9.3 percent of men. Of these women who did receive vocational training, 39 percent did not join the labour force following training (NSDC, 2022). Persisting skill gaps has its qualitative dimensions, an aspect often not highlighted in the public discussions. Studies on the quality of skills and mismatch in demand and supply (FICCI 2006, World Bank, 2007, IAMR, 2010) have brought to fore issues such as lack of marketable skills and low standards of quality. The reasons cited include obsolete and traditional courses, lack of up-gradation of modules, failure to respond to market signals and the consequent lack of functional skills (IAMR, 2011).

It is in this context several studies seek to understand the experience of German dual system as it has historically been cited as a successful model of education and training (Brandt, 1998; Ertl, 2000; Heinz, 2000; Euler, 2013; Dearden et al., 2002) and identify the practical solution for the issue of skill gaps in India by reforming the Indian technical and vocational education system (TVET). Skills training programmes in India have historically been based on traditional gender roles and notions of women's work, mostly restricted to household-related tasks and caregiving (Hirway, 2012). In my MPhil research for instance a finding was that courses for women under Pradhan Mantri

Kaushal Vikas Yojana (PMKVY), for instance, have concentrated on areas like apparel, beauty, wellness, and healthcare—this keeps women out of more remunerative sectors. Another observation during the pilot study was that the National Skill Training Institutes for women offer only 21 courses, while the general Industrial Training Institutes (ITIs), where men predominate, offer 153. Even among the 21, there is a preponderance of courses in occupations that are either outdated or patently stereotypical for women, such as secretarial practice, cosmetology, fashion design, or interior design. 'In the general ITIs, female enrolment is still low, though it has grown from 6 percent in 2014 to 21 percent in 2018' (Poulomi et.al., 2021).

REFERENCES

Afridi, F., Dinkelman, T., & Mahajan, K. (2018). Why are fewer married women joining the work force in rural India? A decomposition analysis over two decades. *Journal of Population Economics*, *31*(3), 783–818. doi:10.100700148-017-0671-y

Allais, S. (2011). What is a National Qualifications Framework?. *Journal of Contemporary Educational Studies/Sodobna Pedagogika, 62*(5).

Allais, S. (2012). Will skills save us? Rethinking the relationships between vocational education, skills development policies, and social policy in South Africa. *International Journal of Educational Development*, *32*(5), 632–642. doi:10.1016/j.ijedudev.2012.01.001

Allais, S. (2019). TVET Reform and Qualifications Frameworks: What Is Known About What They Can and Can't Do? In S. McGrath, M. Mulder, J. Papier, & R. Suart (Eds.), *Handbook of Vocational Education and Training*. Springer., doi:10.1007/978-3-319-94532-3_43

Bertay, N., Carpio, M. A., & Klein, T. J. (2014). *The Effects of Access to Health Insurance for Informally Employed Individuals in Peru.* The Institute for the Study of Labor, Bonn- Germany, Working Paper no: 8709.

Brandt, W. (1998). Change and consensus in vocational education and training: The case of the German 'Dual System. In I. Finlay, N. Stuart, & S. Young (Eds.), *Changing vocational education and training. An International comparative perspective* (pp. 103–120). Routledge.

Cazes, S., & Verick, S. (2013). *Perspectives on Labour Economics for Development*. International Labour Organisation.

Chancel, S. (2022). Women, gender, and the informal economy: An assessment of ILO research and suggested ways forward. International Labour Organisation.

Chand, B., & Srivastav, R. (2014). *Industry Linked Technical Institutes Help Manual.* AICTE India. Www.Aicteindia.Org/Downloads/Aboutaicteciisurvey2015.Pdf?Msclkid=4ff9086fbc1611ec83b8f1906b4b2661

Dearden, L., McIntosh, S., Myck, M., & Vignoles, A. (2002). The Returns to Academic and Vocational Qualifications in Britain. *Bulletin of Economic Research, 54*(3), 249–274. doi:10.1111/1467-8586.00152

Dev, S. M. (2013). Post-2015 Development Agenda: Employment and Growth with Special Reference to India. *IDS Bulletin*, *44*(5-6), 63–71. doi:10.1111/1759-5436.12058

Drèze, J., & Sen, A. (2013). An uncertain glory. In *An uncertain glory*. Princeton University Press.

Eichhorst, W., Planas, N. R., Schmidl, R., & Zimmermann, K. F. (2012). *A Roadmap to Vocational Education and Training Systems Around the World.* Institute for the Study of Labour.

Ertl, J. (2000). The transition of vocational education and training in Eastern Germany: Notes on the role of the European Union Programmes. *Comparative Education Review*, *44*(4), 464–492. doi:10.1086/447630

Euler. (2013). *Achieving gender equality in education: Trends in research and USAID programming (1996-2006); A synthesis report.* MSI.

EY-FICCI. (2013). *Reaping India's promised demographic dividend- industry in driving seat.* EY- FICCI.

Fersterer, J., & Winter-Ebmer, R. (2003a). Are Austrian Returns to Education Falling Over Time? *Labour Economics*, *10*(1), 73–89. doi:10.1016/S0927-5371(02)00105-7

Fersterer, J., & Winter-Ebmer, R. (2003b). Smoking, Discount Rates and the Returns to Education. *Economics of Education Review*, *22*(6), 561–566. doi:10.1016/S0272-7757(02)00072-9

FICCI. (2006). *Implementation of Apprenticeship in India: A Study by FICCI*. FICCI.

Gaidzanwa, F. (2008). *Skills and Skilled Work*. Oxford University Press.

Goldin, M., & Katz, J. (2002). *The Wiley Handbook of Vocational Education and Training*. Wiley Blackwell Publications.

Government of India. (1968). *National Policy on Education*. Ministry of Human Resource and Development.

Government of India. (1986). *National Policy on Education*. Ministry of Human Resource and Development.

Government of India. (2020). National Education Policy. New Delhi: Ministry of Human Resource and Development. Government of India. (1986). National Policy on Education. New Delhi: Ministry of Human Resource and Development.

Government of India. (2023). *Economic Survey 2021-22*. Department of Economic Affairs.

Hirway, I. (2012). Missing labour force: An explanation. *Economic and Political Weekly*, 67–72.

IAMR. (2013). *Low Female Employment in a Period of High Growth: Insights from a Primary Survey in Uttar Pradesh & Gujarat*. IAMR.

ILO. (n.d.). *Women and Men in the Informal Economy: A Statistical Picture*. Geneva: ILO& WEIGO.

International Labour Organization (ILO). (2000). *ABC of women workers' rights and gender equality*. ILO.

Kamdar, D., McAllister, D., & Turban, D. (2006). All in a Day's Work: How Follower Individual Differences and Justice Predict OCB Role Definitions and Behavior. *The Journal of Applied Psychology*, *7654*(4), 841–855. doi:10.1037/0021-9010.91.4.841 PMID:16834509

Kanan, R., & Raveendran, R. (2020). *Women's Economic Empowerment in India*. https://iwwage.org/wp-content/uploads/2020/10/Policy-Landscape-Sudy_Summary-report.pdf

Kane, E. (2004). *Girls' education in Africa: What do we know about strategies that work?* The World Bank.

King, K. (2012). The geopolitics and meanings of India's massive skills development ambitions. *International Journal of Educational Development*, *98765*(5), 665–673. doi:10.1016/j.ijedudev.2012.02.001

King, K., & McGrath, S. (2002). Globalisation, Enterprise and Knowledge: Education, Training and Development in Africa. Oxford: *Symposium Books Ltd*. 10.15730/books.33

King, K., & Palmer, R. (2010). *Planning for Technical and Vocational Skills Development*. UNESCO.

Kingdon, G. G. (1998). Does the labour market explain lower female schooling in India? *The Journal of Development Studies*, *35*(1), 39–65. doi:10.1080/00220389808422554

Kingdon, G. G., & Unni, J. (2001). Education and women's labour market outcomes in India. *Education Economics*, *9*(2), 173–195. doi:10.1080/09645290110056994

Klasen, S., & Pieters, J. (2012). *Push or pull? Drivers of female labor force participation during India's economic boom.*

Klasen, S., & Pieters, J. (2015). What explains the stagnation of female labor force participation in urban India? *The World Bank Economic Review*, *29*(3), 449–478. doi:10.1093/wber/lhv003

Lagarde, C. (2013). Dare the difference. *Finance & Development*, *50*(2).

Malamud, O., & Eleches, C. (2010). General Education versus Vocational Training: Evidence from an Economy in Transition. *The Review of Economics and Statistics*, *92*(1), 43–60. doi:10.1162/rest.2009.11339

Mammen, K., & Paxson, C. (2000). Women's work and economic development. *The Journal of Economic Perspectives*, *14*(4), 141–164. doi:10.1257/jep.14.4.141

Mathur, A., Sharma, S. K., & Saha, P. (2014). The Vocational Training System: A Learner's Perspective. In S. Mehrotra (Ed.), *India's Skills Challenge: Reforming Vocational Education and Training to Harness the Demographic Dividend* (pp. 177–200). Oxford University Press. doi:10.1093/acprof:oso/9780199452774.003.0005

McGrath, S. (2012). Vocational learning for development: A policy in need of a theory? *International Journal of Educational Development, 32*(5), 623–632. doi:10.1016/j.ijedudev.2011.12.001

Mehrotra, S. (2014). *India's Skill Challenge: Reforming Vocational Education and Training to Harness the Demographic Dividend*. Oxford University Press. doi:10.1093/acprof:oso/9780199452774.001.0001

Mehrotra, S., Gandhi, A., & Sahoo, B. K. (2013). Estimating India's Skill Gap: On a Realistic Basis for 2022. *Economic and Political Weekly*, 102–111.

Mehrotra, S., & Ghosh, D. (2012). *The International Experience with National Training Funds: Lessons for India, IAMR Policy Brief No. 1*.

Mehrotra, S., & Parida, J. K. (2017). Why is the labour force participation of women declining in India? *World Development, 98*, 360–380. doi:10.1016/j.worlddev.2017.05.003

Middleton, J., Ziderman, A., & Adams, A. V. (1993). *Skills for Productivity: vocational education and training in developing countries*. Oxford University Press.

Mishra, M. (2014). Vertically integrated skill development and vocational training for socio-economically marginalized youth: The experience at Gram Tarang and Centurion University, India. *Prospects, 44*, 297–316. doi:10.100711125-014-9308-z

MoLE. (2009). *National Skill Development Policy*. Government of India.

Munshi, K., & Rosenzweig, M. (2006). Traditional institutions meet the modern world: Caste, gender, and schooling choice in a globalizing economy. *The American Economic Review, 96*(4), 1225–1252. doi:10.1257/aer.96.4.1225

National Skill Development Corporation (NSDC). (2018). *'Skilling Today for a Brighter Tomorrow' Annual Report 2017-18*. New Delhi.

National Skill Development Corporation (NSDC). (2019). Estimating the Skill Stock In Uttar Pradesh, State Report 2019. New Delhi.

Neff, D. F., Sen, K., & Kling, V. (2012). *The puzzling decline in rural women's labor force participation in India: A reexamination*.

Neff, G. (2012). *Venture labor: Work and the burden of risk in innovative industries*. MIT press. doi:10.7551/mitpress/9780262017480.001.0001

OECD. (2010). *A Family Affair: Inter-generational Social Mobility across OECD Countries.* OECD.

Okada, A. (2012). Skills Development for Youth in India: Challenges and Opportunities. *Kokusai Kyoiku Kyoryoku Ronshu, 879*, 169–193.

Olsen, W., & Mehta, S. (2006). *Female Labour Participation in Rural and Urban India: Does Housewives' Work Count?* Research Gate. https://www.researchgate.net/publication/228461844

Oosterbeek, H., & Webbink, D. (2007). Wage effects of an extra year of basic vocational education. *Economics of Education Review, 7689*(4), 408–411. doi:10.1016/j.econedurev.2006.07.013

Oxfam. (2005). Beyond access for girls and boys: How to achieve good-quality, gender-equitable education. *Education and Gender Equality Series, Programme Insights.* OXFAM.

Pages, C., & Stampini, M. (2007). *No Education, No Good Jobs? Evidence on the Relationship between Education and Labour Market Segmentation.* Institute for Study of Labour.

Pandlier, R. (2017). *Get the Policies Right First: How to get India's Women into the Workforce.* Business Standard. https://www.businessstandard.com/article/opinion/rohini-pande-getting-india-s-women-into-theworkforce-117031601398_1.html

Pischke, J., & Wachter, T. (2008). Zero Returns to Compulsory Schooling in Germany: Evidence and Interpretation. *The Review of Economics and Statistics, 90*(3), 592–598. doi:10.1162/rest.90.3.592

Poulomi, P., Nanda, S., Anand, S., Sharma, S., & Nandi, S. (2020). *Skilling and Non-Traditional Livelihoods.* International Centre for Research on Women. https://assets.ey.com/content/dam/ey-sites/ey-com/en_in/topics/corporate-social-responsibility/icrw-vikalp-policy-report-on-skilling-and-non traditional-livelihoods.pd

Powell, M. (2019). Trends and forecasting of employment intensity of growth in India. *Journal of the Asia Pacific Economy, 765*, 438–459.

Pradhan, B. K., Singh, S. K., & Mitra, A. (2015). Female labour supply in a developing economy: A tale from a primary survey. *Journal of International Development, 27*(1), 99–111. doi:10.1002/jid.2994

Psacharopoulos, G. (1994). Returns to investment in education: A global update. *World Development*, *22*(9), 1325–1343. doi:10.1016/0305-750X(94)90007-8

Psacharopoulos, G., & Tzannatos, Z. (1992). Women's employment and pay in Latin America. *Finance & Development*, *29*, 14–14.

Quintini, G., & Martin, S. (2006). *Starting Well or Losing their Way?: The Position of Youth in the Labour Market. OECD SOCIAL.* Employment And Migration Working Papers.

Rangarajan, C., Seema, & Vibeesh, E. M. (2014). Developments in the Workforce between 2009-10 and 2011-12. *Economic and Political Weekly*, 117–121.

Rao, K., Joshi, S., Mathur, A. K., & Sahoo, B. K. (2014). The Vocational Training System: An Employer's Perspective. In S. Mehrotra (Ed.), *India's Skill Challenge: Reforming Vocational Education and Training to Harness the Demographic Dividend* (pp. 200–223). Oxford University Press. doi:10.1093/acprof:oso/9780199452774.003.0006

Rao, K., Joshi, S., Mathur, A. K., & Sahoo, B. K. (2014). The Vocational Training System: An Employer's Perspective. In S. Mehrotra (Ed.), *India's Skill Challenge: Reforming Vocational Education and Training to Harness the Demographic Dividend* (pp. 200–223). Oxford University Press. doi:10.1093/acprof:oso/9780199452774.003.0006

Rao, M. (2015). Step by step to soft-skills training: How to enhance employability skills in students. *Human Resource Management International Digest*, *76*(6), 34–36. doi:10.1108/HRMID-06-2015-0099

Roemer, J. (1998). *Equality of opportunity*. Harvard University Press. doi:10.4159/9780674042872

Ryan, P. (2001). The School-to-Work Transition: A Cross-National Perspective. *Journal of Economic Literature*, 2345–2365.

Saha, P., & Verick, S. (2017). Casualization and shift of rural workers to non-farm activities. *Rural Labour Mobility in Times of Structural Transformation: Dynamics and Perspectives from Asian Economies*, 127-150.

Saxena, P., & Gandhi, A. (2014). Reforming Apprenticeship Training. In S. Mehrotra (Ed.), *India's Skills Challenge: Reforming Vocational Education and Training to Harness the Demographic Dividend* (pp. 129–177). Oxford University Press. doi:10.1093/acprof:oso/9780199452774.003.0004

Shanmugham, M., & Kishore, S. (2012). Integration of prior learning and assessment in the IGNOU community college system for Skill Development. *Turkish Online Journal of Distance Education*, *765*, 311–321.

Singh, C. K. (2003). Skill, Education and Employment: A Dissenting Essay. *Economic and Political Weekly*, *458*, 3271–3276.

Sinha, A., & Dorschner, J. P. (2010). India: Rising Power or a Mere Revolution of Rising Expectation? *Northeastern Political Science Association*, *2345*(1), 345–367. doi:10.1057/pol.2009.19

Spilerman, A. (2009). Student learning outcomes from a gender perspective: What do international assessments tell us? *Paper presented at the World Bank's Global Symposium - Education: A Critical Path to Gender Equality and Women's Empowerment*, Washington, DC.

Srivastava, M. Z. (2014). Reconsidering women's work in rural India: Analysis of NSSO data, 2004–05 and 2011–12. *Economic and Political Weekly*, *52*(1), 45–52.

Subrahmanian, R. (2005). *Scaling Up" Good Practices in Girls' Education. United Nations Educational, Scientific and Cultural Organization*. UNESCO.

Sudarshan, R. M. (2014). *Enabling women's work*. ILO.

Tansel, A. (1996). Urban male wage earners and moonlighting in Turkey. In *Working paper series/Economic Research Forum; 9601*. Economic Research Forum, Cairo, EG.

Tonder, A. H., & Aspoy, T. M. (2017). When Work Comes First: Young Adults in Vocational Education and Training in Norway. *International Journal for Research in Vocational Education and Training*, *543*(3), 270–288. doi:10.13152/IJRVET.4.3.5

United Nations Economic and Social Council. (2006). *"Economic, social and cultural rights: Girls' right to education." n.p.* United Nations.

United Nations Educational, Scientific and Cultural Organization (UNESCO). (2003). *Gender and education for all: The leap to equality*. UNESCO.

United States Agency for International Development (USAID). (2005). *Education strategy: Improving lives through learning*. USAID.

United States Department of State. (2004). *Advancing the rights of women: An overview of significant progress made by the U.S. in the 10 years since the Beijing conference on women.* State Government. https://www.state.gov/p/io/rls/othr/35882.htm

World Bank. (2007). *Skill Development in India: The Vocational Education and Training System.* Human Development Unit, South Asia Region.

World Bank. (2019). *World Development Report 2019: The Changing Nature of Work. Washington: World Bank. World Bank. (2019). World Development Report 2019: The Changing Nature of Work.* World Bank.

Chapter 6
Corporate Social Responsibility and Rural Development in Gujarat:
A Case Study of Devadthal (Navapura) Village, Ahmedabad

Chetan Rathod
Central University of Gujarat, India

Litty Denis
Central University of Gujarat, India

ABSTRACT

Gujarat is one of the most industrially advanced states in India and consequently accounts for a large pie of CSR investments. Rs.676 crores have been spent in the year 2020-21 and these projects have made a significant contribution to the development of rural communities. In the current study, Devadthal village is selected because several CSR projects are being implemented in the village; in addition, this village was selected for the 'Integrated Tribal Village Development Programme' by different corporates operating in the region. The study attempts to explore different CSR projects undertaken by corporates in Devadthal village and what is the socioeconomic impact of CSR projects on these rural communities. Primary data is collected through interviews and focus group discussions with different stakeholders like CSR officials, NGO implementing partners, Panchayat members, and the community. This study clearly indicates positive outcomes that resulted due to CSR intervention in Devadthal Village by the NGOs, government, and community for the development of the village.

DOI: 10.4018/978-1-6684-6878-4.ch006

INTRODUCTION

A significantly large part of population in India (almost 65% states a World Bank estimate) resides in rural areas and has been developing at a very fast pace with the help of various kinds of investments in social sectors as well as in businesses. Corporate Social Responsibility (CSR) has been one such means that has contributed considerably especially towards creating basic infrastructure and livelihood opportunities. Even though the state is ultimately responsible for the development of the rural areas in the country, partnering with private enterprises certainly help the pace of development. After the amendment made in Companies Act and the addition of Schedule VII, the state has made its intent very clearly visible, to put some onus of enhancing the lives of rural population with improved access to healthcare, sanitation, livelihood, water availability, education etc. onto the corporates through mandatory CSR spending[1]. In India this has been very positively received by the corporates and resultantly increased spending under CSR heads have lead to local area development and improved access to resources while partnering with various stakeholders.

Working with rural communities and partnering with them requires both, an in-depth understanding of the village-level issues and enabling solutions for the pertinent concerns, which can be facilitated through the rural NGOs having relevant community connect and related competencies and strengths. Such organizations act as a bridge between the communities and the stakeholders, helping the rural communities to empower themselves, through their capacity building programs and facilitating them to get access to government rural programs/benefits. Effective rural governance with active citizen participation is a vital tool in making the empowerment happen along with diverse stakeholders like the government, NGOs and corporates through public-private partnerships (PPPs) that are innovative, replicable and scalable models of CSR in rural development (India CSR Report-2018).

Ahmedabad receives the highest CSR funds among all the districts. Devadthal village is selected for the study because of different CSR projects being implemented in the village. The village is having hundred percent tribal pollution and they are still living their lives according to their traditional norms, belief and culture. The current study investigates as to how CSRs partnering with state or civil society organizations contributed to their development. The paper studied what kind of projects were undertaken by corporates in Devadthal village? What is the socio-economic impact of CSR projects on rural communities? How CSR projects are being implemented at the grassroots level?

India lives in its villages and country's vast population is based on agriculture for living. Agriculture covers almost one-fifth of the gross domestic product in India (FAO Report, 2016). The Government has planned several programs pertaining to rural development in India particularly to increase the growth of agriculture sector. Through rural development, government seeks to change the socio-economic structure of the rural community. India is a vast developing country and after its independence in 1947 its economy is growing steadily. But the overall development depends upon development in both the urban as well as rural areas. However, one can still witness a great divide between the rural and urban areas and until rural areas provide infrastructure and opportunities akin to the urban areas, this divide will persist. Most of the population in rural areas depend upon agricultural activities for their livelihood. Lower education rates, poor health conditions, lack of credit facilities, lack of awareness, lack of employment opportunities etc. are major causes of low quality of life in rural areas. Government also makes many policies for improving their quality of life as MGNREGA (Mahatma Gandhi National Rural Employment Guarantee Act), Deendayal *Antyodaya Yojana*, National Rural Livelihood Mission, *Pradhan Mantri Awaas Yojana* etc. But in a large country like India, it is not solely the responsibility of the government but also the responsibility of the corporate sector, to come and contribute towards the development of rural areas. Keeping this view in mind government has passed the Companies Act with mandatory CSR requirements and India has become the first country which legally mandated CSR (Malhotra, Bohra, Upadhyay 2021). As far as rural areas are concerned CSR is considered very important (Maniktala & Punjabi, 2016). Most of the people living in rural areas in India depend upon agriculture or small businesses for their livelihoods. So, the motive of equitable development cannot be fulfilled by concentrating on urban development only. Additionally, it needs to be understood that it is the responsibility of all the stakeholders alike to contribute for the rural development. CSR projects relate with corporate's social responsibility towards society in which they exist and flourish. There are several thousands of companies registered in India and if each one contributes towards change in the society, the rural areas can be developed and the goals of sustainability can be easily achieved. The Government of India makes it mandatory for prescribed companies under Companies Act, 2013 whether private or public, to contribute 2% of its average net profits for CSR activities.

Table 1. CSR spending on rural development in Gujarat State

Year	Total CSR spending (in Cr)	Total CSR spending on Rural development (in Cr)	Total CSR spending on Rural development in Gujarat (in Cr)
2016-17	14394.55	1561.45	77.4
2017-18	17098.26	1724.1	55.56
2018-19	20196.92	2433.44	172.77
2019-20	24954.78	2299.63	88.27
2020-21	25714.65	1847.15	79.04
Total	**1,02,359.16**	**9,865.77**	**473.04**

(Source: CSR.gov.in)

While analysing five years of total CSR spending amounts, close to 10 percent of the total is only spent on rural development out of which 5 percent is spent in Gujarat. Rural development is one of the highest priorities of government (Ministry of Rural Development, 2019) and looking at the total CSR spending, there is still greater possibility of and need of spending in avenues encompassing rural development.

Review of Literature

The pure voluntary flavour of Indian CSR has recently been blended with a mandatory element in it. Unlike in some other countries such as Australia, Denmark, France, Holland, Norway, and Sweden, where only the CSR reporting is mandatory, India is now the only country in the world where both reporting and spending has become mandatory (Deodhar, 2015). The Companies Act, 2013 states that every company, private limited or public limited, which either has a net worth of Rs 500 crore or a turnover of Rs 1,000 crore or net profit of Rs 5 crore, needs to spend at least 2% of its average net profit for the immediately preceding three financial years on corporate social responsibility activities (Corporate Social Responsibility policy, MCA 2013-14).

The concept of CSR cannot be ignored by the corporate firms in the modern market structures and methods of promotions. By keeping in mind, the changing market scenario, business firms have to change their work culture as per the market demands. The concept of corporate social responsibility has gained prominence in all avenues. Companies must realize that government alone will not be able to get success in its endeavor to uplift the downtrodden. The present societal marketing concept of companies is constantly evolving and has given rise to a new concept of Corporate Social Responsibility (Poonam,

2016). Gujarat being home to many industrial projects of several corporates, the state seems to have also emerged as one of the most preferred regions for undertaking corporate social responsibility (CSR) initiatives. Gujarat received the second highest amount of funds spent by publicly traded companies towards CSR in fiscal 2020-21.CSR fund worth Rs 676 crore was spent across Gujarat during the financial year 2020-21. The amount was the second highest after Maharashtra which received CSR expenditure of Rs 1,272 crore according to the abridged India CSR Outlook Report (CSRBOX Report-2021).

A vast majority of the poor in India, people living in villages and towns are in a state of neglect and underdevelopment. The problems of hunger, ignorance, poor health, high mortality and illiteracy are more serious in rural areas than in urban areas. Not only due to lack of equipment and other resources but also because of the defects in our planning investment process and model. India has the potential to meet these challenges in rural areas. However, government efforts may not be sufficient to provide basic services to its citizens. It is increasingly recognized that progress and welfare of society is not only the responsibility of government but also many other stakeholders must be involved to achieve the development goals. The corporate sector has a vital role to play in ensuring that the private investment flows in these rural areas that have been left out of the development process till date and work for sustainable development of rural areas in general (Vastradmath, 2015).

ROLE OF CORPORATE SOCIAL RESPONSIBILITY IN RURAL DEVELOPMENT

Corporates are mostly functioning in rural area for reaping profits but they are at the same time responsible towards the society and its upliftment. If the current opportunity of huge funding in the form of social investments by corporate houses cater to the broad guidelines under the Sustainable Development Goals, then rural areas could benefit from social investments in agricultural system advancement and related livelihoods, community development etc. Agriculture is the mainstay of rural India however it requires tremendous investments to sustain. Similarly, it is important to boost the growth of small and medium scale enterprises for enhancing the economic and social standards of rural areas. Social investments can be made in the area of education and also to increase the application and efficiency of information technology in rural area. CSRs can and are also greatly useful in monitoring and preventing health hazards. Thus, social investments can improve the quality of life be providing access to essential services. However, there are many challenges in delivering these services on ground in the rural India. But it can be made possible if proper planning and appropriate government policies are framed in order to encourage social investments (Patel, 2014).

THEORETICAL FRAMEWORK OF THE RESEARCH

This paper investigates the different kinds of project implementation priorities and methods for CSR and rural development at Devadthal village. This village has used both methods direct implementation as well as through collaborative partnership with social organization along with Community contribution. The paper focuses on the model of collaborative partnerships which has a positive impact on development initiatives. This involves looking at the case analysis under an inter-disciplinary framework focusing on stakeholder theory, legitimacy theory and social contract theory. These theories have a lot of common threads however they offer a rich framework for inquiring about questions on CSR and rural development. These theories would give a clarification on "why companies adopt CSR activities", and "How the impact of CSR activities is useful for rural development".

As per the theoretical framework of CSR and rural development, chart wants to extend the understanding on how CSR and rural development are connected through stakeholder theory. Stakeholder theory is a theory of organizations management and business ethics that deals with principles and values in managing CSR projects (Freeman, 1984)The chart below shows what stakeholders expect from their organizations and how CSR will create a meaningful impact in rural development through its initiatives.

Looking at the significant spending amount under rural development this paper attempts to explore corporate social responsibility projects and its impact on the rural communities.

Research Objectives

1. To explore the CSR projects and activities related to rural development in Devadthal village.
2. To understand the impact of CSR projects at Devadthal Village.

Figure 1. Theoretical framework of corporate social responsibility and rural development

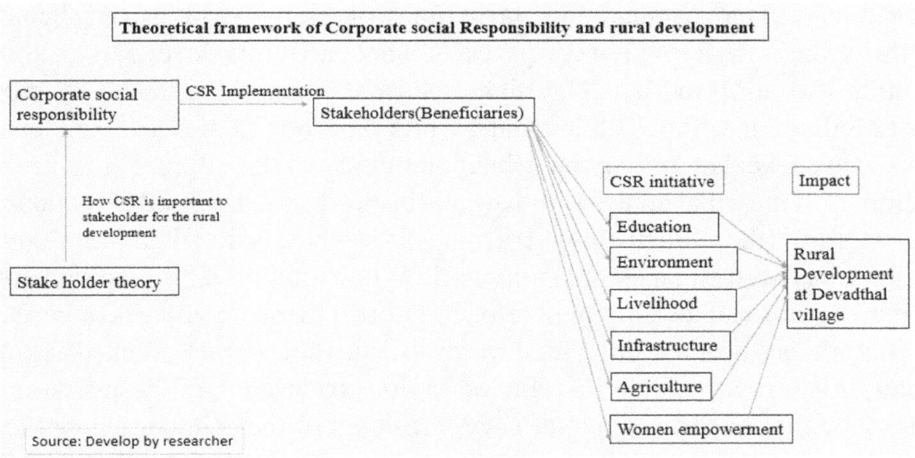

Research Questions

1. What kind of projects are undertaken by corporate in the rural region?
2. What is the socio-economic impact of CSR projects in rural communities?
3. How CSR projects are implemented at the grassroot level?

Research Methodology

To study the CSR and rural development activities and to understand the impact of CSR projects at Devadthal village, primary data was collected through interviews and Focused Group Discussions of different stakeholders: Corporate CSR officials, NGO implementing partners, Panchayat members and community people. Devalthal village has been selected for the study because of various CSR projects being implemented in the village Secondary data was collected from government reports and newspaper articles. Current study has used focus group discussion as a tool to gather impact stories in Devadthal village. The study is descriptive in nature. The data collection process was supported by Dharti Charitable Trust and they readily provided all images in the paper used for academic illustrative purposes.

Brief Introduction of Devadthal Village

Devadthal village is situated in Bavla block of Ahmadabad district. People of this village are living in very peaceful manner. But the level of education is quite low at Devadthal. The highest formal education attained by most in the village is up to 12th standard while only one person is a graduate. This is even weaker among the tribal community of the village. Most of the members of the tribal households have not been educated beyond 5th standard. Agriculture is the main livelihood of this village wherein the tribal community majorly has been engaged in labour work. Whole of Gujarat is reaping fruits of major industrial development reforms but still there are villages or certain communities who are waiting for reforms in education, employment, drinking water, infrastructure, better livelihood options to reach them despite strong efforts by the state to reach out to every resident of the country. The village under study was not able to access these opportunities in the past. Empirically therefore, it becomes important to analyse the implementation of welfare programmes through the experiences of the tribal community residents to understand the perspectives of the beneficiaries for whom such programmes have been designed.

Success Story of the Village

The details of this section are the outcomes recorded through the focus group discussions undertaken for research. Navapara tribal area in Devadthal village was not having its own water supply system and was operated from main Devadthal village which is 2.7 kms far away and was problematic in terms of drinking water resources. For years, families migrated in search of work, eventually leading to children dropping out of schools. Since de-siltation of water body was done with support of Tata Motors Limited & Sumant Moolgaokar Development Foundation (SMDF) it helped in increasing depth and storage capacity of water available and made it more accessible for tribal community. The quality of life of tribal community has improved as there is increase in the availability of water for domestic use and decrease in workload in homes for the women who generally are managing such works for families. This facility has ensured water to households in the village throughout the year and water security even in the years of droughts. De-siltation of the water body also helped in recharging of 60% of the wells in the village. Duration of water availability has increased during summer months & has led to improved farm productivity. One of the most significant achievements is generation of livelihood. It was mentioned that there has been a marked increase in agriculture production and consequently income levels of households. Not only was drinking water a problem but also insufficient water for irrigation purpose. Prior to this intervention crops used to suffer during deficient rain seasons and therefore productivity and production would be low. As drought was a regular phenomenon, many families would migrate to neighbouring places in search of sustenance. This situation has changed tremendously with the availability of sufficient water for farming. Since last ten years paddy crop were harvested only in 40 ha. due to unavailability of water. Productivity & yield of paddy crop was only 20% due to infrequent rains & less water. Farmers suffered severe losses and earned meagre income. After this intervention there was considerable increase in area of cultivation from 40 to 212 ha. The productivity & yield of paddy crops has increased from 20 to 100% owing to the availability of additional water. In 2022, the percent change in the area of cultivation and productivity & yield of paddy crops has considerably increased. There is drastic change in the productivity of paddy grown in rainy season along with the area under cultivation. Farmers have earned income of more than Rs crore from paddy crops (in 2022). The employment and income of tribal households have increased substantially. Now farmers will be able to harvest wheat also in the coming years during winters. The farmers can now harvest around three crops in a year. This will eventually decline the tribal migrating outward due to a rise in employment opportunities. This intervention is a blessing for the tribal villagers as it has increased earnings and prosperity in the village.

Dam Construction and Livelihood Generation

This is a unique project wherein a stakeholder participatory model can be observed. The local government has provided the land for the dam construction, TATA Motors Ltd. and Sumant Moolgaokar Development Foundation has funded the project, Dharti Charitable Trust, a civil society organisation has implemented the project while the community was engaged in the construction of the dam and majority labour was provided by them. After this intervention there was considerable increase in area of cultivation from 40 to 212 ha. The productivity & yield of paddy crops has increased from 20 to 100% owing to the availability of additional water. In 2022, the percent change in the area of cultivation and productivity & yield of paddy crops has considerably increased. There is drastic change in the productivity of paddy grown in rainy season along with the area under cultivation. The employment and income of tribal has increased substantially. The project has enormously impacted the lives of the rural community. The water stored with the help of check dam is being used for agricultural activity and fisheries. This has also resolved the issues of water for domestic requirements and for cattle. The household income has almost doubled of these community.

Figure 2. CSR Company - TATA Motors Ltd & Sumant Moolgaokar Development Foundation (SMDF), Implementing Partner - Dharti Charitable Trust

Skill Development for Women

Skill development projects for young women is being supported by TATA company and implemented by DCT. Under this CSR project young women between the age of 18 to 35 are trained for basic stitching and sewing skills.

Under the project total 40 young women have been trained and consequent to the skill training there has been improvement in the socio-economic status of these women. 32 out of 40 women who earlier had no employment are now able to earn through working in a garment factory and others are earning through self-employment. The project has not only helped these young women to become independent but has also improved their social status in the family as well as in the community.

Figure 3. CSR Company - TATA MOTORS LTD, Implementing Partner - Dharti Charitable Trust (DCT)

Reconstruction of Primary School

Under this project government primary school is being reconstructed with the support of a non-government organization. The primary school construction program aims to provide quality education as well as holistic development to the underprivileged children in the rural areas. It is designed to empower students to explore, question, reason and communicate effectively. It also encourages them to connect with their community and stay rooted to their local culture. Also, the construction has an element of BALA (Building as a Learning Aid). It is expected to reduce the school drop-out ratio and also helped in improvising the quality of teaching and learning activities and all necessary approvals are facilitated by the concerned government department. This is one best practice recorded for improving steps towards enhanced quality of education in rural areas. As all partners are concerned with making people aware and educated, it will directly benefit to the community at large.

Figure 4. Implementing partner - Round Table India

Model Anganwadi (Play School)

The aim of this program is to provide non-formal pre-school education on one hand and also breaking the vicious cycle of malnutrition, morbidity and mortality among mothers and children on the other hand. An Anganwadi is the focal point for the delivery of many services to the community.

The Anganwadi program adds to the larger goal of socially empowering women in the community. Many women from the village have been able to sustain their daily lives and more importantly take part in activities outside the home for work while also contributing to the family income. This has uplifted the socio-economic status of women in the village as they find true respect from their families and village community for their contributions. Many mothers from the village have been able to leave their children at the Anganwadi which is generally hygienic and safe places as they work at other places without worries of their children being taken care off. This has added to their well-being. It has been a major provider of some leisure time to the women of the community. This progress on both fronts, economic and social for the women of the village has been possible through platforms and associations. The said project has fully funded the reconstruction of the Anganwadi which in turn helped in reducing malnutrition among children with the support from Integrated Child Development Scheme (ICDS).

Figure 5. CSR company - Zydas Cadila Pharmaceuticals, implementing partner - Dharti Charitable Trust

Organic Farming, Kitchen Garden & Tree Plantation

In this project organization created awareness about organic farming and also took up some specific intervention to promote organic farming and development of kitchen garden for good health of the people of the village. In the village, more than 35 kitchen gardens have been prepared every year to produce organic vegetables which the residents of the village used for self-consumption only. Organic farming has been undertaken in some parts of the village. It is will take time to make people aware about the benefits and impact of organic farming. 7000 to 10000 saplings were distributed by Dharti Charitable Trust with the support of Tata Motors Ltd. and Forest Department to support Integrated Tribal Village Development Project in 2021.

Figure 6. Implementing partner: Dharti Charitable Trust CSR Company: Tata Motors Ltd

Findings

The CSR programme in Devadthal has impacted more than 175 households by enhancing their livelihood opportunities for farming and fisheries. The village residents got more than rupees one crore of income in 2022 from farming by using the water from the dam built under the CSR project. Dam water is very helpful to villager for cultivation of fisheries which tribal population are expert to do this work. After intervention of CSRs in Devadthal, the village community got employment in village itself. It has directly impacted the livelihoods and well-being of the residents of Devadthal. Likewise, the school building was constructed by CSR fund which is inspiring people to get education as well as other organizations to contribute towards making impact on education. Now the village has a well-equipped primary school building where children of the village are getting their education without any disturbance. The village is having a newly constructed Anganwadi which provides safe and happy space for children to play while also getting the right kind of nutrition at the same place. The kitchen garden project is providing the additional nutrition and good health to people who have implemented and used it. Tailoring classes have enabled women to do at least stitching work for their own household requirements while for many it has provided productive employment in or around the village. Major institutional contributions in the village development have come from Tata Motors Limited, Dharti Charitable Trust, Zydus Cadila Pharmaceuticals, Round Table India. CSR projects in Devadthal have used both the methods, direct implementation as well as through collaborative partnerships with social organizations, along with community participation. These organizations have been working here in collaboration with the state and the community for sustainable rural development. Thus, as we try to analyse the activities and projects implemented under the ambit of CSR, one can strongly connect to the significance of stakeholder participation as advocated by Freeman's Stakeholder Theory.

Suggestions and Challenges

The government can encourage and incentivize big companies to take into account the social and economic issues of the rural areas. Social audits should be regularly conducted by the third party to evaluate the performance and impact on rural community. CSR projects help to eradicate problems in the rural areas as well as take rural areas on path of development with the financial and social support of organization-based setup at that location. There are but many challenges too to participate effectively in rural areas for CSR activities. People in the rural areas do not have much knowledge about CSR activities so they do not show enough interest in participation and contribution towards it. A major challenge is always that some of the people only favour individual benefit as against that of whole community. This attitude poses a great hurdle in prioritizing and implementation. Major challenges in rural areas mainly comprises of better education, pure drinking water, good health facilities and strengthened road network in areas.

CONCLUSION

During this study we clearly get to know about the joint interventions of CSRs, NGOs and Government at Devadthal Village as well as community support and community intervention or contribution towards the development of village. Projects being managed at Devadthal village are covered under "Integrated Tribal Village Development" and under this there are sub projects named "Promoting Education", working on constructing new school building for this village and proving necessary resources to students, "Livelihood Generation" by constructing dam for doing farming of fish, "Organic Farming and Kitchen Garden" to save environment and making good health, these all sub projects are running very smoothly to provide as much benefit to the residents of the village and when one enters into this village one can witness a very positive impact of CSR. Corporate Social Responsibility projects have made a significant contribution for the socio-economic development of the rural community. The major areas of improvement identified are skill development, education, malnutrition, women empowerment and livelihood opportunities.

REFERENCES

Damor, K. (2021). Gujarat ranks second in CSR funds received. *Times of India.* https://timesofindia.indiatimes.com/city/ahmedabad/gujarat-ranks-second-in-csr-funds-received/articleshow/87897669.cms

Freeman, R. E. (1984). *Strategic management: A stakeholder approach.* Pitman Publishing Inc.

Malhotra, R. K., Bohra, N. S., & Upadhyay, R. (2021). An Investigation Of Sustainable Development Within CSR For Rural Development In India, *Ilkogretim Online Elementary Education. Online (Bergheim)*, *20*(01).

Maniktala, J., & Punjabi, L.C. (2016). Corporate Social Responsibility: Perspectives and Challenges in Rural India. *IOSR Journal of Business and Management* (IOSR-JBM) pp. 41-46.

MCA. (2013). *The Companies Act, 2013.* Ministry of Corporate Affairs. https://www.mca.gov.in/Ministry/pdf/CompaniesAct2013.pdf

MCA. (2014). *General Circular No 21/2014.* Ministry of Corporate Affairs. https://www.mca.gov.in/Ministry/pdf/General_Circular_21_2014.pdf

Ministry of Rural Development. (2019). *Development of Rural Areas is one of the Priorities of the Modi Government.* Rural NIC. https://rural.nic.in/en/press-release/development-rural-areas-one-priorities-modi-government-narendra-singh-tomar

Patel, J.R. (2014). Role of corporate social responsibility in rural development. *Research Hub-International Multidisciplinary Research Journal*, *1*(2).

Poonam. (2016), Corporate Social Responsibility in Rural Development Sector: An Introduction, *International Journal of Scientific and Research Publications*, *5*(10).

Prasad, R. N. (2015). Theoretical Counter on CSR, Trusteeship, Corporate Social Responsibility & Peace.

Report, F. A. O. (2016). *India at a glance*. Food and Agricultural Organisation of the UN. Retrieved from https://www.fao.org/india/fao-in-india/india-at-a-glance/en/

Report, I. (2022). *National Family Health Survey 2019-21 (NFHS-5)*. International Institute of Population Studies. https://ruralindiaonline.org/en/library/resource/national-family-health-survey-nfhs-5-2019-21-india/

Vastradmath, N. (2015). The Role of Corporate Social Responsibility for an Inclusive Growth in the Society. *International Journal of Scientific and Research Publications*, *5*(10).

World Bank Report. (2018). Rural population (% of total population)-India. World Bank. https://data.worldbank.org/indicator/SP.RUR.TOTL.ZS?locations=IN

ENDNOTE

1 The Indian Companies Act amended in 2013, under section 135 has made it mandatory for corporates of India to make CSR investments in priority areas as envisaged by the government. Any company with a net worth of more than Rs.500 cr., or turnover of Rs.1000 cr. or more, or net profit of Rs. 5 cr. or more in the preceding financial year needs to spend a minimum of 2 percent of the average net profits of the preceding previous 3 financial years in CSR activities.

Chapter 7
Feminization of Migration

Neema Gnanadev
Bangalore University, India

ABSTRACT

The migration of women has emerged as an important field of research within the larger domain of migration studies and is being explored under various disciplines. Despite the growing proportion of women in the global migration pattern, the contribution of women to the migrant labour force has been largely overlooked. The paper highlights the fact that the feminization of migration has undoubtedly increased the visibility of women in the migration, but much more needs to be done in terms of evolving policies for ensuring their protection and security, and above all empowering them and increasing their participation in the labour market. The findings of the study also suggest that though females accompany their spouses, their economic role need not be undermined. The work participation rate of female migrants as compared to female non-migrants increases in rural-urban migration over a period of time as is evident from the data. In a nutshell, the significance of economic factors in determining female migration should be given greater importance in migration studies.

DOI: 10.4018/978-1-6684-6878-4.ch007

INTRODUCTION

The migration of women has emerged as an important field of research within the larger domain of migration studies and is being explored under various disciplines. Despite the growing proportion of women in the global migration pattern, the contribution of women to the migrant labour force has been largely overlooked.

The neglect of research on women's migration is attributed to a number of factors. The existing economic theories of migration view migration as male phenomenon for economic reasons and look at female migration for family-related reasons rather than economic considerations. Several researchers have concluded that migration of females is largely caused by marriage considering them as dependents (Bose, 1973; Rele, 1969). This kind of gender bias in the analysis of migration patterns is often explained in the context of India's institutional and socio-cultural norms characterising women playing secondary role to those of men. Due to this male-centric preference, the dynamics underlying female migration remains unexplored.

Feminization of Migration: Meaning

Of late there is a trend towards an increasing proportion of women amongst migrant workers. The high share of female migrants to total female population is termed as 'feminization' of migration '(Oishi, 2005).

The objectives of the present paper are as follows:

- To understand the patterns and determinants, of female migration in India and
- To examine the challenges of feminization of migration.

Sources of Data

For analysing the trends and patterns of female migration, Census of India (1971 to 2001) is used.

Feminization Of Migration in India: Magnitude

According to 2001 Census, of 309 million migrants (based on place of last residence,) female migrants constitute 218 million while it is 91 million for male. Migrants constitute around 30 per cent of the total population; whereas male and female migrants constitute 18 per cent and 45 per cent of their population respectively.

Unlike the world trend, the migration rate of women in India has been considerably greater than that of males for decades. As per the Periodic Labour Force Survey (PLFS) of 2020-21, the female migration rate was 47.9%, which was 37.2 percentage points greater than the males Not only in terms of magnitude but also from the perspective of development, internal migration of women is an important factor influencing socio-economic development of the country. Internal migration such as intra district migration, inter district migration and inter-state migration has greater potential for reducing poverty especially feminisation of poverty and also for meeting the Development Goals.

The main reasons for migration of women in general include the following:

- lack of viable opportunities in the home country,
- widespread poverty in the family,
- desire for a better future
- a higher remuneration in the destination country
- factors such as the harsh realities of family life,
- alcoholism of the male members of the family and
- oppressive social systems, playing a crucial role in influencing a woman's decision to migrate.
- Other causes for migration being natural disasters, conflicts and violence.

Traditionally the women in India played a secondary role in the family depending on menfolk for running the family. But the following factors have influenced mobility pattern of Indian women in recent times.

- transformation of the Indian economy,
- transport and communication facilities,
- improvement in the levels of education at primary, secondary and higher levels,
- shifting of workforce from agriculture to tertiary activities,
- shift in job pattern,
- shift in government policy.

Feminization of Migration: Sri Lanka, Bangladesh, Nepal

The feminization of migration is largely associated with the migration of women from Sri Lanka. About 80 to 90 per cent of women from Sri Lanka migrate to work as domestic workers (SLBFE 2009). In the present decade, the migration of women workers from Sri Lanka is inextricably linked with the employment of domestic workers in Western Asia. Sri Lankan women migrants are predominantly Sinhalese and Muslim; the number of Tamils is much lower. While migrants were drawn primarily from the urban areas surrounding the capital city of Colombo in the late 1970s, they were from all over the island, including the western districts of Colombo, Kurunegala and Gampaha.

Prior to the current rise of women's international migration, women migrants were mainly working in plantations or in free trade zones (Kottegoda, 2006) and comprised a higher workforce participation rate. The vibrant garment industry spread across Sri Lanka also boosted the number of women migrant workers as many women trained in these factories have found jobs in garment factories overseas Despite liberalization, unemployment remained a major problem and the standard of living of the population further worsened with the withdrawal of the decades-long food subsidy programme in 1979. The increased demand for workers in Western Asia gave the Government of Sri Lanka an avenue to overcome the low economic growth. In this context, the historical legacies of women employment outside the household also helped women from Sri Lanka to migrate in large scale (Oishi, 2005).

Women's migration from Nepal presents a different trajectory. Migration before the 1990s often meant male migration in which women accompanied their spouses, parents or relatives. Patriarchal attitudes coupled with a lack of reliable and available networks as well as money to support migrant initiatives hindered the independent movement of women migrant workers (Adhikari, 2006). As in the cases of Sri Lanka and Nepal, widespread poverty, unemployment at home, and wage differences at the destination country triggered international labour migration from India to Western Asia

Though female migration from Bangladesh continues to be low, there has been a gradual uptrend from the less than 1 per cent share of females in the annual labour flow that prevailed until 2000. It is ironic that the social situation that inhibits women's migration also tends to be a major factor pushing female migration. As indicated in studies by IOM and the International Research and Training Institute for the Advancement of Women (INSTRAW) (2000) women who face unhappy social situations, including difficult marriages, harassment and violence, see migration primarily as a quest for independence and a means of realizing their self-worth.

Academic literature on international labour migration in India is largely focused on male migration with invisibility of women migrants in data. This seems ironic in the case of Kerala which records high levels of labour migration of women, particularly nurses, to Western Asia.

It is evident from various case studies that women's migration is now taking place increasingly for employment purposes (Singh, 1984; Sharma, 1986; Shanti, 1991; Sundari, 2004; Premi, 2001). Technological developments in agriculture have displaced many women from agricultural work. Economic hardships in the form of poverty and lack of employment opportunities force them to migrate for survival. Therefore, women are compelled to migrate owing to their economic hardships. On the other hand, the emergence of gender segregated labour markets due to globalisation creates demand for females' labourers in export processing zones, garment industries, jute processing etc. which act as a pull factor for females to migrate. Thus women are no longer passive agents; rather they are influenced by various socio-economic factors in the context of development reforms occurring in the country.

Growth of Migrants

Unlike the world, the migration rate of women in India has been considerably greater than that of males for decades. As per the Periodic Labour Force Survey (PLFS) of 2020-21, the female migration rate was 47.9%, which was 37.2 percentage points greater than the males.

The table shows migrants having less than 5 years of migration duration, it shows a negative growth rate indicating a sharp reduction during the decade.1981-1991 It might be due to the fact that the process of globalisation had a greater impact on the mobility pattern, thereby reducing the spatial mobility of people and increasing the capital mobility, but the post economic reform (1991-2001) period shows a spurt in the growth of migration both for males and females.

Table clearly shows that the magnitude of female migration increases over a period of time.). The female-male ratio as revealed from the table implies that the growth rate of female migration is higher than that of male migration. A variety of factors such as globalization, emergence of gender specific labour market, extreme poverty, mechanization of agriculture, environmental degradation etc. are responsible for increasing the growth of female's migration (Sundari, 2004; Arya et al, 2005). Table-2 presents the percentage distribution of migrants by sex and below 5-year duration of It might be that the process of globalisation has a greater impact on the mobility pattern, thereby reducing the spatial mobility of people and increasing the capital mobility, but the post economic reform period shows a spurt in the growth of migration both for males and females.

Table 1. Growth of migrants (<5 years)

Census year	Male	female	Total
1971-81	14.02	9.79	17.20
1981-1991	-7.71	-17.75	-0.70
1991-2001	20.63	21.34	20.22

Table 2. Internal migrants in India – percentage of migrants to total population

Census	Female	Male	Total persons
1971	43.1	19	30.6
1981	43.9	17.6	30.3
1991	41.2	14.6	27.4
2001	44.6	17.5	30.6

Source: Census of India 1971-2001

Patterns of Female Migration: Insights From Census

The migration data in India are classified into four different types of migration with the help of administrative boundaries of a district and state:

1. *Intra-district Migrants: women migrate* to various blocks but born within the district.
2. *Inter-district Migrants: Women* born in another district of the same state migrate to other districts.
3. *Interstate Migrants:* Those women born in one state migrate to other states preferably in search of jobs. For example, laborers from Orissa and Jharkhand migrated to TamilNadu and worked as labourers for laying

down roads under National Highways scheme. Workers from Nagaland migrated to preambular in Tamil Nādu and work as labourers in the Guest house o run by companies

4. *International Migrants Women migrate to various countries in search of job or for pursuing higher education*

.In 1991, among intra-district migrants, 3,643 females were found per 1,000 males. During the year 2001 in case of inter district, interstate the sex ratio was 663, 1102 respectively.

Table 3. Sex-ratio of migrants by migration type (males per 1000 females), 1971-2001, duration <5yr

Census/type	1971	1981	1991	2001
Intra district	596	571	460	427
Inter district	898	815	675	663
Inter state	1283	938	975	1102

Source: Census of India 1971-2001

This growing trend in international migration can be attributed to some major developments such as rising numbers of women migrants, growth of women-centric occupations, migration of women in an independent capacity, women-related legislations and growth of gendered perspectives on various issues. These factors together increased the visibility of women in the migration process and have given rise to what has been termed the 'feminization of migration'

Determinants of Female Migration

The data on reason for migration are useful to understand the motivational factors behind the movement of women

The reasons for migration were classified into five broad groups — employment,

- education,
- family movement,
- marriage and

- others.

The scope of data was further increased in the 1991 census, as additional categories of

- business and
- natural calamities such as flood, drought, and so on were made. Others include movement due to displacement and retirement, which was not covered by employment, business, education, family movement, marriage, natural

Table-4 shows the sex-ratio of migrants across various distance categories. It is evident from the table that there has been predominance of females in all distance categories except in the case of interstate migration. In the below -5 year duration of residence, male dominance was higher in 1971 and 2001. While the growth rate of female migrants is higher during 1991-2001 decade as compared to earlier decades.

Table 4. Female-male ratio in the census

Census	Female-male ratio
1971	2.22
1981	2.41
1991	2.71
2001	2.41

Source: Census of India 1971-2001

This growing trend can be attributed to some major developments in international migration such as rising numbers of women migrants, growth of women-centric occupations, migration of women in an independent capacity, women-related legislations and growth of gendered perspectives on various issues. These factors together increased the visibility of women in the migration process and have given rise to what has been termed the 'feminization of migration'

Table 5. Spatial pattern percentage distribution of female migrants by migration streams, 1971-2001

Migration stream	1971	1981	1991	2001
Rural to rural	36.3	62.92	63.36	63.78
Rural to urban	21.42	15.65	16.65	16.72
Urban to rural	10.82	7.8	7.39	6.39
Urban to urban	31.46	13.59	12.6	13.11

Source: Census of India 1971-2001

The above table shows that there is predominance of females in the rural-rural stream followed by the rural to urban, urban-urban and urban-rural streams respectively. Although the rural stream constitutes the dominant category, the emerging migration pattern indicates that rural to urban and urban to urban migration is becoming more pronounced. Many studies point out that the gender-specific demand for labour, particularly in export industries, has resulted in the out migration of females (Roberts, 1997; Pandey, 1998) Regional disparities of development along with socio-economic transformations have brought about a shift in the distribution of rural-urban migration.

Table 6. Work participation rate of female migrants

Work status of female migrants	Work participation rate
Migrants	36.47
Non migrants	14.80

Source: Census of India 2001

Challenges

This paper explores the various nuances of the feminization of migration and aspects of female migration focusing on India. It begins with an overview of the growing numbers of women in the migratory flows. Despite the rising numbers and increased participation of women in the developmental migration, they remain increasingly vulnerable and exposed to exploitation. While migration can be a source of economic empowerment and progress for women migrants and their families, the existing system of migration poses many challenges for women who want to benefit from migration and the potential employment opportunities. Some of the possible consequences under this system are as follows:

- cases of physical violence,
- sexual abuse,
- withholding of passports, restrictions on mobility and communications and
- even death while trying to escape (Migrant Forum in Asia 2004).

Migrant women who escape at exploitative work setting and bring legal action against their employers rarely succeed. The lack of access to legal services and redress systems by appropriate authorities leads them to be deported and lose their employment income, jeopardizing the livelihood of their families back home. As such, many women migrant workers choose to continue to work in their places of employment no matter the level of abuse and exploitation in absence of a better alternative. Despite these challenges, recent trends suggest that more women workers will go overseas in the search of better employment opportunities in the future

The paper highlights the fact that that feminization of migration has undoubtedly increased the visibility of women in the migration but much more needs to be done in terms of evolving policies for ensuring their protection and security and above all empowering them and increasing their participation in the labour market.

The findings of the study also suggest that though females accompany their spouses, their economic role need not be undermined. The work participation rate of female migrants as compared to female non-migrants increases in rural- urban migration over a period of time as is evident from the data, in a nutshell, the significance of economic factors in determining female migration should be given greater importance in migration studies.

REFERENCES

Adhikari, J. (2006). Poverty, globalisation and gendered labour migration in Nepal. *Women and migration in Asia: Poverty, gender and migration, 2*, 87-106.

Bose, A. (1973). *Studies in India's Urbanistation: 1901-1971*. Tata-Mcgraw Hill.

Kottegoda, S. (2006). *Bringing home the money: Migration and poverty in gender politics in Sri Lanka. Poverty, gender and migration*, 49-71.

Oishi, N. (2005). *Women in motion: Globalization, state policies, and labor migration in Asia*. Stanford University Press. doi:10.1515/9780804766906

Pandey, D. (1998). Migrant labour, employment and gender dimensions. *The Indian Journal of Social Work*, *62*(1), 743–765.

Premi, M. K. (2001). Who Migrates to Delhi? *Demography India*, *30*(1), 49–59.

Rele, J. R. (1969). Trends and Significance of Internal Migration in India. *Sankhya Series B*, *31*(3-4), 501–508.

Roberts, K. D. (1997). China's Tidal Wave of Migrant Labour: What can we learn from Mexican Undocumented Migration to United States. *The International Migration Review*, *31*(2), 249–293. PMID:12292872

Shanti, K (1991). Issues relating to economic migration of females. *The Indian journal of labour Economics, 34* (4), 335-46.

Sharma, U. (1986). *Women's work, Class and the Urban Household: A study of Shimla, North India*. Tavistock Publications.

Singh, A. M. (1984). Rural to Urban migration of women in India: Patterns and Implications. In J T Fawcett et al (eds), Women in the Cities of South Asia: Migration and Urban Adaptation. Boulder, Colorado: West view press

Sundari, S. (2004). *Migrant Women and Urban labour Market: Concepts and Case studies of problems, gains and losses*. Deep and Deep.

Chapter 8
The Impacts of Lavender Gardens on Rural Tourism

Serkan Bertan
Pamukkale University, Turkey

ABSTRACT

In this study, the impacts of lavender gardens in terms of rural tourism were examined. For this purpose, data was collected by interview form in Gözler Neighborhood of Pamukkale district of Denizli province. When the data were analyzed, the economic, environmental, and socio-cultural effects of lavender gardens were determined. It has been determined that lavender gardens support rural development by increasing the number of products, entrepreneurship, job opportunities, investment, and quality of life. Social relations have increased in the region, leisure and tourism awareness has been created, and loyalty, participation, and solidarity have increased. The importance of natural resources has been understood, ecological awareness has been created, environmental protection and environmental awareness have increased, the importance of lavender in agricultural areas has increased, and the importance of a sustainable environment has emerged.

INTRODUCTION

Sustainable development which is not to harm the ecological balance in meeting the current needs in order to meet the needs in the future covers the concepts of development and protection (Erdem and Bozan, 2021: Yavuz and Zığındere, 2000). Rural tourism, whose importance has increased with the

DOI: 10.4018/978-1-6684-6878-4.ch008

epidemic, which includes touristic activities in rural areas, provides added value for the regions and especially supports sustainable development (Bozok and Karaman, 2018). With the differentiation of tourism experiences in recent years, tourism has been diversified and the demand for rural tourism has increased (Aytuğar and Aydoğdu, 2021; Ongun et al., 2018).

Definition of rural tourism, effects of rural tourism, effects of covid 19 epidemic on rural tourism, rural tourism stakeholders, rural tourism management and performance, rural tourism theory and methods, rural tourism marketing, rural tourism market segment, rural tourism products, rural tourism image, tourist satisfaction and behavior in rural tourism, rural tourism policies, rural tourism and technologies, tourist motivations in rural tourism and rural tourism potential are discussed in researches on rural tourism (Karali, et. al., 2021; Rosalina, et al., 2021; Vaishar and Šťastna, 2022; Silva, 2022). In this study, the effects of lavender gardens in Denizli Province, Pamukkale District, Gözler Neighborhood in terms of rural tourism were examined.

Literature Review

Rural tourism, which has been associated with eco-tourism, agro-tourism, cultural tourism and other types of tourism, is very important in terms of rural development in recent years (Soykan, 2003; Yazgan and Kadanalı, 2012; Albayrak and Tuzukan, 2020; Torun, 2013). Rural tourism is a tourism activity carried out in rural areas where the underpopulation and exposed to migration due to economic problems (Cengiz and Akkuş, 2012; Çeken et al., 2012). Rural tourism, which provides the revival of rural areas, can be done in all seasons, integrates with other types of tourism, contributes to the protection of the natural environment and cultural heritage, serves the understanding of sustainable tourism and an important factor in the promotion of the country, which is in direct contact with the local community and its social and economic life, provides local products, natural and cultural heritage (Badulescu vd., 2015; Soykan, 2003; Cengiz and Akkuş, 2012).

Rural tourism provides rural development, provides employment to women in rural areas, prevents migration by stimulating local economies, prevents the disappearance of rural culture by developing rural areas, protects the natural environment, plays a role in the protection of cultural heritage, local development and increasing the social and economic quality of life of the people of the region, development of infrastructure, health and education services, solution to the immigration problem by providing new job opportunities, creates income and new jobs for the rural community from various sources, slows down migration, employs women, raises awareness of protecting and owning the culture of the local people, and develops the entrepreneurial spirit of the rural society, prevented that nature and the rural environment remain uncontrolled due to deprivation (Baykal and Ataberk, 2020; Torun, 2013; Kodaş and Sibel; 2012; Yazgan and Kadanalı, 2012, Emekli et. al., 2007; Demircioğlu, 1993).

Rural tourism is a very advantageous type of tourism because it can be done in smaller groups after the COVID-19 epidemic, and hygiene can be provided with social distance (Arslan and Kendir, 2020). Rural development, which aims to balance the differences between the city and the countryside, is what needs to be done to increase the welfare level of people living in rural areas (Sezen and Boz, 2021). Rural tourism is strengthens the economic structure in rural areas, leading people to be overwhelmed by the urban lifestyle, participating in holiday activities with different motives, wanting to have different experiences, tourists wanting to go to calmer and natural environments, experiencing rural life (Kodaş and Sibel, 2012; Çeken, et. al., 2012).

As a type of agricultural tourism, which is important in ensuring rural development and sustainability, bee tourism is a viable type of tourism in Turkey, providing important opportunities for activating rural areas, forming new lines of business and supporting rural areas with tradition and culture (Uzun et. al., 2022). With the development of rural tourism, the incomes of small businesses have increased, and in order for rural tourism to be sustainable, the local people should be made aware of tourism and should be encouraged, it is necessary to develop tourism by realizing superstructure investments and raise awareness for rural tourism (Dalgın and Yemenoğlu, 2020).

Since the local people's perspectives on tourism activities are related to the development of that region in terms of tourism, rural tourism contributes to the local people (Akkaşoğlu et. al., 2019). Handicrafts also have great potential in terms of rural tourism as they are a touristic product (Kaya and Erol, 2021). Since the inclusion of rural tourism in development items is important for the regional economy, rural tourism should be included in rural development (Yılmaz and Gürol, 2012).

The scale, which was developed to determine the perceptions of farmers about agritourism management, was examined under 9 factors: factor 1 environmental ımpact (ı think agro tourism will cause air pollution; land development for agro tourism will cause more; ı think that mass development will increase temperatures and spoil the agriculture business; ı think that agro tourism will increase the temperature of this place; ı think agricultural pesticides and fertilizers will cause pollutşon of the environment), factor 2 accessibility (ı think that the steep slope of the road will affect tourist's access to my farm; ı think that the width of the road will affect tourist's access to my farm; ı think my farm's location, far from the main road, will stop tourists from coming; ı think the road is the biggest constraint that stops tourists coming to my farm), factor 3 economic benefit (agro tourism generates more income for my farm; agro tourism increases my land value; ı think the agro tourism business will bring additional which can lead to the disturbance of the farmers' daily income; agro tourism strengthens the local economy; agro tourism provides enough good jobs to the local community; factor 4 entrepreneurial knowledge (ı think ı have enough experience to run an agro tourism business; ı think ı have enough knowledge to run an agro natural environment, tourist visits). tourism business), factor 4 socio-cultural benefits (ı like learning about tourists' countries and cultures; ı love interacting with tourists; my interactions with tourists are positive and useful), factor 6 crowding (tourism causes crowding and congestion in this area; tourism increases traffic jams), factor 7 awareness (ı think that agro tourism is a business based on agriculture; ı think agro tourism needs a natural environment; ı think that if ı develop the land, it will attract more tourists to my farm; ı think that agro tourism is an activity where tourists visit farms), factor 8 constraints (ı think that the destruction, by the visitors to the plants in my farm, is one of the constraints that stop me being involved in agro tourism; seasonality of tourist arrival stops me from being involved in agro tourism; ı think that tourists visiting to my farm will disturb my daily life schedule), factor 9 land ıssues (ı think that limited land size will stop tourists coming to my farm; ı think the size of my land is too small to run an agrotourism business) (Kunasekaran et. al., 2011). Collaboration of local people, private sector and government is necessary for product development, diversification and marketing in agricultural tourism (Eshun and Tichaawa, 2020).

Farms operating in the field of farm tourism, which has started to become popular in recent years, a sub-branch of rural tourism and entered the development process, are small-scale units that make organic agriculture based on ecological principles, carry out nature-friendly production, and at the same time continue the rural life, traditions and customs of the region they are located in. aims to transfer its current values to future generations without losing its traditional texture (Tuncer and Bakırcı, 2021).

When the studies on lavender are examined, it has been revealed that the main purpose of the visits is to share photos of lavender gardens and holiday for rural experience, especially the visuality of lavender and social media posts are important factors in the decision of the visitors (Giray et. al., 2019). In the study, which deals with the lavender tourism potential of Kastamonu Province, it has been stated that lavender gardens are suitable in terms of climate and geography and can be a preferred destination center for lavender visitors (Aytuğar and Aydoğdu, 2021) . SWOT analysis within the scope of rural tourism of lavender cultivation in Isparta province Kuyucak Village, which is important in terms of rural tourism and especially lavender production, has been presented suggestions for the development of lavender tourism (Bozok and Karaman, 2018). In another study, the medicinal effects and usage areas of lavender, which is highly demanded in the world and in our country, were examined (Demir, 2019). Lavender is used in many of the foods and beverages in Kuyucak Village of Keçiborlu District of Isparta; It is thought that positive impressions are formed when visitors taste these flavors and contribute to gastronomy tourism (Akşap, 2018). In the study of Ongun et al. (2018), the importance of lavender gardens in Kuyucak Village in terms of rural tourism was emphasized, the contributions of lavender and the expectations of the local people were revealed. In the study conducted by Tarhan et al. (2019), Kuyucak Village was discussed in terms of rural development, and the views of the local people were evaluated, and it is understood that the visitors prefer lavender coffee and lavender crown first, and it is understood that the region is advantageous in terms of development. Previous studies mainly focus on the important of lavender for rural areas.

METHODOLGY

In this study, data were collected by semi-structured interview for individuals' perspectives on the effects of lavender. Interviews were held with lavender garden owners and people who have knowledge about lavender. Before starting the interview, the purpose of the study was explained and information was given about the study.

In the interview form, first of all, it contains information about the purpose of the study, who will be interviewed, the duration of the interview, and the data will be used for scientific purposes only. In order to determine the effects of lavender tourism in Denizli Province Pamukkale District Gözler

Neighborhood in terms of rural tourism, detailed questions were asked in order to obtain more explanation and information about the effects of lavender gardens in the semi-structured interview, and the interviews lasted an average of 1 hour and 20 minutes. Along with the interview, the researcher observed the lavender gardens. First of all, a pilot test was conducted to understand whether the questions in the interview form were understood, and it was concluded that the statements were appropriate, clear, easy and correctly understood. After the pilot study, interviews were held with lavender garden owners and people who knew about lavender.

In the coding formed by collecting the data in categories (Creswell, 2013), common expressions that are meaningful and similar to each other by examining more than once are discussed under the same theme under certain headings, taking into account their meanings in the sentence. The determined themes were shared with the people and experts interviewed about lavender in Gözler neighborhood, and their opinions were taken and evaluated.

Finding

In this study, which was conducted to examine the effects of lavender gardens in terms of rural tourism, 16 people were interviewed in Pamukkale District, Gözler Neighborhood. Thyme was planted for the first time in the region in 1994. The region started to be known as the center of Medicinal and Aromatic plants. It started planting sage in 2004 and lavender in 2008. Lavender seedlings were cultivated in the region. In 2019, lavender saplings were planted for tourism purposes.

Table 1. Lavender related products

Lavender ice cream	Lavender bunch	Cream
Lavender soda	Lavender crown	Lavender oil
Lavender honey	Lavender sapling	Cologne oil
Lavender jam	Lavender sachet	Lavender water
Lavender coffee	Lavender pillow	Soap
Lavender tea		Shampoo

Regarding lavender in Gözler Neighborhood, lavender honey, lavender jam, lavender coffee, lavender tea, lavender ice cream, lavender soda, lavender bunch, lavender crown, lavender sapling, lavender sachet, lavender oil, dried lavender, cologne, lavender water, cream, soap, shampoo and lavender pillow are offered to the visitors as souvenirs. In addition, since thyme and sage are produced in the region, thyme, thyme juice, thyme oil, thyme honey and sage are offered.

The distribution of themes in evaluating the effects of lavender tourism within the scope of rural tourism is shown in the table below.

Table 2. Distribution of themes

Economic	Entrepreneurship Employment Investment Sapling Life Promotion Unity Product Income	Socio -cultural	Traditional Social Regional Meals Events Recreation Consciousness Loyalty Participation Solidarity
Environmental	Natural resource ecological awareness environmental protection environmental awareness Agriculture biodiversity		

It has been emphasized that the most important theme in the effects of lavender gardens is economy. After the theme of economy, socio-cultural and environmental impact are the most emphasized themes, respectively. When the words related to economy are evaluated; emphasis was placed on the words entrepreneurship, employment, investment, sapling, quality of life, promotion, unity, product and income. Lavender increased entrepreneurship, created job opportunities, increased the number of lavender gardens, increased investment, increased seedling production increased quality of life, provided promotion, established a medical and aromatic producers' association, lavender-related products, and provided support to rural development by increasing income. In the theme of socio-cultural impact; regional identity, traditional culture, social relations, local products, food, cultural activities, recreation, tourism awareness, loyalty, participation and solidarity are emphasized. With lavender gardens, traditional culture was given importance, social relations increased, local products and dishes emerged, the number of cultural activities increased, recreation and tourism awareness were created, place attachemnt, loyalty, participation and solidarity with lavender increased. In the environmental impact theme, the words natural resources, ecological awareness, environmental protection, environmental awareness, agriculture, biodiversity are emphasized. With lavender gardens, the importance of natural resources has been understood, ecological awareness has been created, environmental protection and environmental awareness have increased, the importance of lavender in agricultural areas has increased and biodiversity has been achieved.

Results

Thyme was planted in 1994, sage in 2004, lavender in 2008, and lavender gardens were created for tourism purposes in 2019 in Gözler Neighborhood. Lavender honey, jam, coffee, tea, ice cream, soda, oil, dried, water, cream, soap and shampoo are offered as souvenirs in the lavender gardens.

Three themes emerged in this study: economic, socio -cultural and environmental impact. In the theme of economy, lavender tourism increased entrepreneurship, created job opportunities, increased the number of gardens, increased the production of saplings, increased the quality of life, promoted, established a medical and aromatic producers association, produced lavender-related products and provided support to local development by increasing income. In the theme of socio-cultural impact, traditional culture was given importance, social relations increased, local products and foods were offered, the number of cultural activities increased, the importance of social effects was emphasized by adopting lavender by creating a recreation and tourism awareness. The importance of natural resources has been understood, ecological awareness has been created, environmental protection and environmental awareness have increased, the importance of lavender in agricultural areas has increased and the importance of sustainable environment has emerged.

Gözler Neighborhood, high demand for lavender gardens began to occur, medicinal and aromatic plant production increased, lavender products gained fame with recognition, demand for lavender plants emerged, and farmers began to turn into investors. Thanks to the lavender gardens, the region has started to develop in terms of tourism, tourism has been diversified, the local people have provided economic gain, the region has been promoted, the demand for the products grown by the local people has increased, and the cultivation of lavender seedlings has increased.

Since the awareness of lavender in the region has increased in recent years, in order to increase the number of lavender gardens, Support should be given for lavender planting areas in large areas, taking into account the visuality. In order to increase awareness, national and international promotions and events should be planned through social media and television advertisements. For this purpose, a lavender festival should be held every year. Access roads to lavender gardens should be improved and the number of signboards should be increased. Lavender should be used in the landscape planning of Gözler Neighborhood, especially at the entrances of the neighborhood, lavender should be planted for visual appeal. It is necessary to create tour routes for lavender gardens. A lavender route should be created that includes Eski Gözler, waterfall, canyon and lavender gardens. In order for lavender-related products to generate better income, e-commerce should be established and marketed through cooperatives. For photography, the positions of the objects in the lavender garden should be planned both in terms of background and sunlight angles. Local dishes should be emphasized in the food and beverages given to the guests in the lavender gardens. In this study, Denizli Province, Pamukkale District, Gözler Neighborhood is discussed. In future studies, different destinations can be considered in terms of lavender .

REFERENCES

Akkaşoğlu, S., Telbalkan, M., Yılmaz, E. Z., & Ulama, Ş. (2019). Yerel Halkın Kırsal Turizme Bakış Açısı: Samsun Kızılırmak Deltası Örneği. *Lnternational Journal Of Geography And Geography Education*, (40), 295–310. doi:10.32003/iggei.557902

Akşap, Y. (2018). Gastronomik Bir Değer Olarak Lavanta. *Uluslararası Global Turizm Araştırmaları Dergisi*, *2*(1), 32–41.

Albayrak, A., and Tuzunkan, D. (2020). Kırsal Turizm Ve Türlerine Yönelik Hazırlanan Lisansüstü Tezlerin Bibliyometrik Analizi. *Turkish Studies- Social, 15*(1), 845-859.

Arslan, E., & Kendir, H. (2020). COVID-19 salgını sonrası yükselen trend kırsal turizm: Zile örneği. *Türk Turizm Araştırmaları Dergisi*, *4*(4), 3668–3683. doi:10.26677/TR1010.2020.584

Aytuğar, S., & Aydoğdu, A. (2021). Kırsal Turizm Çekiciliği Olarak Lavanta ve Kastamonu İli Lavanta Turizmi Potansiyeli. *Uluslararası Türk Dünyası Turizm Araştırmaları Dergisi*, *6*(1), 72–89.

Badulescu, D., Giurgiu, A., Istudor, N., & Badulescu, A. (2015). Rural tourism development and financing in Romania: A supply-side analysis. *Agricultural Economics*, *61*(2), 72–82.

Baykal, F., & Ataberk, E. (2020). Kozbeyli'de (Foça/İzmir) Kırsal Turizmin Geliştirilmesi Hakkında Yerel Halkın Görüşleri. *Ege Coğrafya Dergisi*, *29*(1), 1–17.

Bozok, D., & Karaman, R. (2018). Isparta lavantasının kırsal turizm kapsamında swot analizi yöntemiyle değerlendirilmesi: Kuyucak köyü örneği. *International Journal of Social and Economic Sciences*, *8*(2), 27–33.

Çeken, H., Dalgın, T., & Çakır, N. (2012). Bir Alternatif Turizm Türü Olarak Kırsal Turizmin Gelişimini Etkileyen Faktörler Ve Kırsal Turizmin Etkileri. *International Journal Of Social And Economic Sciences*, *2*(2), 11–16.

Cengiz, G., & Akkuş, Ç. (2012). Kırsal Turizm Kapsamında Yöre Halkının Kalkındırılması: Erzurum Örneği. *Karamanoğlu Mehmetbey Üniversitesi Sosyal Ve Ekonomik Araştırmalar Dergisi*, *2012*(1), 61–74.

Creswell, J. W. (2018). *Nitel Araştırma Yöntemleri: Beş Yaklaşıma Göre Nitel Araştırma ve Araştırma Deseni, (Çeviri: Mesut Bütün ve Selçuk Beşir Demir)*. Siyasal Yayınevi.

Dalgın, T., & And Yemenoğlu, E. (2020). Buldan İlçesi'nin Kırsal Turizm Potansiyelinin Belirlenmesine Yönelik Nitel Bir Araştırma. *Turar Turizm ve Araştırma Dergisi*, *9*(2), 121–143.

Demir, C. (2019). Kokunun En Şifalı Hali: Lavanta. Göller Bölgesi Aylık Hakemli Ekonomi ve Kültür Dergisi. *Ayrıntı Dergisi*, *7*(77), 7–10.

Demircioğlu, G. (1993). Kırsal Turizm Nedir? *Anatolia: Turizm Araştırmaları Dergisi*, *4*(5), 8–10.

Emekli, G., Südaş, İ., & Soykan, F. (2007). Göç, kırsal kalkınma-kırsal turizm ve Türkiye. *Uluslararası Asya ve Kuzey Afrika Çalışmaları Kongresi*, *38*, 10–15.

Erdem, M. S., & Bozan, M. Türkiye'de Sürdürülebilir Kalkınma Çerçevesinde Ekolojik Turizmin Kalkınma Planları İçerisinde Değerlendirilmesi, *Sinop Üniversitesi Sosyal Bilimler Dergisi, 5*(1), 67-90.

Eshun, G., & Tichaawa, T. M. (2020). Developing agro-tourism tours on the cocoa sector in africa: emerging issues from Ghana. *EuroEconomica, 39*(1).

Giray, F. H., Kadakoğlu, B., Çetin, F., & Bamoi, A. G. A. (2019). Rural tourism marketing: Lavender tourism in Turkey. *Ciência Rural*, *49*(2), 49. doi:10.1590/0103-8478cr20180651

Karali, A., Das, S., & Roy, H. (2021). Forty years of the rural tourism research: Reviewing the trend, pattern and future agenda. *Tourism Recreation Research*, 1–28. doi:10.1080/02508281.2021.1961065

Kaya, M., & Erol, N. (2021). El sanatları ürünlerinin kırsal turizm kapsamında değerlendirilmesi: Espiye-Akkaya Köyü Örneği. *Journal of Humanities and Tourism Research*, *11*(1), 226–240. doi:10.14230/johut991

Kodaş, D., & Sibel, S. Ü. (2012). Kırsal Turizm İle Kültürel Turizmin Bütünleşmesi. *Karamanoğlu Mehmetbey Üniversitesi Sosyal Ve Ekonomik Araştırmalar Dergisi*, *2012*(1), 169–174.

Kunasekaran, P., Ramachandran, S., Yacob, M. R., & Shuib, A. (2011). Development of farmers' perception scale on agro tourism in Cameron Highlands, Malaysia. *World Applied Sciences Journal*, *12*, 10–18.

Nguyen, N. T. H., Suwanno, S., Thongma, W., & Visuthismajarn, P. (2018). The attitudes of residents towards agro-tourism impacts and its effects on participation in agro-tourism development: The case study of Vietnam. *African Journal of Hospitality, Tourism and Leisure*, *7*(4), 1–18.

Ongun, U., & Erbaş, E. (2020). Sosyal Medyanın Destinasyon Gelişimindeki Rolü: Lavanta Kokulu Kuyucak Köyü Örneği. *Journal of Tourism and Gastronomy Studies*, *8*(4), 3129–3154. doi:10.21325/jotags.2020.755

Ongun, U., Gövder, B., & Kösekahyaoğlu, L. (2018). Kırsal turizm kapsamında yerel halkın beklentileri: Isparta Kuyucak Lavanta Vadisi örneği. *Turar Turizm ve Araştırma Dergisi*, *7*(2), 43–58.

Rosalina, P. D., Dupre, K., & Wang, Y. (2021). Rural tourism: A systematic literature review on definitions and challenges. *Journal of Hospitality and Tourism Management*, *47*, 134–149. doi:10.1016/j.jhtm.2021.03.001

Sezen, B., & Boz, İ. (2021). Ziyaretçilerin Kırsal Turizm Faaliyetlerinden Memnuniyet Düzeyi: Cumalıkızık Köyü Örneği. *Black Sea Journal of Public and Social Science, 4*(1), 24–33. doi:10.52704/bssocialscience.779509

Silva, L. (2022). The impact of the COVID-19 pandemic on rural tourism: A case study from Portugal. *Anatolia, 33*(1), 157–159. doi:10.1080/13032917.2021.1875015

Soykan, F. (2003). Kirsal Turizm Ve Türkiye Turizmi İçin Önemi. *Ege Coğrafya Dergisi, 12*(1), 1–11.

Tarhan, Y., Açıksöz, S., & Çelik, D. (2019). Lavanta Tarımı Ve Sürdürülebilir Kalkınma: Isparta/Keçiborlu-Kuyucak Köyü Örneği. *Bartın University International Journal of Natural and Applied Sciences, 2*(2), 216–227.

Torun, E. (2013). Kırsal Turizmin Bölge İnsanına Katkıları. *Karamanoğlu Mehmetbey Üniversitesi Sosyal Ve Ekonomik Araştırmalar Dergisi, 2013*(1), 31–37.

Tuncer, B., & Bakırcı, M. (2021). Ekolojik Çiftliklerin Entegre Kırsal Turizm Bağlamında Analizi: Muğla İli Örneği. *Coğrafya Dergisi, 0*(42), 85–100. doi:10.26650/JGEOG2020-824039

Uzun, B., Dalgın, T., Çeken, H., & Özer, Ç. 82022). Arı Turizminin Kırsal Kalkınma Üzerindeki Etkisi: Marmaris Örneği. *Asya Studies, 6*(22), 179-192.

Vaishar, A., & Šťastná, M. (2022). Impact of the COVID-19 pandemic on rural tourism in Czechia Preliminary considerations. *Current Issues in Tourism, 25*(2), 187–191. doi:10.1080/13683500.2020.1839027

Yavuz, E., & Zığındere, Y. Ö. (2000). Sürdürülebilir Kalkınmanın Turizme Etkisi. *Balıkesir Üniversitesi Sosyal Bilimler Enstitüsü Dergisi, 3*(4), 322–336.

Yazgan, Ş., & Kadanalı, E. (2012). Ağrı İlinin Kırsal Turizm Potansiyelinin Değerlendirilmesi. *Karamanoğlu Mehmetbey Üniversitesi Sosyal Ve Ekonomik Araştırmalar Dergisi, 2012*(1), 5–10.

Yılmaz, G. Ö., & Gürol, N. K. (2012). Balıkesir ilinin kırsal turizm potansiyelinin değerlendirilmesi. *Karamanoğlu Mehmetbey Üniversitesi Sosyal ve Ekonomik Araştırmalar Dergisi, 2012*(2), 23–32.

Chapter 9
Agriculture and Farmer's Plight in the Backward Region of Uttar Pradesh After 75 Years of Independence

Kavita Baliyan
Giri Institute of Development Studies, Lucknow, India

ABSTRACT

This chapter portrays the constraints faced by the farmers in Uttar Pradesh in terms of infrastructure, production, marketing, irrigation, and finance. Apart from this, a few natural constraints are also responsible for low productivity in agriculture. Hence, the present study was undertaken in the selected eastern districts of Uttar Pradesh to identify the institutional, social, and economic constraints hampering the growth of agriculture in the selected districts. It analyses the farmers' perception regarding constraints which is responsible for low agricultural productivity.

INTRODUCTION

U.P. is predominantly an agrarian economy and the performance of agriculture and allied activities is critical in determining the growth rate of the State. The state is the largest producer of food grain in India and offers a diverse agro climatic condition which is conducive for agricultural production. Uttar Pradesh is a highly populous state in India and is divided into four economic

DOI: 10.4018/978-1-6684-6878-4.ch009

region namely Western, Eastern, Central and Bundelkhand. However, the problem of poverty and economic backwardness in Eastern UP has attracted the attention of scholars and policy makers in the past. The region has favorable conditions for agricultural development in terms of fertile land, water and climate but is marred with low productivity, small and fragmented size of landholdings etc. The region has not reached its full agricultural potential and the yields levels are relatively low. Numerous studies reveal that farmers in Uttar Pradesh especially eastern UP face many problems from preliminary stage of production up till the sale of products in the market. As a result, agriculture as an occupation has become unprofitable.

The agriculture in UP has many constraints like periodic failure of monsoons, drought conditions and crop failure. Out of the 240.93 lakh hectares geographical area of the State, about 73.06 lakh hectares is flood prone and around 27 lakh hectares are annually affected due to floods. another major disaster affecting the State is drought. Annual loss due to drought in the State varies depending on the severity of the drought (Nath et al., 2006). Moreover, farmers in UP also face problems related to infrastructure, production, marketing, irrigation and finance to a large extent.

Further, the problem of poverty and economic backwardness of Eastern UP has attracted the attention of scholars and policy makers in the past. One of the first efforts in this direction was the Report of The Joint Study Team of the Planning Commission which studied four districts of the region and came out with a number of suggestions (Planning Commission, 1964). Moreover, the Government of UP also declared East UP as a backward region along with Bundelkhand and Hill Division in the 1950s so that special consideration is paid to the development of these regions. Later a committee was appointed by the Reserve bank of India under the chairmanship of Dr. S.R. Sen to look into the issue of agricultural productivity in eastern India (RBI 1984). The study covered the states of West Bengal, Orissa, Bihar and East UP. and provides a valuable collection of factual data on various aspects of agrarian structure as well as on input use, productivity and growth in the agricultural sector of different eastern Indian states and their regions. The existence of considerable diversity within the region in all these respects is clearly brought out, with east Uttar Pradesh stood better off in terms of most indices as compared to the rest of the region and Bihar being generally the worst off (Vaidyanathan, 1987). Nevertheless, the committee also found the constraints to agricultural growth in east UP like the small size of holding, uncertainty of rainfall, drought, floods, water logging, sub-standard arrangements for distribution of quality seeds and agricultural inputs, weak cooperative credit structure, poor extension and marketing services, lack of coordination among departments, problems related to irrigation and research. The committee suggested that substantial public investment and credit from banks as well as a better coordinated administrative structure are required for increasing agricultural growth in the region.

A study conducted by Singh (1981) analysed in detail comparative economic development of western and eastern regions of UP during the period 1951 to 1975. The study pointed out that apart from factors like floods and droughts, small size of holdings and low land man ratio, underdevelopment of the region in terms of credit and marketing institutions and lack of assured means of irrigation, shortage of capital and social customs are accountable for agricultural backwardness of east UP. In recent times, Tanwar et al. (2017) conducted a study on assessment of agricultural development in eastern Uttar Pradesh and found wide inequalities in the level of agricultural development among different districts of eastern UP. Besides, some studies conducted to analyse the agriculture productivity in specific districts based on primary surveys are: Sultanpur (Subas, 1984), Jaunpur (Singh, 1974), Jhanshi (Prakash and Singh, 2013), Mirzapur (Tirth, 2015).

The existing literature found that most of the studies are based on secondary data only and doesn't reveal the constraints at farm level. Also, there is dearth of comprehensive district level analysis of agricultural performance especially in Eastern part of UP and Bundelkhand region. Adequate literature is unavailable especially on the convergence/divergence of the performance in agriculture in Eastern Uttar Pradesh and on the role of financial institutions on agricultural performance in Uttar Pradesh. Detailed studies are required to identify the areas of low level of agricultural growth and for enhancing agricultural performance. It is in this background that the study is undertaken to identify the reasons of low agricultural productivity in the Eastern Uttar Pradesh and for accelerating agricultural growth and performance in the region based on its potential.

The present paper is prearranged into 5 sections. Section I presents the background of the paper. Section II describes the objective of the paper and research methodology. Section III discusses the flood and drought related problems of sampled farmers. In section IV, major constraints faced by farmers other than natural calamities are discussed. The final section summarizes the findings of the paper and suggestions to overcome the problems.

Research Methodology

Objectives: The present study was conducted in the selected eastern districts of Uttar Pradesh to ascertain institutional, social and economic constraints that impedes the development and growth of agriculture in the selected districts. At district level, the primary data analysis is based on farmers' perception regarding constraints related with low agricultural productivity.

Source of Data: The present paper is based on the primary data collected through field survey for the detailed project during 2019-20. For collecting primary data, stratified random sampling design was used. First stage consists of three agro-climatic zones of the Eastern region covering North-Eastern zone (11districts), Eastern plain zone (12 districts) and Vindhyachal zone (3 districts). Further, selection of 2 districts from north-eastern zone, 2 districts from eastern plain zone and 1 district from Vindhyachal zone has been done. From each of the selected district, two blocks were selected-one from relatively developed block and one from relatively less developed block. From each block, two villages were randomly selected (one with better access to roads and one away main road). From each village, 25 farm households were randomly selected from different size group holdings, i.e., marginal, small, medium and large. Thus, the total sample size contains 5 districts, 10 blocks, 20 villages and 500 farm households.

In selecting districts from different zones of east U.P., the selected indicators of agricultural development were taken into account. The study proceeds with the assumption that agricultural development of districts mainly depend on the indicators like percentage of GSA to NSA, % of gross irrigated area to gross area sown, % irrigated area by tube wells and wells, productivity of total food grains(qtl per hectare), % of area under commercial crops to gross sown area, distribution of total fertilizers per hectare of gross sown area, number of tractors per 1000 hectare gross area sown, consumption of electricity in agriculture, consumption of electricity in Agriculture (consumption- L.W.H. per 000 hectare of GSA), Gross value of agricultural Produce per hectare of gross area sown, number of regulated *mandis* per lakh hectare of gross area sown, number of agriculture Marketing center per lakh hectare net area sown. A PCA method has been used to calculate the agriculture development index for the districts. The table 1 describes the factor score of selected districts of agro climatic zones of Eastern Uttar Pradesh. Mau and Siddharth Nagar are selected as developed districts having 1st and 3rd rank respectively on factor basis. Sonbhadra and Balrampur selected as a less developed districts and Jaunpur also selected as developing districts for comparison.

Table 1. Sample distribution district, block and village based on selected indicators

S. No.	Districts	Status of District	Block Name	Statusof Block	Village 1 (on road)	Village 2 (Interior)
1	Sonbhadra	Less dev	Ghorawal	High dev.	Barawan	Ortha
			Myorepur	Less dev.	Khairahi	Raspahari
2	Jaunpur	Less dev	Karanjakala	High dev.	SaloniMahimapur	Patahani
			Sujanganj	Less dev.	Bara	Sabeli
3	Siddhartnagar	High dev.	Itwa	High dev	Mahadev	Ganvariya
			Jogiya	Less dev.	Sirsiya	Lakhanapar
4	Balrampur	Less dev.	Utraila	High dev	Kohiniya	Rasoolpur
			GaidasBujurg	Less dev.	Dudhara	Sahiyapur
5	Mau	High dev.	Raanipur	High dev	Pirwa	Gokulpura
			Muhamdabad Gohna	Less dev.	Galibpur	Jamin Narauni

Source: Authors calculation. Note: Districts were selected on basis of highly developed and less developed

Computation Method of Aggregate Weighted Score (AWS)

To find out the major problems faced by the farmers, the aggregate weighted score of each problem is calculated. The perception and views expressed in terms of major problems are related to institutional, financial, technological, marketing, infrastructure, storage, warehouses and other post-harvest management areas. Ten-point Likert Scale has been selected to measure the extent of problems. The range of scale is 1 to 10. The weighted average score has been calculated by assigning weights like 10 to rank 1 means major problem and 1 to rank 10 i.e. minor problems. On the basis of frequency of ratings for each problem, average weighted scores are calculated with the help of following formula:

Figure 1.

$$x = \frac{\sum_{i=1}^{n} (x_i * w_i)}{\sum_{i=1}^{n} w_i}$$

Where, x = Average weighted score W = Weights given to the problem i = Number of respondents who attached weights to the problem. Highest score showing more problem and lower score showing that problem faced by the farmers is lower or minimum.

Background of the Study Area

The study is limited to eastern Uttar Pradesh which is among the most backward regions of the country, having an area of 85845 sq. km. (35.6 percent of state area). As per 2011 Census, the population of the region is 40 percent of state population. The density of population is as high as 930 persons per sq. km. in the region. Moreover, poverty levels are also very high in the region. As per NSS 2009-10 round, head count poverty ratio in Eastern U.P. was 44.39% against the state average of 41.24%. Eastern U.P. accounted for nearly half of the poor in the state. Nearly 88 percent population in the region lives in the rural areas. Agriculture remains the chief occupation of the people of the region. According to Census 2011, nearly 64 percent of workers in Eastern U.P. were engaged in agriculture as compared to 59% at the state level. The Government of U.P. also declared East U.P. a backward region along with Bundelkhand and Hill Division in the 1950s so that special attention is paid to the development of this region.

RESULTS AND DISCUSSIONS

Flood and Drought Situation

The agriculture sector is particularly exposed to risks of floods and droughts, which may become more frequent and severe due to climate change in the context of increased demand for food and urban space (OECD, 2016). Annually about 27 lakh hectare land is affected by floods in UP. About 432 crores of rupees is the estimated annual loss due to floods (Nath et al., 2006). During the survey, 45.6 percent sampled farmers reported about drought and flood related problems during the last three years. This includes 70 percent respondent from Mau, 53 percent from Balrampur, 47 percent from Sonbhadra, 38 percent from Siddharth Nagar and only 20 percent from Jaunpur (Figure 2).

Figure 2. Distribution of HH, faced any kind of flood/ drought situation in last 3 years

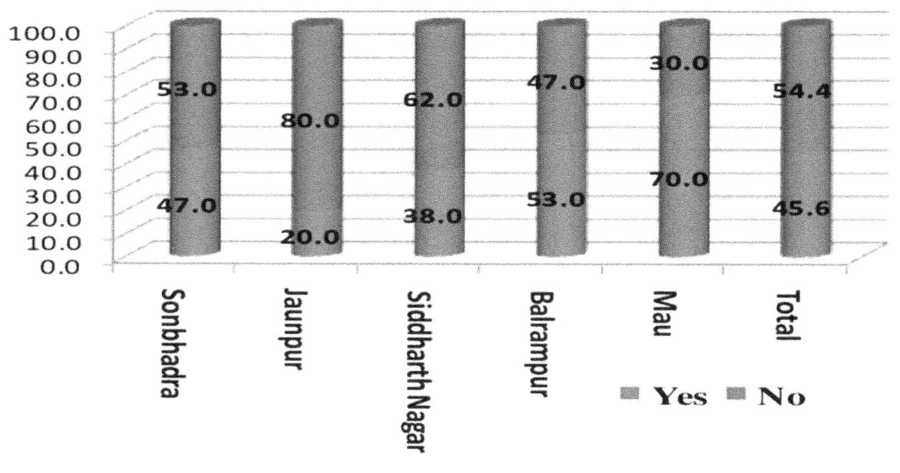

The analysis reveals that impact of drought and flood on agriculture is alarming in the sampled districts. Table 1 depicts average area sown affected by flood/drought during three periods of time. On an average, percent share of affected area to gross sown area (GSA) is found 44.71 percent in selected districts. Significant impact of drought or flood in percent share of affected area to GSA has been found in Siddharth Nagar. Agriculture area which is largely affected by flood or drought is Mau (approximately 2.02 acre), however the percentage of gross sown area highly affected by drought/flood is in Siddhartha Nagar (65.17 percent) while Sonbhadra (32.45 percent) is least affected among the sampled districts.

Economic impacts caused by drought affects agriculture through losses in crop yields and livestock production, but also through increased insect infestations, plant diseases and wind erosion (European Commission, 2007). In recent years, the year 2017, 2018 & 2019 were crucial in terms of drought/ flood, with loss to crop, animals and physical assets. The average loss related to crops, animals and physical assets in terms of rupees was Rs.60416,

Rs.650549 and Rs. 274047 respectively. It can be asserted that economic costs of droughts and floods in agriculture can be direct or indirect. Direct (short) losses normally consist of crop, livestock and physical asset related losses (as discussed in the table 2). Contrary to this, direct and long-term effects of flood and drought contain losses of productive assets like machinery and buildings and declines in land value, which lessens productivity in the long run and could entail important resources for improvement in agricultural productivity.

Table 3 shows loss happened due to flood and drought in crops, animals and physical assets i.e. damage in houses, animal shed, others household durables etc., in value terms (in Rupees). It is observed that percent share of loss in physical assets is higher as compared to loss related to animal and crops. In value terms, the highest loss is noticed in Mau (Rs.1, 78,248) and Jaunpur (Rs.1, 45,893), indicating the better status of agriculture in these districts. Balrampur registered the lowest loss in terms of rupees.

Table 2. Loss in agriculture due to flood/ drought situation in last 3 years

District		2017	2018	2019	TE Average
Sonbhadra	Average Area sown (acre)	2.52	2.68	1.73	2.31
	Affected area (Acre)	.85	.91	.49	.75
	% share of Affected area to GSA	(33.78)	(33.80)	(28.41)	(32.45)
Jaunpur	Average Area sown (acre)	1.16	2.25	1.67	1.69
	Affected area (Acre)	1.16	.92	.37	.81
	% share of Affected area to GSA	(100.00)	(40.70)	(21.92)	(48.09)
Siddhartha Nagar	Average Area sown (acre)	1.45	1.77	1.70	1.64
	Affected area (Acre)	1.00	.98	1.23	1.07
	% share of Affected area to GSA	(68.84)	(55.51)	(72.05)	(65.17)
Balrampur	Average Area sown (acre)	.95	.77	.77	.83
	Affected area (Acre)	.25	.39	.37	.34
	% share of Affected area to GSA	(26.32)	(51.07)	(47.91)	(40.65)
Mau	Average Area sown (acre)	8.38	2.44	3.23	4.68
	Affected area (Acre)	3.39	1.18	1.49	2.02
	% share of Affected area to GSA	(40.50)	(48.19)	(45.97)	(43.09)
Total	Average Area sown (acre)	14.45	9.91	9.10	11.15
	Affected area (Acre)	6.65	4.37	3.94	4.99
	% share of Affected area to GSA	(46.01)	(44.13)	(43.28)	(44.71)

Hence, there are two natural reasons (drought and flood) that may lead to poor performance and production in agriculture. Table 3 depicts that agricultural loss due to drought and flood in the selected sampled districts separately. It has been observed that floods account for huge economic loss than drought. Loss of animals and crops are included in the economic loss as loss of crops (due to effected land) and loss of animals is linked directly to agricultural productivity.

Table 3. Loss due to flood/drought situation during last 3 years (value in Rs.)

Year	Type of Loss	2017	2018	2019	TE Average Loss	% Share
Sonbhadra	Crops	21436	7825	5748	11670	19.0
	Animals	45000	8500		26750	43.5
	Others (Physical Assets)	3500	75000	17600	32033	52.1
	Total	**69936**	**91325**	**23348**	**61536**	**100.0**
Jaunpur	Crops	8000	14260	5920	9393	6.4
	Animals	9500		15000	12250	8.4
	Others (Physical Assets)	30000	255000	100000	128333	88.0
	Total	**47500**	**269260**	**120920**	**145893**	**100.0**
Siddhartha Nagar	Crops	11978	10492	13513	11994	28.2
	Animals	50000	10000	-	30000	70.5
	Others (Physical Assets)	31667	-	-	31667	74.4
	Total	**93644**	**20492**	**13513**	**42550**	**100.0**
Balrampur	Crops	4100	8813	6444	6452	20.1
	Animals	0	8222	0	2741	8.5
	Others (Physical Assets)	0	18750	50000	22917	71.4
	Total	**4100**	**35785**	**56444**	**32110**	**100.0**
Mau	Crops	28933	14845	18942	20907	11.7
	Animals	150000	50000	31400	77133	43.3
	Others (Physical Assets)	150000		90625	120313	67.5
	Total	**328933**	**64845**	**140967**	**178248**	**100.0**
All	Crops	74447	56234	50567	60416	6.1
	Animals	587859	890743	473044	650549	66.0
	Others (Physical Assets)	215167	348750	258225	274047	27.8
	Total	**877473**	**1295727**	**781836**	**985012**	**100.0**

Loss due to flood is found higher as compared to loss from drought in the study area (Table3). Siddharth Nagar and Balrampur reported high loss of crops (reported by 90.24 percent and 97.06 percent farmers) due to flood, whereas Jaunpur registered highest crop loss due to drought, as reported by 78.26 percent farmers. As far as loss of animals due to flood is concerned Balrampur district registered maximum loss as mentioned by all the sampled farmers. Contrary to this, Jaunpur and Sonbhadra have reported highest loss (i.e. 71.43% and 66.67% respectively) of animals due to drought. Thus, loss due to drought and flood in these districts varies depending on the severity of drought and flood.

Table 4. Reason of loss in sampled households since last 3 years

	Reason for loss of Crops			
	Flood	**Draught**	**Others**	**Total**
Sonbhadra	40.00	54.55	5.45	100
Jaunpur	8.70	78.26	13.04	100
Siddharth Nagar	90.24	7.32	0.00	100
Balrampur	97.06	0.00	2.94	100
Mau	48.68	46.05	5.26	100
All	62.36	32.70	4.56	100
	Reason for loss of Animals			
Sonbhadra	14.29	71.43	14.29	100
Jaunpur	0.00	66.67	33.33	100
Siddharth Nagar	33.33	33.33	33.33	100
Balrampur	100.00	0.00	0.00	100
Mau	57.14	14.29	28.57	100
All	51.72	31.03	17.24	100
	Reason for loss of Others			
Sonbhadra	50.00	25.00	25.00	100
Jaunpur	25.00	0.00	75.00	100
Siddharth Nagar	100.00	0.00	0.00	100
Balrampur	100.00	0.00	0.00	100
Mau	20.00	0.00	80.00	100
All	51.61	6.45	41.94	100

Source: Primary Survey 2019

Flood is considered as one of the most important reason of loss of crops (62.36%) and loss of animals (51.72%). So, planners and government's attention should be towards improvement in effective measures of flood management. The economic growth of flood prone areas is seriously hampered and special measures are required to be taken for their economic development. Therefore, chronically flood prone and drought prone areas should be treated as backward areas and special status and measures should be adopted for promoting agricultural development in those areas.

Other Problems and Constraints

Besides climatic problems, agriculture sector faces a variety of problems like social and institutional, irrigation and electricity, marketing & selling, infrastructure and storage, debt and finance, post-harvest management and technology related problems that affects agricultural income of farmers and institutional risks. The relative importance and combination of these constraints can vary across selected districts. The impact of droughts and floods on farmers' income should be considered as serious problem. Drought & flood conditions intensify the risk of crop and animal loss, and thus aggravate agricultural losses.

According to table 5, problems related to selling & marketing is reported by 90.4 percent of sampled farmers followed by post-harvest problems (reported by 88.6 percent respondents) and storage related problems (80.6 percent sample farmers).

Table 5. Distribution of farmers by their problems in agriculture (multiple responses)

Districts	Sonbhadra	Jaunpur	Siddharth Nagar	Balrampur	Mau	Total
Finance Related	49.0	54.0	53.0	66.0	57.0	55.8
Infrastructure Related	59.0	59.0	83.0	68.0	66.0	67.0
Selling & Marketing	79.0	85.0	97.0	94.0	97.0	90.4
Social Institutional	53.0	55.0	97.0	65.0	68.0	67.6
Technological	69.0	62.0	11.0	79.0	75.0	59.2
Post-Harvest problems	93.0	93.0	76.0	87.0	94.0	88.6
Storage Related	75.0	83.0	75.0	73.0	97.0	80.6

Source: Primary Survey 2019

For identification of actual, concrete and major problems among the sampled farmers in selected eastern districts, Percentage Aggregate Weighted Score (PAWS) of Rank have been computed for each problem of the farmers and the method for calculating PAWS has been explained in the next section.

Social and Institutional Problem

Percentage Average Weighted Scores (AWS) showing the level of problems that are faced by the farmers in different districts is depicted in Table5. Social and Institutional problem contains large use of traditional farming, small land holdings, paucity of hired labour, non-acceptance of new technology, lack of family labour, inferior quality of seeds and fertilizer, lack of cooperative societies /financial institutions and corruption in subsidy distribution.

The table5 reveals that respondents are facing major problems such as Small and fragmented land holdings (14.48) followed by lack of hired labour (12.82 percent). AWS of 10.76 percent for resistance in adoption of new technology indicates that due to fear of failure most of the sampled farmers don't use modern technology. In general, these problems are more or less similar in five selected districts as indicated by mean value of AWS, however majority of problems are related to small and fragmented land holdings and modern technology adoption as depicted in Figure 2.

Table 6. District-wise aggregate weighted score (%) of social and institutional problem

Reasons	Sonbhadra	Jaunpur	Siddharth Nagar	Balrampur	Mau
Attachment to Traditional farming	8.93	9.33	10.21	10.35	10.73
Small and fragmented land holding	13.11	14.10	15.11	14.76	14.48
Lack of hired Labour	10.92	11.96	14.84	12.89	12.82
Resistance in adoption of new technology	12.83	12.52	12.78	13.15	10.76
Lack of Family labour due to Migration	12.09	10.27	11.24	9.69	9.55
Poor quality of seeds& fertilizer	12.66	11.19	9.87	10.42	10.38
Lack of cooperative societies	10.35	9.82	9.23	9.51	9.90
Lack of Financial institutions	10.08	11.53	8.40	8.90	10.66
Bribery in Subsidies	8.51	8.55	6.78	9.72	10.11
Others	0.53	0.73	1.54	0.61	0.61
Mean value of AWS	9.87	9.52	8.78	9.53	9.74

Source: Primary Survey 2019

Irrigation and Electricity Related Problems

The problem related to irrigation and electricity is discussed in this section. Few respondents (13 percent) reported decreasing level of river water as an important problem of irrigation.

District-wise average weighted score for different problems related to irrigation are shown in table Problem of low voltage (17.42 percent) and lack of electricity supply (16.42 percent) are the major problems related to irrigation reported by farmers in Mau. The decreasing level of ground water (15.77 percent) high cost of maintenance (15.09 percent) is high in Sonbhadra whereas in Jaunpur decreasing level of ground water (15.81 percent) along with high cost of irrigation (15 93 percent) and maintenance of irrigation equipment's (15.59 percent) are the main constraints that were reported during the survey. In Siddarth Nagar, high cost of irrigation (16.55 percent) and unavailability of irrigation facility on time (15.65 percent) are main constraints of sampled farmers (Table 6). High cost of irrigation as well as maintenance is also reported by sampled farmers in Balrampur district.

It is pertinent to note that irrigation is an important input which contributes the most to increase crop production, farmer's income and other socio-economic conditions of the farmers. Hence, to improve the irrigation related problems, increase the efficiency, availability, technology, and awareness of modern methods of irrigation is needed.

Table 7. District-wise aggregate weighted score (%) of irrigation and electricity related problem

Reasons	Sonbhadra	Jaunpur	Siddharth Nagar	Balrampur	Mau
Lack of electricity supply	14.71	13.90	11.48	12.70	16.42
Low voltage	14.17	12.90	14.60	13.85	17.42
Decreasing Level of Ground Water	15.77	15.81	14.32	12.33	13.55
Decreasing Level of River Water	13.28	11.65	14.88	13.17	13.83
High cost of irrigation	15.09	15.93	16.55	17.03	12.33
Unavailability of irrigation facility on time	13.90	14.21	15.65	14.58	13.54
High cost of maintenance	13.08	15.59	12.52	16.35	12.91
Total	100.00	100.00	100.00	100.00	100.00

Source: Primary Survey 2019

Marketing and Selling Related Problem

It is well known that agricultural market in Uttar Pradesh is full of uncertainties and fears. The farmers are unable to obtain a reasonable share in the price which is paid by the buyers. In this section, problems related to marketing and selling faced by sampled farmers are discussed. Before asking bproblem, farmers were asked that where they sold their produce and why and then asked wht problem/s thay have faced related to selling and marketing.

The sampled farmers face more of the marketing related problems like late payment, low price of agricultural produce (12 percent), lack of standardization (10 percent) and inadequate transport facilities (10 percent). They also face problems related to unorganized marketing system (8 percent), inappropriate cut in price of produce in mandi (10%), many middlemen, corrupt policies of *mandies* (10 percent), lack of awareness of market information (7 percent), and lack of selling centers (6 percent). Problem related to marketing and selling is almost similar in all the districts as shown in the table 8.

Table 8. District-wise aggregate weighted score (%) of marketing and selling related problem

Reasons	Sonbhadra	Jaunpur	Siddharth Nagar	Balrampur	Mau
Unorganized marketing system	6.83	7.84	9.04	9.28	10.23
Late payment	9.18	9.13	12.48	14.03	13.02
Inadequate transport facilities	8.83	9.75	11.80	11.16	10.49
Lack of standardization	10.04	9.04	11.66	9.55	11.12
Low price of produce	11.77	11.95	11.84	11.75	12.90
Un-appropriated cut in produce in mandi	9.62	11.01	10.68	10.53	8.42
Too many middlemen	9.80	10.50	9.10	9.38	8.84
Corrupt policies of Mandies	8.52	7.89	8.02	7.52	7.76
High Marketing costs	7.85	8.94	7.28	7.38	6.73
Lack of awareness of market information	9.26	7.47	5.38	4.70	5.22
Lack of selling centers	8.28	6.50	2.72	4.71	5.27
Total	100.00	100.00	100.00	100.00	100.00

Source: Primary Survey 2019

Post-Harvest Management Problems

Post-harvest management has the potential to create rural industries in developing countries like India, where 70 per cent of the people live in villages and 65 per cent of them depend on agriculture (Planning commission, 2007). Efficient techniques for harvesting, transportation, storage, processing/ preservation, packaging, labeling etc., are the components of post-harvest management. Reports of farmers destroying their crops of tomato, cabbage and other vegetables in the field are due to awful returns of their produce. Hence, it is poor post-harvest management of farm produce, and not plentiful production (Farm distress, 2018).

In eastern UP, lack of transport facilities (16%), loss of produce (16%), lack of storage (14%), problems related to packaging and labeling (12%) and lack of adequate container to keep the produce (13%) emerged as major problems among the sampled farmers in selected districts. They also face some grading and processing (14%) related issues. Postharvest losses in all the districts are high due to inadequate transport facilities and loss of output on field due to natural calamities. Post-harvest losses are faced by all the farmers in India as pointed out by the Report on assessment of quantitative harvest and post-harvest losses (2016) that Indian farmers incur Rs 92,651 crore per year in post-harvest losses, the primary cause of which are poor storage and transportation facilities (Jha et al., 2016)

Table 9. District-wise aggregate weighted score (in %) of post-harvest management problem

Reasons	Sonbhadra	Jaunpur	Siddharth Nagar	Balrampur	Mau
Lack of transportations facilities	14.98	14.35	17.59	17.19	16.77
Loss of produce on field due to calamities	15.80	15.85	15.37	15.28	16.73
Grading problem	13.83	14.60	14.67	13.33	12.41
Lack of Storage	14.41	14.51	14.80	14.31	13.85
Problem of packaging and labelling	12.37	12.35	12.75	11.96	13.18
Processing problem	15.15	14.11	12.92	13.86	12.02
Lack of quality Container to fill the produce	13.16	14.23	9.76	12.52	13.95
Others	0.30	0.00	2.15	1.55	1.10
Total	100.00	100.00	100.00	100.00	100.00

Source: Primary Survey 2019

The problem related to post-harvest losses of sampled farmers in the selected districts can be reduced by the practice of optimal crop aspects, decrease of losses in handling, packaging, labeling, transportation and storage with improved infrastructure. The success of post-harvest management will depend on the integrated approach so that nothing goes waste and there will be full utilization of the agriculture produce.

Infrastructural Related Problem

Infrastructure in the agriculture sector implies those facilities that help farmers in the processes of sowing to selling namely, irrigation, road connectivity, electrification, storage and telecommunication (Garg, 2019).

As far as infrastructure related problems are concerned, lack of irrigation facilities (14 percent), irregular transport facilities (13 percent), poor road (13 percent),lack of training centers (13 percent), lack of fertilizer and seed sailing center (12 percent) and lack of cold storage (11 percent)are the main problems of farmers.

AWS found high in case of Siddhartha Nagar where problems related to poor road condition show high score i.e. 17.14 percent followed by Balrampur (15.31 percent) as compared to other districts under study (table12). Other problems related to infrastructure are almost similar in all the districts as shown in the table12. Hence, there is urgent need to revamp infrastructural

Table 10. District-wise aggregate weighted score (in %) infrastructural related problem

Reasons	Sonbhadra	Jaunpur	Siddharth Nagar	Balrampur	Mau
Bad Road condition	10.90	9.66	17.14	15.31	14.46
Irregular Transport facility	11.49	12.45	14.93	14.22	14.22
Lack of cold storage	11.20	10.22	12.51	10.50	12.29
Lack of irrigation facilities	14.80	14.34	13.52	12.73	11.59
Lack of seed and fertilizers selling center	13.26	12.51	11.49	11.88	11.72
Lack of selling centers	12.99	12.83	12.12	11.58	10.67
Electricity problem	12.75	12.28	9.29	9.99	12.03
Lack of training centers	12.63	15.56	7.74	13.66	12.73
Others	0.00	0.16	1.26	0.13	0.30
Total	100.00	100.00	100.00	100.00	100.00

Source: Primary Survey 2019

constraints particularly in rural infrastructure, especially by the government. This will help in reduced costs, better productivity, increase in income and capacity building.

Storages Related Problem

The main concern of farmers is to sell their produce as early as possible due to lack of appropriate storage facilities. Proper storage not only increases the life of crops but also keep them safe from early decay. However, in the study area, the storage problem show high weighted Score (AWS) as compared to other problems discussed earlier.

Table 11. District-wise aggregate weighted score (%) of storages related problem

Reasons	Sonbhadra	Jaunpur	Siddharth Nagar	Balrampur	Mau
Lack of cold storages	19.13	19.04	19.79	19.95	20.81
High cost of storages	19.84	19.74	19.14	19.25	20.74
High cost of transportation	18.56	19.45	19.69	21.31	18.91
Lack of care	19.72	19.68	18.38	19.40	18.36
Low storage capacities	22.18	21.17	20.28	19.74	17.34
Others	0.58	0.93	2.71	0.34	3.85
Total	100.00	100.00	100.00	100.00	100.00

Source: Primary Survey 2019

Table 11 reveals that high cost of storage (20 percent), low storage capacities (20 percent), high cost of transportation (19 percent) and lack of care (19 percent) emerged as the major problems faced by large number of famers in the selected districts under study. Cold storage technology is highly necessary as a part of post harvesting management of farm produce as it increases the life and storability of the products.

TECHNOLOGICAL PROBLEM

Table 12 show the various types of technological related problems faced by the farmers in the selected districts. The main problems reported in case of technology are difficulties related with the use of machinery in small holdings and lack of modern machinery and equipment. The other problems related to technology reported by farmers is lack of information for HYV seeds and its availability, lack of technology for weather forecasting and uncertain rain variability.

The problems related to technology are similar in the selected eastern districts (Table 12). Thus, major common problem reported by sampled farmer was scarcity of machinery and agriculture equipment's.

Lack of irrigation facilities is the major constraints in front of farmers to adopt the new technologies. Apart of this, small size of land holdings is also major hurdle in adoption of the new farming technique. Thus, some problem are the interrelated to each other. One hurdle create another hurdle and finally create major constraints in agriculture development in eastern Uttar Pradesh. This is in all selected districts either developed or less developed.

Table 12. District-wise aggregate weighted score (in %) of technological problem

Reasons	Sonbhadra	Jaunpur	Siddharth Nagar	Balrampur	Mau
Difficulties in use of machinery in small holdings	13.86	12.71	11.86	13.33	13.97
Difficulties in to get the fertilizers	13.34	13.05	14.24	12.72	14.70
Lack of modern machinery and equipment	17.30	16.48	15.47	15.93	14.83
Lack of information for HYV seeds	13.68	12.40	15.21	13.08	12.89
Lack of high yielding varieties seeds	14.75	15.30	14.24	13.36	12.93
No technology for weather forecasting	13.19	14.78	14.36	15.03	15.05
Uncertain rain variability	13.65	15.26	12.96	13.56	14.61
Others	0.23	0.00	1.68	2.99	1.02
Total	100.0	100.0	100.0	100.0	100.0

Source: Primary Survey 2019

Indebtedness and Financial Problem

It is said that a farmer is born in debt, lives in debt and ultimately dies in debt. Still, after seventy years of planning in India, majority of farmers in rural areas are bearing the burden of debt to a large extent. Hence in this section, the problem of indebtedness of sampled farmers in the selected districts is examined. About 52.2 percent farmers (majority in Mau i.e. 71 percent) reported to have taken loan. Majority (56.7 percent) of them had taken loan from Kisan credit card followed by 32.2 percent from relatives (Table 13). The remaining indebted farmers had taken loan from different non-institutional sources like bank, money lenders, SHGs, co-operative societies and big farmers.

Table 13. Number of farmers reporting loans from different sources

District	% of HHs taken Loan	% share in different Sources (% to total Indebted Farmers)						
		Large Farmers	Money Lenders	Cooperative Society	Bank	Kisan Credit Card	Self Help Groups	Relatives
Sonbhadra	42.0	2.4	2.4	9.5	9.5	54.8	9.5	21.4
Jaunpur	58.0	0.0	1.7	1.7	6.9	62.1	1.7	29.3
Siddharth Nagar	40.0	2.5	0.0	0.0	0.0	72.5	0.0	25.0
Balrampur	50.0	2.0	2.0	0.0	4.0	56.0	0.0	40.0
Mau	71.0	1.4	4.2	0.0	19.7	45.1	1.4	39.4
Total	52.2	1.5	2.3	1.9	9.2	56.7	2.3	32.2
No. of HHs	261	4	3	2	24	148	6	84

Source: Primary Survey 2019

Table16 shows the purpose of loan reported by the sampled farmers. Most of farmers reported that thay have taken loan for agriculture (73.4 percent). This percentage is highest in case of Jaunpur districts followed by Siddharth Nagar.10.2 percent loan was used for marriage purposes, while 8 percent of the loan was used for education, 4.4 percent loan for construction purpose

Table 14. Distribution of loan by purpose (%) multiple responses

Purpose for loan	Agriculture	Construction	Marriage	Personal Use	Education	Total
Sonbhadra	78.2	2.2	13.0	2.2	4.3	42 (100.0)
Jaunpur	83.3	5.0	6.7	0.0	5.0	58 (100.0)
Siddharth Nagar	80.0	0.0	12.5	7.5	0.0	40(100.0)
Balrampur	74.0	2.0	12.0	8.0	4.0	50 (100.0)
Mau	59.5	8.9	8.9	3.8	19.0	71 (100.0)
Total	73.4	4.4	10.2	4.0	8.0	261 (100.0)

Source: Primary Survey 2019

and 4 percent was taken for personal use. It was quite interesting that in Mau district, 20 percent farmers taken loan for education. Hence, it appears from table 14 that most part of the loan from institutional and non-institutional sources is used for productive purposes.

No. of farmers reporting that they have faced many problem in availing loan not only institutional sources even from the non-institutional sources. The major problems reported by the farmers are summarized in table 15. The major problem from the co-operatives societies are Demand for Collateral and long process while problem of Non-Cooperation of Officials and Non-Availability on time are faced availing loan from the KKCs. This may be the reason that farmers have to move to loan from the non-institutional sources which provide loan at a very high interest rate.

Table 15. Problem in availing loan (%) multiple responses

Problems in Availing loan	Large Farmers	Money Lenders	Cooperative Society	Bank	KKCs	SHGs	Relatives	Total
Inadequate loan	4.9	2.0	1.0	4.4	19.5	5.4	0.5	37.6
Non-Availability on time	2.0	1.0	0.0	7.3	24.9	2.9	4.9	42.9
High Rate of Interest	0.5	5.9	4.4	15.1	18.0	0.0	33.2	77.1
Demand for Collateral	1.0	3.9	30.7	8.8	1.5	4.4	1.5	51.7
Long Process	0.5	3.9	60.5	6.3	1.0	0.0	0.0	72.2
Non-Cooperation of Officials	0.5	0.0	1.0	7.3	44.9	1.0	0.0	54.6

Source: Primary Survey 2019

Thus, it is clear from the above analysis that majority of farmers faced problems in obtaining loan due to high rate of interest .Secondly, these financial institutions don't give loan to the farmers without collateral (security). So, it becomes a big barrier in getting loan from the bank and other financial institutions. As a result, many marginal and small farmers do not get the facility of agriculture loan from the banks. Consequently, high interest rate, long process and non-cooperative attitude /behavior of bank official and demand for security are the main constraints in availing loan as reported by the sampled farmers (Baliyan 2022).

But further to show the relationship between institutional credit and size of land, regression analysis has been done. The table 16 shows that there is significant and positive relationship between amount of loan from institutional sources and size of land. It means as per size of land increased amount of loan also increased and vice versa. This association clearly seen in the figure 3 which shows the concentration of small loan around the small size of land. It implies that marginal and small farmers are reaching to the institutional credit but the size of loan they are getting is very small. Because, institutional loan is directly related to the size of land and more than 70 percent sampled

Table 16. Relationship between amount of loan from institution sources and size of land

Model Summary and Parameter Estimates							
Dependent Variable: Institutional Credit							
Equation	Model Summary					Parameter Estimates	
	R Square	F	df1	df2	Sig.	Constant	b1
Linear	.270	183.781	1	498	.000	626.670	27193.499
The independent variable is Net sown area in Acre.							

Figure 3.

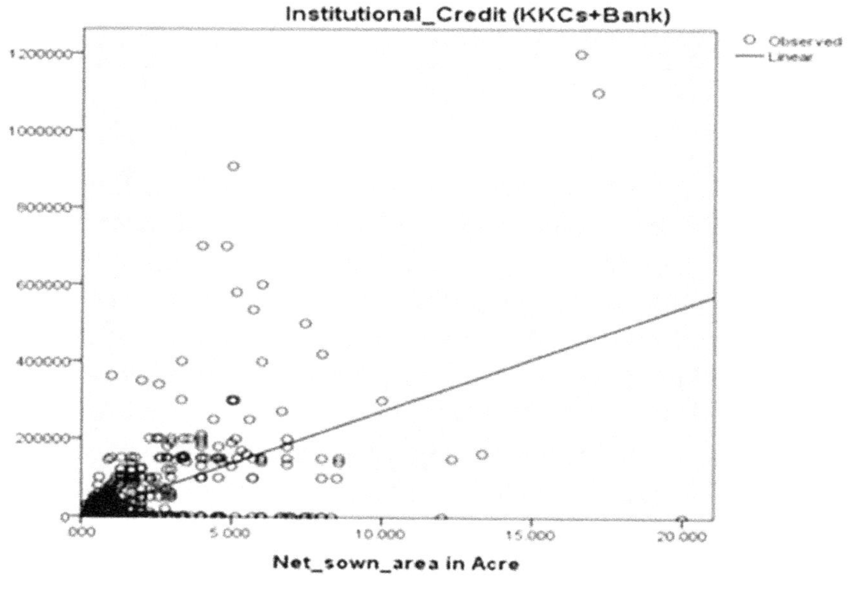

population having land less than 5 acre only. So, this can be concluded that small farmers is reaching to the institutional credit but due to small size of land they are not able to get sufficient amount of loan. It proves that small holding is a major constraints in the credit facilities. This is also found in the table 16 which shows the major problems in the availing loan.

Different problems faced by the farmers in availing bank loan facility are summarized rank-wise in the following table. The farmers selected for the study are confronting problems related to inadequate loan(37.6%), non-availability of loan on time(42.9%), high rate of interest(77.1%), demand for collateral (51.7%), long process (72.2%)and non-cooperative behavior of officials(54.6%) etc.

Thus, it is clear from the above analysis that majority of farmers faced problems in obtaining loan due to high rate of interest .Secondly, these financial institutions don't give loan to the farmers without collateral (security). So, it becomes a big barrier in getting loan from the bank and other financial institutions. As a result, many marginal and small farmers do not get the facility of agriculture loan from the banks. Consequently, high interest rate, long process and non-cooperative attitude /behavior of bank official and demand for security are the main constraints in availing loan as reported by the sampled farmers.

Insurance Details

Table18 shows the district wise details about insurance of crops, as reported by the sampled farmers. Out of 500 sample farmers, only 12 farmers reported about crop insurance. Out of 12, 9 farmers mentioned that they need to take the insurance amount for their crop. But only three farmers out of 9, got the insurance amount of Rs.1,17,800 consists of average amount of Rs.10,000 in Sonbhadra, 7800 in Siddhartha Nagar and Rs.10000 in Mau. Thus, very few farmers have insured their crop in the selected districts. It is to be noted that these farmers insured their crops by themselves as they were not aware about the KKCs crop insurance scheme. So, nobody has claimed against the KKC insurance when they required.

Table 17. District-wise details of insurance reporting by the farmers (no.)

District	Is any of your crop/crops is insured?	Did you need to take the insurance amount?	Did you get the insurance amount?	If yes, then how much (average amount in Rs)
	Yes	Yes	Yes	Amount
Sonbhadra	3	3	1	10000
Jaunpur	2	2	0	-
Siddharth Nagar	1	-	-	-
Balrampur	1	1	1	7800
Mau	5	3	1	10000
Total	**12**	**9**	**3**	**117800**

Source: Primary Survey 2019

CONCLUSION

It is clear from above analysis that besides climatic problems like drought and flood, the agriculture sector faces a variety of problems related to social and institutional issues, irrigation and electricity constraints, marketing & selling issues, infrastructure and storage issues, debt and finance, post-harvest management and technology related problems that can affect agricultural product, income of farmers and institutional risks. The study shows that farmers are facing various problems related to agriculture in the selected districts. Problems related to irrigation, infrastructure and market have emerged as a major problem among sampled farmers. The main problems related to irrigation is high cost of irrigation. The most important problem related to social institutional reported by farmers was small and fragmented land holdings. The farmers also faced problems in obtaining loan due to high rate of interest. Irregular transport facilities is another area of concern for the farmers. Low price of their produce emerged as the main marketing problem. Lack of cold storage, high cost of storage, lack of modern machinery and equipment and loss of produce on field due to calamity were also mentioned as major problems that are faced by a large number of farmers. These problems and constraints are major areas of concern for government and policy makers .To tackle these problems, effective delivery mechanisms are needed that can translate into effective facilitation in terms of increasing productivity or decreasing cost at the ground level.

Though there are a number of schemes aimed to bring development in agriculture at national and state level, but, our analysis clearly exhibits the reality that the various government programs and scheme introduced for the benefit of farmers are not effectively reaching to the majority of farmers. Hence, there is clear need of revamping these programs and the delivery system at the grass route level so that the problems faced by the farmers are effectively dealt with. Thus, agriculture sector of eastern UP requires very innovative ideas for uplifting the agrarian sector.

REFERENCES

Garg, D. (2019). The Agriculture Infrastructure in India– Connecting Dots to Paint a Bigger Picture. *Indian Folk*. https://www.indianfolk.com/agriculture-infrastructure-india-connecting-dots-paint-bigger-picture/

Jha, S. N., Vishwakarma, R.K., Ahmad T.R.A., & Dixit, A.K. (2016). *Assessment of Quantitative Harvest and Post-Harvest Losses of Major Crops/ Commodities in India*. Technical Report of Ministry of Food Processing Industries, Government of India and Indian Council of Agricultural Research (ICAR)/ ICAR-CIPHET, PAU, Ludhiyana.

Planning Commission. (1964). Report of the Joint Study Team on Eastern Districts. Planning Commission.

Planning Commission. (2007). *Scenario of the Village*. Planning Commission. http://planningcommission.nic.in/plans/stateplan/.../sdr_orich16.doc

Prakash, S., & Singh, B. (2013). Economics and Constraints Analysis of Rice Production in Jhansi District Of Uttar Pradesh, India. *Plant Archives, 13*(2), 865–869.

Reserve Bank of India. (1984). *Agricultural Productivity in Eastern India*. RBI.

Singh, A. K. (1981). *Patterns of Regional Development: A Comparative Study*. Sterling Publishers.

Singh, S. (2019). Determinants of Agriculture Production in Uttar Pradesh, India: A regional analysis. *Research Review International journal of Multidisciplinary, 4*(1).

Subas, R. (1984). Dynamics of Agrarian Relations in Sultanpur East Uttar Pradesh. *Social Scientist, 12*(7), 57-63.

Tanwar, N., Tripathi, R. K., Hooda, E., Khan, M., & Godara, P. (2017). Assessment of Agricultural Development in Eastern Uttar Pradesh. *Annals of Biology*, *33*(1), 139–144.

Tirth, R., Badal, P. S., Singh, O. P., & Singh, R. (2015). Constraints to agricultural Diversification in Mirzapur District of Uttar Pradesh. *Economic affairs, 60*(2), 273-276.

Nath, P., Verma, A., Dhusia, N., & More, N. (2006). Study on Impact of Natural Disasters And Its Relationship With Rainfall Distribution in The State of Uttar Pradesh During, 2006-2010. *Conference Paper.*

European Commission. (2007). Mediterranean water scarcity and drought report. Technical report on water scarcity and drought management in the Mediterranean and the Water Framework Directive. Mediterranean Water Scarcity and Drought Working Group, Brussels.

Vaidyanathan, A. (1987). Agricultural Development in Eastern India. *Economic and Political Weekly*, *22*(52), 2259–2263. https://www.jstor.org/stable/4377916

Chapter 10
Construction Industry:
A Case of Rural Inclusiveness at the Workplace in the Indian Perspective

Gaganpreet Kaur
Independent Researcher, India

Nandita Mishra
Linkoping University, Sweden

Puja Singhal
National Center for School Leadership (NIEPA), India

ABSTRACT

The construction industry has always been a major pillar in the overall development of any economy. The boons of this industry are not only restricted to the structural development of the nation, but it is a major role player in the economic development of any nation. The hidden benefits this industry has provided cannot be ignored. Generating maximum employment, which is not only for the educated section but also for the uneducated section of society, regardless of the skilled or unskilled people, is worth discussing. This industry is a perfect example of the amalgamation of diversity as well as equity within the workplace. This chapter tries to focus on the variables that play a major role when the issues and benefits of diversity and equity are discussed in the context of the construction industry. The data from 450 workers were collected and a questionnaire was prepared to know the exact situation of diversity and equity in the construction industry at prevailing times.

DOI: 10.4018/978-1-6684-6878-4.ch010

INTRODUCTION

According to the Construction Industry development Council 2003, construction industry showing an annual growth of 10 per cent is one of India's fastest growing sectors among other sectors of the country. After agriculture, this industry is the second largest employment generating industry which includes the female count as well, (Baruah, 2010). Construction workers are made to work under challenging conditions such as hostile weather conditions due to which the chances of having health-related trouble to these workers are higher than any other industry. There is a chain which is linked to the various worker's related plights such as the relatively less developed areas encourage local people to move out of their comfort area and hence starts the journey of challenging path starts. Moving to the developed areas such as big metropolises, working as low paid jobs and even as unorganized sectors which further escalates the prevailing problem as they have to live in poor living conditions and have to even compromise with unsafe working conditions. With reduced wages, they fail to maintain the basic standard of living and thus such situations make them prone to health problems.

Construction workers suffer a major plight which is payment of low wages for their work. Although the presence of Minimum Wages Act assures the workers for being rightly paid it fails to cover the unorganised sector. The present situation depicts the pictures that both skilled as well as unskilled construction workers work for low wages. The workers are generally supplied by labour contractor on a commission basis, which means labours are being paid after deduction of commission charges. Since beginning the industrial workers are treated as machines having long working hours, no interval for rest and working without having any demand for wages. In the lieu of earning heavy profits, owners of the industry have developed an attitude towards the workers to work for them untiringly, on low wages even should not complain about working in unhygienic conditions.

Female workers also face the dilemma of being less paid because of migration. The foremost reason for migration of female workers is marriages. Also, when they get employed in migratory construction sites; they are treated as assistants to their husband. This leads to the situation where only men get paid and women are devoid of their rights of 'full-time' wages.

Especially focusing on construction industry it seems that India is not the only country in which the entry of female workers is subject to some restrictions. The percentages of this restriction may be up or down in some countries but problem remains same. Either being a developed country or being a developing country this industry defined a clear cut segmentation of two genders where female workers are placed at the bottom.

The positions, as well as situations, have not changed enough with regards to construction industry entertaining women labourers. Even today construction industry stands at second place to hold the least number of female employers after mining and quarrying (the activities which involve the extraction of building stone or slate from an open surface quarry). The reasons for this can be recruitment practices, the sexist attitudes, the education criteria or maybe the image of this industry and even it's working environment.

As a result, female are more prone to accidents and injuries at the site. They are more common victims of feet injury, skin infection, head injury and many others. This is common when female workers are not provided with safety equipment but when provided, they hesitate to wear them.

ISSUES WITH WORKING WOMEN

There is no question to this fact that after agriculture construction industry ranks second to employ women for its working. In spite of knowing to this fact that it includes the most dangerous, difficult jobs to be performed in it. It has been ranked as the most perilous also includes activities that are prone to accidents by an International Labour Organization (ILO). There are number of problems associated with women labour. Mentioning few of them are like an iceberg where the hidden problems are far more major than the outer one. They face the most common problem of gender discrimination. The construction industry is male considered to be a male-driven industry. The female worker is subjugated at every genre of industry; they are considered as a helper to men.

This scenario of gender discrimination enables an employer a chance to exploit them and to pay them fewer wages than that of the men. All the female workers are made to work unskilled work and the main work allotted to them includes work like shifting of building material to the place of site.

LACK OF CRECHES

Working women are not only overburdened with the work pressure but there are a lot more other things that need to be considered. Apart from women in the construction sites, they handle their babies as well due to the lack of availability of crèches are forced to roam around at the construction sites and sometimes be the victims of accidents. The employers on being questioned about the presence of children on the construction site put the blame on the women workers. Women are held solely liable for any miss happening occurring to them or to their young ones at the construction sites.

The rules under "The Building and Other Construction Workers' (Regulation of Employment and Conditions of Service) Act (BOCW) 1996", makes it compulsory for the employers to follow the guidelines provided under it related to various measures. Any construction site employing more than 50 women labours are required to provide the facilities of crèches to them. But these benefits tend to reach the workers only if they are registered.

POOR SANITATION AT LABOUR COLONIES

At some construction sites, the workers are provided with the labour colonies in which they live and these are mostly adjacent to the working sites. But the conditions prevailing in them are not at all close to satisfactory and are totally unhygienic. Lack of basic facilities like sanitation, water, electricity, medical facilities, and non- availability of shops to buy basic amenities, the conditions of these facilities available are pathetic. Having no separate washing area for women and even lack of gynaecologic for the female workers makes the situation, even more, worst for female workers.

SEXUAL HARASSMENT OF WOMEN AT WORKPLACES

Women today hold a very important and strong place in society. The importance of her role can be judged from the fact that she has touched and excelled in all the fields of the modern world the same as men. But talking of her participation in a few years back was not as it is today. They were lacking in many fields due to their non- participation and if they were involved their number was almost negligible. Apart from their involvement being less in number they were respected by men. But in today's world, although their number has increased incredibly, they are disrespected by men.

Women are being objectified by the male dominating society which develops the feeling of lack of confidence and self-esteem as well. The unwanted sexual advances which are mostly traced in the form of promises or threats, explicit or implicit, inappropriate questions or remarks person's sex life, making sexual remarks, sending offensive pictures, MMS, caressing, kissing or fondling someone against her will, falsely accusing a person behind closed doors are some of the ways of sexually harassing a person. The impact of sexual harassment is highly negative on the victim. It not only affects the victim mentally but also affects productivity. To overcome this traumatic stress there is an increase in the number of absenteeism which ultimately decreases the opportunities for promotion and loss of pay as well. The victim becomes a subject to gossip and is scrutinised at work and its impact is that there is a feeling of shame, guilt and start blaming her of the situation. It becomes difficult for her to concentrate due to lack of motivation due to the feeling of betrayed and violated. She has been facing sexual harassment at workplace in innumerable forms.

OBJECTIVE OF THE STUDY

1. To study whether female workers are paid equally paid as of male workers.
2. Do the companies provide basic sanitation facilities to female workers.

LITERATURE REVIEW

Working women in the construction industry has faced the maximum discrimination in this industry. Women are under-represented in all construction occupations and professions, (Sang & Powell, 2012). Although formally no discrimination exists against women worker, wage differentials and gender discrimination does happen in a job market, both in organized and unorganized industries, (Kumar,2013). The female workers are paid less wages as compared to the male workers, (Tiwary & Gangopadhyay, 2011). Women workers are basically called as the unskilled workers of the construction industry. They are responsible for sweeping, picking up and throwing away the rubble from the site, assisting mistris by carrying and handling out bricks and making the cement mix, (Dalmia, 2012). Migrant women have to face the problems twice than the other working women as they have not only have to navigate their roles as migrants but further have to face the issues of gender discrimination, (Moyce & Schenker, 2018). The issues of women workers are still not adequately addressed both by the employer and the law makers, (Kulkarni G., 2007). Lack of family support and social security make them a vulnerable to violence, (Chawada, Gharat, Bansal, & Kantharia, 2012). The laws which are meant for working women are paradoxically turned against their interest by unscrupulous employers, (Mahalakshmi, 2015). There is a difference in the employment pattern as well, only 55% of women are employed for full time positions in contrast to 95% for men, (Fielden et al., 2000). Women workers face harassment at workplace as well as home, and they are discriminated in promotion and wages, (Kumar, 2013). Barriers to women working and entering the construction arising from: image of the industry, career knowledge, criteria of selection and male dominated courses, practices of recruitment and procedures, sexist attitude, culture and the working environment, (Fielden et al., 2000). Pertaining to gender bias women are not promoted as masons and women workers are not given an equal opportunity to be trained informally like men in the construction industry, (Kumar, 2013).

Setting the hypothesis for objectives:

1. To study whether female workers are paid equally paid as of male workers.
   Setting the objectives for first objective:
   H01= (Null hypothesis) Male and female workers are equally paid with regards to overtime done by them.
2. Do the companies provide basic sanitation facilities to female workers.
   Setting the hypothesis for second objective:-
   H02= (Null hypothesis) Female workers are provided with all the basic sanitation facilities required at the sites by the companies.

RESEARCH METHODOLOGY

Social research informs understanding of the human condition and contributes to predictive theoretical models rests on qualities that range from research methodology and sample selection, (Davis & Ruddle, 2010). There are mainly 3 sectors which are contributing towards the Gross Domestic growth of Indian economy. The aim of researcher for selecting the secondary sector was due to the fact that ever since 1950 the secondary sector has shown and remained stagnant towards the GDP contribution till the year 2013. In the first few years of independence, it has been the agriculture sector which was leading ahead for its contribution and followed after that was the industry sector and the last was the service sector. But the service sector has shown tremendous growth in itself and now stands the first position in the GDP contribution.

QUESTIONNAIRE DESIGNING

The study essentially focuses on collecting of data from the construction sites of Delhi, Noida and Gurugram through primary source. Framing of questionnaire was done and a total of 450 respondents were considered, out of which 315 were male and 135 female workers. The questionnaire was designed in a semi-structured form.

DATA ANALYSIS

1. To study whether female workers are paid equally as of male workers. H01= (Null hypothesis) Male and female workers are equally paid with regards to overtime done by them.

To test this **Chi-square test** was applied with variables taken into consideration being

1. Gender
2. Overtime paid

From table-1 the results which came out was that there were total of 138 male respondents which said no to the question asked which was that they are not given overtime for their work. But the expected answer which was supposed was 155, on further study there were 177 male workers who said yes and they are being paid overtime.

Table 1. Crosstabulation table for variables gender and overtime

			Do you get overtime?		Total
			No	Yes	
Gender	MALE	Count	138	177	315
		Expected Count	155.4	159.6	315.0
	FEMALE	Count	84	51	135
		Expected Count	66.6	68.4	135.0
Total		Count	222	228	450
		Expected Count	222.0	228.0	450.0

Source: Researcher's own calculation through SPSS

Table 2. Chi-Square Tests for variables gender and overtime

	Value	Df	Asymp. Sig. (2-sided)	Exact Sig. (2-sided)	Exact Sig. (1-sided)
Pearson Chi-Square	12.818[a]	1	.000		
Continuity Correction	12.091	1	.001		
Likelihood Ratio	12.910	1	.000		
Fisher's Exact Test				.000	.000
N of Valid Cases	450				
a. 0 cells (.0%) have expected count less than 5. The minimum expected count is 66.60.					
b. Computed only for a 2x2 table					

Source: Researcher's own calculation through SPSS

In table-2 the P value of the Pearson Chi-Square test comes out to be 0.000 which is less than 0.05 hence, **rejecting the null hypothesis.**

P (0.000) < 0.05

Null hypothesis is rejected which further means than male and female workers are not being paid equally for the overtime done by them.

In the above table there is a low but negative relationship among the variables taken under study.

2. Do the companies provide basic sanitation facilities to female worker.

Setting the hypothesis for second objective:-

H02= (Null hypothesis) Female workers are provided with all the basic sanitation facilities required at the sites by the companies.

Table 3. Symmetric measures for variables gender and overtime

		Value	Approx. Sig.
Nominal by Nominal	Phi	-.169	.000
	Cramer's V	.169	.000
N of Valid Cases		450	

Source: Researcher's own calculation through SPSS

To test the above hypothesis **T-Test** was applied but before the application of the t-test the test to see the normality of the data was applied on the two variables:

1. Gender
2. Do these toilets have proper and easy accessibility on site.

From the above test it became clear that the sanitation facility given to the workers was not up to the mark according to the workers. Further it was important to study that whether the sanitation facility which was given to the workers was equally utilized by the male and the female workers at the site.

Table 4. Tests of normality for variables gender and accessibility of toilets

	Gender	Kolmogorov-Smirnov[a]			Shapiro-Wilk		
		Statistic	Df	Sig.	Statistic	df	Sig.
Do these toilets have proper and easy accessibility on sites?	MALE	.352	315	.000	.712	315	.000
	FEMALE	.423	135	.000	.580	135	.000
a. Lilliefors Significance Correction							

Source: Researcher's own calculation through SPSS

Under the table-4 the value of the Kolmogorov- Smirnov was 0.000 which was less than 0.05 which indicates that the data is not normally distributed. Therefore the **Mann-Whitney U Test** was applied to check the hypothesis.

Table 5. Ranks table for variables designation and sanitation

	Gender	N	Mean Rank	Sum of Ranks
Do these toilets have proper and easy accessibility on sites?	MALE	315	215.90	68009.00
	FEMALE	135	247.90	33466.00
	Total	450		

Source: Researcher's own calculation through SPSS

Table 6. Test statistics for variables designation and sanitation

	Do these toilets have proper and easy accessibility on sites?
Mann-Whitney U	18239.000
Wilcoxon W	68009.000
Z	-2.790
Asymp. Sig. (2-tailed)	.005
a. Grouping Variable: Gender	

Source: Researcher's own calculation through SPSS

In the above table the significant value is coming more than 0.05 hence we fail to reject the null hypothesis.

P value (0.005) < 0.05

Hence there was a difference in the accessibility of the toilets at the site for male and female workers. **The result of the test rejected the null hypothesis** set and stated that yes there was a difference between the accessibility of the toilets at the site provided on the site. Even though the facility of toilets was given at the site, yet they were not equally utilised by the female and the male workers. The reason behind this was the conditions of the toilets they were using. Many of the toilets were not having the doors which made uncomfortable for the female user. Moreover there were other big issues:

- Toilets without doors
- No separate toilets for male and female workers.
- Privacy issues between the two toilets connected from within.
- Providing the toilets away from the site in remote area.

Were the few reasons which restricted the female workers from using the sanitation facility as male workers.

PROVIDING SOLUTION

From the above study it is inevitable that construction workers are compounded by illiteracy, lack of infrastructures, security, poor working conditions and have inadequate health facilities, (Patel, Moitra, Momin, & Kantharia, 2012). Workers must be given health education; moreover female workers must be given education regarding the importance of hygiene. Provision of various welfare facilities like availability of toilets on sites, separate toilets of male and female workers, provision of crèches for female workers must be provided. There is a need to provide proper training and induction programs to workers without any gender discrimination. There is also a need to educate / contractors and other male masons to train and accept women masons and pay them equally without gender discrimination, (Kumar, 2013). Male workers must discourage the environment of ill- treating the women co- workers at workplace In India, as workers are mostly illiterate, it is desirable to impart health education to them, to apprise them of the ill effects of work and remedial measures, (Tiwary & Gangopadhyay, 2011). It becomes the duty of the workers to avoid going for sanitation in open. Compromising with the situation is no solutions to any worker relate issues.

LIMITATION AND FUTURE RESEARCH

This study is conducted from the 15 construction sites of Delhi, Noida and Gurugram, hence there is a wide scope for the upcoming researcher to study similar working conditions in other parts of the country.

REFERENCES

Baruah, B. (2010, February). Women and globalosation: Challenges and opportunities facing construction workers in contemporary India. *Development in Practice*, *20*(1), 31–44. doi:10.1080/09614520903436935

Chawada, B., Bansal, R., & Kantharia, S. (2012). Plight of female construction workers of Surat city. *Indian Journal of Community Health*, *24*(1), 19–22.

Chawada, B., Gharat, V., Bansal, R., & Kantharia, S. (2012). Plight of female construction workers of Surat city. *Indian Journal of Community Health*, 19–22.

Dalmia, A. J. (2012, June). Strong women, weak bodies, muted voices. *Women construction workers in Delhi, 47*(26), pp. 249-255.

Davis, A., & Ruddle, K. (2010). Constructing Confidence: Rational skepticism and systematic enquiry in local ecological knowledge research. *Ecological Applications*, *20*(3), 880–894. doi:10.1890/09-0422.1 PMID:20437971

Fielden, S. L., Davidson, M. J., Gale, A. W., & Davey, C. L. (2000). Women in construction: The untapped resource. *Construction Management and Economics*, *18*(1), 113–121. doi:10.1080/014461900371004

Kulkarni, G. (2007). Construction industry: More needs to be done. *Indian Journal of Occupational and Environmental Medicine*, *11*(1), 1. doi:10.4103/0019-5278.32455 PMID:21957363

Kumar, B. (2013). Gender discrimination among construction workers with reference to Vijaywada. *Journal of sociology ans social work, 1*(1), 42-53.

Kumar, B. R. (2013, June). Gender discrimination among construction workers with reference to Vijayawada. *Journal of Sociology and Social Work*, *1*(1), 42–53.

Mahalakshmi, J. (2015). Protection to women in India: A judicial Perspective. *Labour Law Journal*, 29-33.

Moyce, S. C., & Schenker, M. (2018). Migrant workers and their occupational health and safety. *Annual Review of Public Health*, *39*(1), 351–365. doi:10.1146/annurev-publhealth-040617-013714 PMID:29400993

Patel, H. C., Moitra, M., Momin, M. I., & Kantharia, S. L. (2012). Working conditions of male construction worker and it's impact on their life: A cross sectional study in Surat city. *National Journal of Community Medicine*, *3*(4), 652–656.

Sang, K., & Powell, A. (2012). Gender inequality in the construction industry: Lessons from Pierre Bourdieu. *In Proceedings of the 28th Annual ARCOM Conference* (pp. 237-247). Edinburgh, UK: Association of Researchers in Construction Management.

Tiwary, G., & Gangopadhyay, P. (2011). A review on the occupational health and social security of unorganized workers in the construction industry. *Indian Journal of Occupational and Environmental Medicine*, *15*(1), 18. doi:10.4103/0019-5278.83003 PMID:21808496

Tiwary, G., & Gangopadhyay, P. K. (2011, April). A review on the occupational health and social security of unorganized workers in the construction industry. *Indian Journal of Occupational and Environmental Medicine*, *15*(1), 18. doi:10.4103/0019-5278.83003 PMID:21808496

Chapter 11
Climate Change:
Its Impact on Equity, Diversity, and Livelihood of the Rural Population

Nisha Saini
Arun Jaitley National Institute of Financial Management, India

ABSTRACT

Climate change is universally a shift in the existing flora and fauna and those natural systems that make the atmosphere congenial for the existence of humans and biodiversity. In this context a lot of research work is going on sustainable development for example: SDG Goals 2030 are a step forward in this direction, IPCC reports, conferences, and workshops. If we look at a scenario of the world from the past up till today, it has various divisions on account of settlements such as rural, suburban, and urban. All these divisions are crucial as they are interdependent on each other. According to these divisions, the availability of resources to the population in these areas differ at all levels as per their economic stability. But the climate has the power to change and impact this economic stability, the cycle of availability of resources, production, manufacturing, preservation, and consumption of goods and services in the short as well as long term.

Climate change is the single greatest threat to a sustainable future but at the same time addressing the climate challenge presents a golden opportunity to promote prosperity, security and a brighter future for all. ~ Ban Ki-Moon, Former Secretary-General of UN

DOI: 10.4018/978-1-6684-6878-4.ch011

INTRODUCTION

Climate change is amalgamation of two words but its connotation and influence are at an enormous scale and long-lasting which could be both positive and negative. If we analyse the terminology from geographical dimension climate change take place at slow pace with life changing phenomena. Many factors are responsible for climate change. They could be natural, man-made and presence of gases like methane, carbon dioxide in large quantity which does impact the environment and climate at great extent. According to Carbon Brief and study published in journal Nature, greenhouse gases from industrial era began warming the world oceans in the beginning of 1830.

The beginning of production-manufacturing and consumption cycle of humans is also the reason of growth and unsustainable development. As the development characteristic matured among the world, we began sacrificing the sustainable development. We did not stop at one solution but build the complex structure of economy around us based on factors of production. This eventually gave rise to many other dimensions such as economic, political, social, behavioural and technological. Due to which the engine of growth got boost and it is growing at not ever culminating swiftness and nonentity can recognize what is going to be its final result!

One of the major features that are left far behind is to achieve right balance of atmospheric lifecycle for existence of humans and other living beings. The living groups with whom we share the planet are playing their role by creating flora and fauna through their activities. If we observe the actions of all living beings, one can state that these living beings utilise the resources made available by the mother earth for their basic needs and return it back in a more fruitful way that is good for the planet. We humans do not do so. We are exploiting resources in the amount that is not even available in nature.

We must think where are we going after all? All this creates a huge instability and imbalance in all aspects. That's the reason why we all are leading discontent lives despite being blessed by nature. Climate change is beginning of the result of our past activities. Let's have a glance at literature review and research methodology before we explore the different aspects of this chapter in brief yet in detail manner.

Literature Review

Sea level rise globally by ADB elucidates about the GDP loss by year 2100 from 0.3 to 9.3 percent. The paper also give insight about strategies to prevent land loss and migration of the people due to climate change. The accommodation plan give detail about limit the damage by flood proofing or raising structures. In general community acceptance of sea level rise strategies will be significant to strengthen the vulnerable areas (Asuncion & Lee, 2017).

How individual can contribute to prevent climate change by adapting effective steps to their activities which can help in achieving a balance in temperatures of the earth. People as a citizen and a consumer both have to take initiatives to save the world from the repercussions of climate. (Ortiz, 2018)

Climate change not only impacts the environment but also the health and safety of workers. The rise in temperatures will increase heat related stress and heat related disorders for example expose to hazardous chemicals and its adverse effects on the health of workers. Rise in global temperature will give influence to the natural phenomena's that will affect the life cycle of all living beings. In this context what all steps should be taken is also discussed to support the health of indoor and outdoor workers (Levy & Roelofs, 2019).

The report by ILO elucidates about three main topics firstly, negative effects of climate change and extreme weather events on climate change. Secondly, adaptation measures can create jobs and protect workers and income. Thirdly, accompanying and enabling policies to maximize the positive employment effect of the transition to a climate-resilient economy. All these dimensions are crucial to study the impact of climate change and issues regarding labour and employment (Maitre et al., 2023).

An article written in Global Citizens describes on how war impact climate change and the environment. It further describes about three key facts about how war impacts the climate crisis and the environment. Also, how warfare releases greenhouse gas emission, pollution, destroy wildlife and biodiversity. In the end it assesses what can be done by global citizen to help? This article is explores the new aspect which do needs a focus and analysis at present (McCarthy, 2022).

United Nation Climate Change (2023), The website give knowledge about the Paris agreement along with its meaning, how it works, nationally determined contributions, long term strategies, how countries are supporting each other, its tracking progress and achievement so far as per the agreement.

IPCC, working group I have focused on various aspects of climate change in its reports such as Climate Change:The IPCC 1990 and 1992 assessment, SAR climate change 1995,TAR climate change 2001,AR4 climate change 2007,Managing the risk of extreme events and disaster to advance climate change adaptation 2012,AR5 climate change 2013,Global warming of 1.5degree Celsius 2018,Climate and land 2019, The ocean and cryosphere in changing climate 2019 and AR6 Climate Change 2021.

Research Methodology

The following questions will be researched to write this chapter: -

1. To explore the historical dimension of climate change phenomena.
2. For Understanding Agreements framed and implemented in the context of climate change.
3. Which factors are responsible for climate change?
4. To understand the impact of climate change on diversity of rural population, equity and livelihood.
5. What all initiatives have been taken by the government for climate change?
6. Suggestions as solutions to reverse the effects of climate change.

By reviewing secondary data sources, the study for the chapter would employ both qualitative, quantitative and analytical approach.

To understand how climate change impact the diversity, equity and livelihood? We need to primarily understand the historical dimension of temperature transformation (climate change).

History of Climate Change

Environment, climate, weather, atmosphere are different names of one of the major aspect due to which life is possible. As human civilization came into existence it began to understand things around them and gradually as the requirement of humans grew the cycle of economic activity also grew with it. As per United Nations, World Meteorological Organization was the organization limited to operational activities.

Natural resources are essential requirement for the economic growth of countries whether they are developed or developing. In year 1949 (Lake

Success, New York, 17 August to 6 September) the United Nation Scientific Conference on the conservation and utilization of resources was the first to address the depletion of those resources. Until 1968 environmental issues did not receive attention by any major UN organs. The Economic and Social Council was the first to include environmental issues in its agenda as a specific item and decided by the general assembly later to hold the first United Nation Conference on the human environment.

Similarly, in year 1972 from 5 to 16 June, the United Nation Scientific Conference was held in Stockholm, Sweden, also known as the first Earth Summit. In this summit a declaration was adopted that set out principles for the conservation and enrichment of the human environment with the action plan containing recommendations for international environmental action. The declaration raised the issue of climate change for the first-time warning governments to be aware of activities that will evaluate the likelihood and magnitude of climatic effects. This conference also proposed the establishment of stations to monitor long term trends present in the atmosphere. All these programmes were coordinated by World Meteorological Organizations to help the world community to develop understanding regarding the causes of climate change.

The Conference also called for the convening of a second meeting on the environment and established the Governing Council of the United Nations Environment Programme (UNEP), with its secretariat in Nairobi, Kenya, the Environment Fund and the Environment Coordination Board. Water resources, marine mammals, renewable energy resources, desertification, forests, environmental legal framework and the issue of environment and development became the main focus.

In 1979, the UNEP governing council asked its executive director, under the earth watch programme, to monitor and evaluate the range of air pollutants and first international instrument on climate the Convention on Long-Range Transboundary Air Pollution -- was then adopted. This initiative took to next level in year 1980, when its governing council expressed concern at the damage to the ozone layer and recommended measures to limit the production and use of chlorofluorocarbons F-11and F-12.

This further led to the negotiation and adoption of Vienna Convention in 1985 for the protection of the ozone layer and recommended measures to limit the production along with the conclusion of the protocol to 1979 Transboundary Air Pollution Convention, which aimed at reducing sulphur emissions by 30 percent. One of the side effects of climate change which was faced in the beginning in Europe and North America was "acid rain". Due to this various programme were initiated by UNEP and WMO for keeping this phenomenon to analyse the change further.

Ultimately, it was 1987 the UN general assembly emphasised on environmental issues when it adopted the environmental outlook for the year 2000 and beyond. It's a framework that guides national action and international cooperation on policies and programmes directed at attaining ecologically sound development. This perspective introduced the notion of "Sustainable Development".

Even depletion of ozone layer and global warming became increasingly prominent in international public debates and political agenda in year 1988. An internal seminar was organized by UNEP to classify environmental sectors that are sensitive to climate change. From here the Intergovernmental Panel on Climate Change (IPCC), a forum for the examination of greenhouse warming and global climate change, was established and met for the first time in November.

After all these initiatives, another first significant global effort was taken in year 1989, the General Assembly recommended the UNEP Governing Council's request to commence arrangements with WMO for discussions on a structure resolution on climate change; regional action was also being taken. In addition, the Maldives conducted the text of the Male Declaration on Global Warming, Sea Level Rise to the UN Secretary-General; the Helsinki Declaration on the Protection of the Ozone Layer was adopted on 2 May. Also in 1989, the Montreal Protocol on Substances that Deplete the Ozone Layer entered into force.

At the same time, year 1990 marked as effort to raise awareness on the effects of climate change at second world climate conference held from 29 October to 7 November 1990. Further in 1992 the urgency for stronger international action on the environment including climate change expanded, the General Assembly in Rio de Janeiro, Brazil, the United Nations Conference on Environment and Development. The Earth summit set a new framework for seeking international agreements to protect the integrity of the global environment in Rio Declaration and Agenda 21. Chapter 9 of Agenda 21 consist of the protection of the atmosphere, establishing the link between science, sustainable development, energy development and consumption, transportation, industrial development, stratospheric ozone depletion and transboundary atmospheric pollution.

The most significant event during the Conference was the opening for signature of the United Nations Framework Convention on Climate Change (UNFCCC); by the end of 1992, 158 States had signed it. It entered into force in 1994, and in March 1995, the first Conference of the Parties to the Convention adopted the Berlin Mandate, launching talks on a protocol or other legal instrument containing stronger commitments for developed countries and those in transition.

Therefore, climate change action was, therefore, the adoption in Japan in December 1997 of the Kyoto Protocol to the UNFCCC, the most significant climate change achievement so far taken. It aimed to reduce the industrialized countries' overall emissions of carbon dioxide and other greenhouse gases by at least 5 per cent below the 1990 levels in the commitment period of 2008 to 2012. The Protocol, which opened for signature in March 1998, came into force on 16 February 2005, seven years after it was negotiated by over 160 nations. At present, countries have taken many initiatives and are taking to reverse the effects of climate change but the change is slow and not enough for what is lost due to development and other activities.

However, we should keep working towards a sustainable world. After the brief history of climate change, it becomes crucial to know about the agreement without which it will be incomplete to understand the whole framework about initiatives taken in context of climate change.

The Kyoto Protocol

The Kyoto protocol takes into account United Nations Framework Conventions on Climate Change by obliging industrialised countries to reduce green house gases emanations in agreement targets assumed by the nations.

The Paris Agreement

This agreement is a legally mandatory international treaty on climate change. It was adopted by 196 countries at COP 21 in Paris, on 12 December 2015 and came into force on 4 November 2016. Its objective is to limit the global warming to well below 2 to 1.5 degrees Celsius. To accomplish this long-term temperature goal, country's main objective is to reach global peaking of greenhouse gas emissions as soon as possible to attain a climate neutral world by mid-century.

The implementation of this Paris Agreement requires economic and social transformation. The Paris Agreement works on a five-year cycle of progressive ambitious climate action carried out by countries. It was year

2020, when countries had to submit their report or plans for climate action known as nationally determined contributions (NDCs).

In National Determined Contributions countries actions will take to reduce their greenhouse gas emissions and steps to build resilience to adapt to the impact of rising temperatures. Beside all this the Paris Agreement provides a framework for financial, technical and capacity building support to those countries who require support in these terms. The pillars which support this agreement are finance, technology, capacity building.

Finance, Capacity Building, and Technology

In terms of finance Paris Agreement should take into account developed countries to lead in providing financial assistance for countries that are less capable and more vulnerable. Climate finance is necessary and needed for modification, because large-scale investments are required to significantly reduce emissions.

Climate finance is correspondingly important for adaptation, as substantial financial resources for all. Secondly, technology which is necessary for improving resilience and reducing greenhouse gas emission through technology framework to provide overarching guidance to the well-functioning technology mechanism and transfer or sharing of policy and implementation arms to other countries.

As all developing countries do not have sufficient capacities to deal with many of the challenges brought by the climate change. Due to this the Paris Agreement places great emphasis on climate-related capacity-building for developing countries. Also, this agreement enhances transparency framework that will begin in year 2024.This will make countries liable to report actions taken and progress made towards climate change. This will further add into the global stocktake which will assess the collective progress towards the long-term climate goals. With the analyses of what is done and what is to be done will be suggested for the next round. If technology is utilised to some extent some issues of climate change can be solved. We need to develop such technologies through Artificial Intelligence which can support the initiatives for climate change and help humans to retore what has been lost due to development.

Hence, all the countries are gradually moving towards this direction by introducing zero carbon solutions. This trend is noticeable in the power and transport sectors and has created many new business opportunities for early movers too. By 2030, zero carbon emission could be competitive in sectors representing over 70% of global emissions. All this information describes how climate change began and what all has been done till yet. To add meaning to this chapter lets know what all activities trigger climate change below.

Factors Responsible for Climate Change

Figure 1. Human and natural influences on global temperature
Source: U.S. Global Change Research Program, Fourth National Climate Assessment, *Chapter 2: Our Changing Climate EXIT EPA WEBSITE*, 2017.

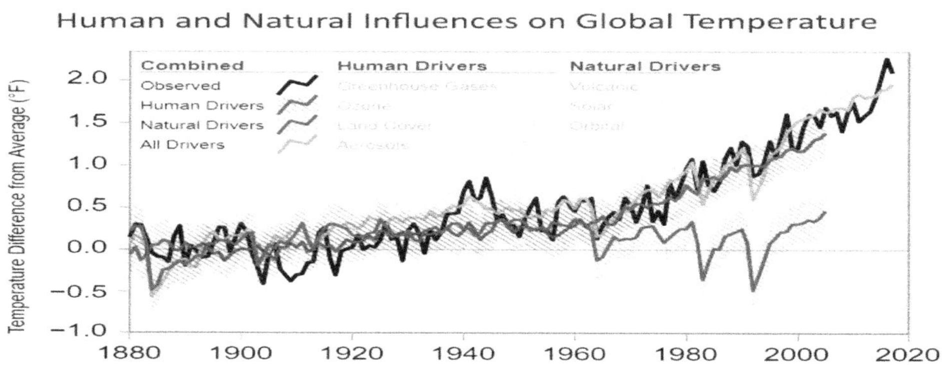

As per the "United States Environment Protection Agency" though there are many factors responsible for change in climatic conditions but according to them human activities are majorly responsible for it. However, climate change takes place by both manmade and natural activities that impact the atmosphere and environment around us. The points below explain all the aspects geographical, biological and artificial. They are: -

1. Greenhouse gas emanation.
2. Concentration and reflection of sun energy.
3. Deviations in the earth's orbit and rotation.
4. Alterations in earth reflectivity.
5. Volcanic activity.
6. Modifications in Naturally Occurring Carbon Dioxide Concentrations.
7. War and armaments are also contributing to climate change.
8. Rise in Sea Level.

1. Greenhouse Gas Emanation

Figure 2. Greenhouse gas
Source: - https://climatechange.lta.org/get-started/learn/co2-methane-greenhouse-effect/

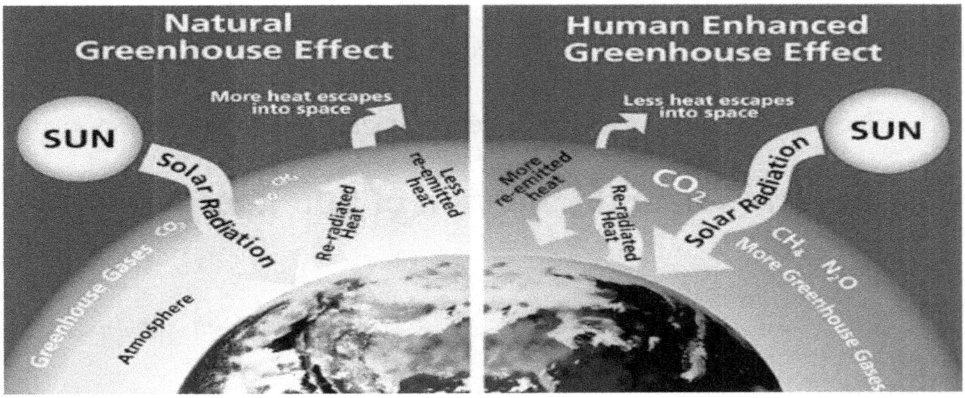

We all know a large mass of carbon emission comes from greenhouse gases but it is crucial to understand what these greenhouse gases are? Greenhouse's gases are generally those which trap heat in earth atmosphere. As per Scientific American newsletter the study began over 200 years ago in 1824 by Joseph Fourier, a French mathematician and physicist on greenhouse gases. In a way we can say that these gases act as a glass ceiling which trap the heat and make the earth temperature warmer. The irony is after discovering the side effects of greenhouse gases still implementation of sustainable alternative is quite sluggish in the world accepts few countries. Who are utilizing energy based renewable sources of energy as a solution to greenhouse effects. We all know mostly these gases in earth atmosphere are carbon dioxide (CO2), methane (CH4), nitrous oxide (N2O). Similarly, Industrial gases are hydrofluorocarbons (HFCs) perfluorocarbons (PFCs) sulfur hexafluoride (SF6) nitrogen trifluoride (NF3). According to national academy of sciences (2020) greenhouse gases are one of the major reasons for increasing the temperatures. Human activities are considered the major reason for increasing the amount of greenhouse gases. Some examples in this context are burning fossil fuels, solid waste, cement manufacturing and the way land resources are utilised by cutting trees and plants which absorb carbon dioxide. These activities also impact the marine life which crucial for healthy water bodies. On this note another gas which impacts the environment severely is methane.

According to scientist methane has more power to make earth warmer than the carbon dioxide. On the other hand, Carbon dioxide gas has long-lasting effect than methane. But methane adds to already existing problem by increasing its rapidity of warming up the earth surface. Methane is emitted by natural wetlands, agricultural activities, and fossil fuel extraction, oil, gas and transport. To solve this issue one can, take help of technology available today. This technology must be shared among the nations for the welfare and existence of the world altogether. Let's have glance on concentration and reflection of sun energy. How it gets impacted due to human activity?

2. Concentration and reflection of Sun Energy

Figure 3. Concentration and reflection of Sun Energy
Source:-https://courses.lumenlearning.com/suny-environmentalbiology/chapter/10-4-climate-change/

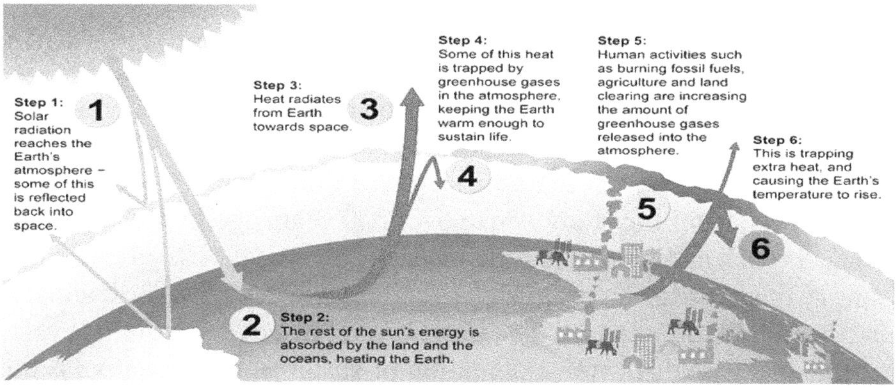

Absorption and reflection of sun energy gets impacted when activities like road construction, agriculture, deforestation and all those activities other than mentioned here disturb the cycle of phenomena's which are essential for earth surface. Growth in population than the resources available for utilization is another issue which interrupts the cycle of environment. All the countries are divided in rural and urban areas. According to experts, urban areas are today warmer than rest of the surroundings. They do not replicate sunlight back in the atmosphere as the natural surfaces get involve with the procedure. In short, we can say that land use does bring changes in atmosphere of the earth and eventually in temperatures. Now after having a brief view on this let's have a glance on deviations in earth orbit and rotation.

3. Deviations in Earth Orbit and Rotation

Earth revolves around the sun and it possesses its own system of reservations for climate change too. The seasons, temperatures, weather changes due to earth rotation and variations in its orbit. Geographically, longitudes and latitudes along with equator, tropic of cancer and tropic of Capricorn play a crucial role in bringing relevant changes in the atmosphere.

Figure 4.
Source: - https://ugc.berkeley.edu/what-is-global-change/infographic/

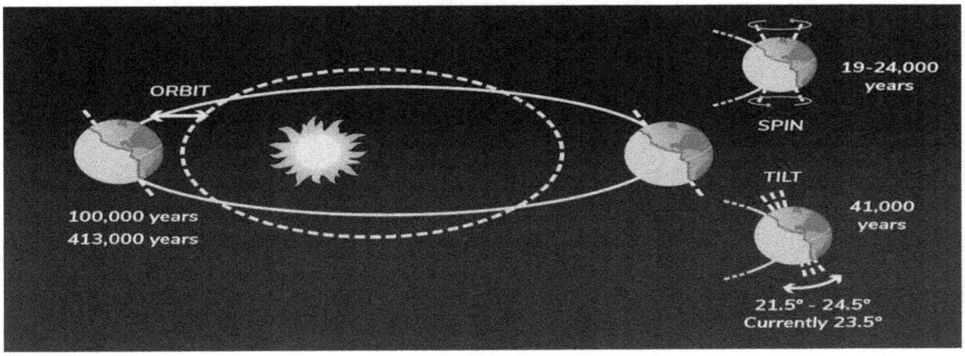

It is always claimed that there was long period of ice age and short period of warm temperatures too and the average global temperature during that period was about 2-degree Fahrenheit which is considered warmer than today's temperature. In similar direction other changes could be related to alteration in earth reflectivity, volcanic activity, and carbon dioxide concentration. In a similar way alterations in earth's reflectivity another natural phenomenon which do impact climate change but not to the extent which human activities impact.

4. Alterations in the Earth's Reflectivity

It is scientifically proven that dark object and surfaces absorb more heat than the light objects and surfaces. Most of sunlight which reaches the earth is absorbed by these dark objects namely oceans, forests and soil. Whereas the surfaces like snow and clouds reflect the sun light. But due to rise in temperatures the glaciers are melting, which will eventually give rise to sea level and other natural changes with whom human have to live and adjust to survive. With this point comes the volcanic activity.

5. Volcanic Activity

Figure 5.
Source: - https://www.enchantedlearning.com/subjects/volcano/

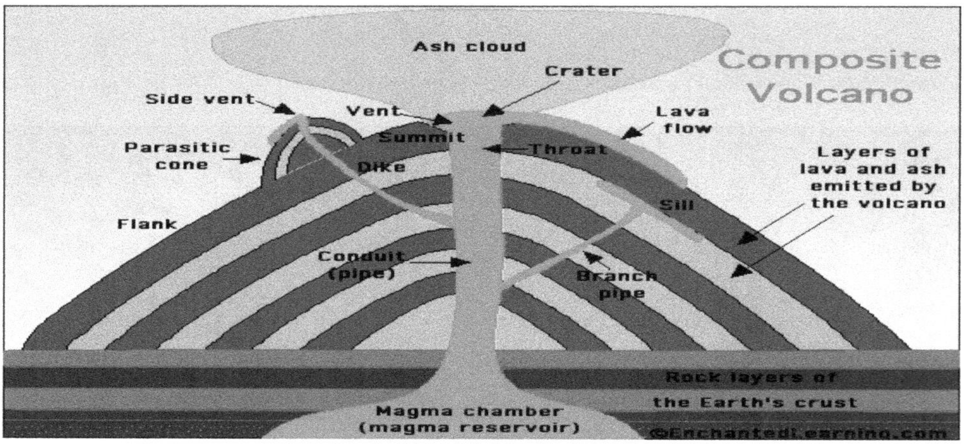

This activity is natural with its own advantages and disadvantages. We already know when the volcano erupts lot of gases, smoke, ash and many others elements are released. In the end it also produces molten lava which forms most fertile soil on earth. We cannot blame volcanic eruption totally because it an ages old geographical feature on earth which has been functioning since long time. At the same time the particles released in atmosphere remains for a shorter time than gas emissions. Yes, the amount of carbon dioxide it released does play a role in change of climate but not more than human activities that are releasing carbon dioxide which emit more than 100 times as much carbon dioxide as volcanoes each year. Beside this the carbon dioxide level too has a role to play that can be read in next point.

6. Modifications in Naturally Occurring Carbon Dioxide Concentrations

Figure 6. Carbon cycle
Source: - https://www.researchgate.net/figure/The-Carbon-Cycle-Source-Alamy-2020-The-Carbon-Cycle-8_fig2_343185753

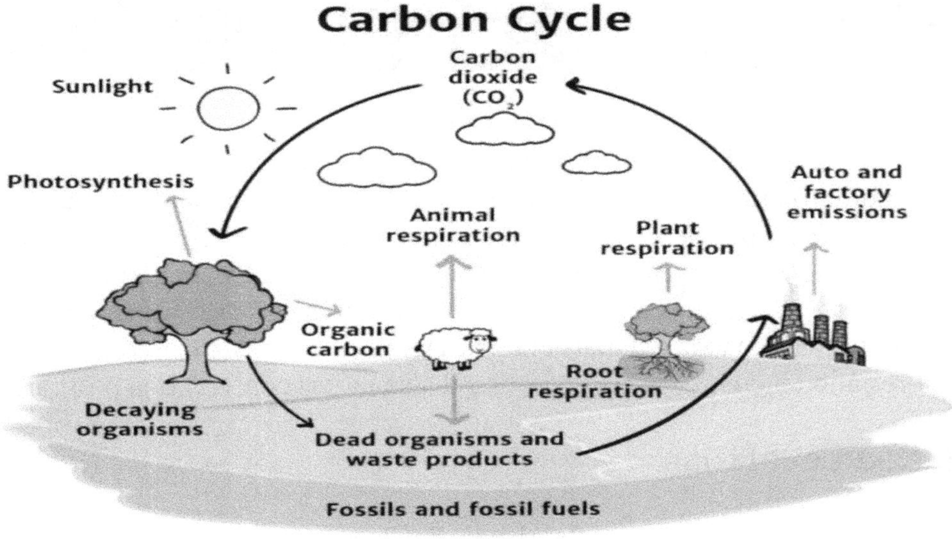

Carbon dioxide level varies according to temperatures. When the temperatures are warm carbon dioxide levels are higher and during cool temperatures period carbon dioxide levels are lower. Therefore, heating or cooling of the earth's surface and oceans can cause variations in the natural sources and sinks of these gases, and thus change greenhouse gas absorptions in the atmosphere. These exchanging concentrations have acted as a positive climate feedback, amplifying the temperature changes caused by long-term shifts in the earth's orbit. Other than these activities there is more that adds to the climate change that is war.

7. War Impact Climate Change

According to McCarthy (2022), militaries consume massive amounts of fossil fuels, which contributes directly to global warming. Bombings and other methods of modern warfare directly harm wildlife and biodiversity.

Figure 7.
Source: - https://environmentalchangewestern.wordpress.com/2014/11/20/the-earth-at-gunpoint-how-does-war-affect-ecosystems/

The collateral damage of conflict can kill up to 90% of large animals in an area. Pollution from war contaminates bodies of water, soil, and air, making areas unsafe for people to inhabit. In addition to this sea level rise is another side of atmosphere which does have huge impact on climate and it's after effects that be read in brief below. Beside this large scale of war scrap may be produced or abandoned that contains a range of polluting materials. Even deforestation increases during conflict. It also harms conservation program.

8. Sea Level Rise

One of the major reasons for the rise in sea level is melting of glaciers, ice caps and ice sheets due to rise in temperatures regionally and globally both. This rise will adversely affect the coastal areas.

Figure 8. Future sea level predictions
Source: - https://www.nrdc.org/experts/rob-moore/new-ipcc-report-sea-level-rise-challenges-are-growing

The National Aeronautics and Space Administration reported that (February 2016) had the highest increase in sea height variation at 74.8 millimetres (mm) since 1993 and the global mean sea level change is at 3.4 mm per year. Several studies confirm that increased air temperatures cause thermal expansion of oceans as they absorb 85% of the excess heat trapped by the atmosphere and were the main driver of global SLR for 75–100 years after the start of the industrialization (Cazenave and Llovel 2010; Levitus et al. 2009; Levitus, Antonov, and Boyer 2005; Levitus et al. 2001).

On the other hand, the most vulnerable to SLR are mostly small island states and atoll countries. For example, close to the highlighted and anticipated impact of SLR are: one is Kiribati, an island in the Pacific, and another is the city-state of Singapore, where notably, the impact of SLR is slowly being felt in market and nonmarket areas. According to the World Bank (2013), Kiribati is one of the world's most vulnerable countries to climate change and extreme weather. Kiribati is one of the first Pacific islands that will be in danger of becoming uninhabitable due to climate change. Now, after reading the main causes of climate change. Let's look on the impact of climate change on diversity of rural population.

Impact of Climate Change on Diversity of Rural Population

All the countries along with its population whether rural or urban are going to deal with the effects of the climate change according to the resources and adaptability of environment they possess. Those resources could be indigenous or shared sustainable technologies. Climate change is going to impact the environment in three ways that could be one for long time, two short terms and three permanent effects. These effects will depend on geographical dimension of the particular place. At the same time, this change won't be easy to bring back the normalcy until and unless strong steps for keeping the balance in environment and atmosphere are not taken by the people and representatives of the states and nations.

In a way we can analyse as the rural areas depend more on the nature for their growth and prosperity. Rural economy is an agrarian based; variation in climate will change the cropping pattern, crops sowing and harvesting period. Similarly, how livestock will survive with changing environment will completely depend upon the immunity they are carrying which can adapt according to the present atmosphere. On the other hand, economically in rural areas too household assets and liabilities matter for taking care of their basic requirements to great extent for survival. The rural people dependency upon forest resources makes them vulnerable income group. Those who have more resources will have more chances to survive the aftermath of changes in atmosphere but people with low income are going to be the most affected group. Yet all these are assumption, one never knows which group of rural people will be able to cope up with the climate change well.

Beside this, other occupations will also get impacted due to climate change. As per the International Labour Organization, (Maitre et al., 2023), climate change will bring massive changes the way we are working today. In its report "Working on a warmer planet "by 2030 in the succeeding two decades the entire world will see the 2% loss in output due to upsurge in temperatures. As per ILO about 80 million jobs will be at stake across the world, if we did not take enough measures to keep the temperature under control. Even now, the extreme weather conditions such as extreme precipitation, augmentation in air pollution, the spread of vector borne diseases and other health hazard can result in dislocation of workers, shift in working hours, opportunities might decrease in areas of fishing, renewable energy, conservation, costal protection will increase and disruption of public and private infrastructure such as structures, equipment, manufacturing sites, raw materials and supply chains will get affected in short and long run too,(Levy & Reolofs,2019).

Let's have a glance on what kind of impact equity will have due to climate change.

Impact of Climate Change on Equity

Equity generally means accountability & responsibility for those benefiting from the root causes that drive climate change. It can also be defined as just and fair inclusion into a society in which all can participate, prosper, and reach their full potential. In other words, we can explain it as equality of outcomes not equality of opportunity. Starting from different places requires different mechanisms to reach equality. Now, we will analyse the equity in economy.

The economy of every country differs as per their systems of finance and banking rules. Hence, the impact on equity due to effects of climate change is going to be immense for long term investment in the economy. As there will be no security of any aspect related to equity and only risk involved in economic scenario. At the same time if we analyse the historical impact of climate change. It shows that natural climatic disasters cause human distress along with large economic and ecological damage. These types of damages add additional costs on equity. This means that loss of life, property and interruption in economic activity will be main side effects of climate change.

On the other hand, climate change will impact the low-income groups more and disadvantaged population. These aspects might shift many people to poverty. This will further lead to migration of people to other places if they could survive the changes occurring in the climate pattern.

This will lower the investment and make the area vulnerable for investors.

Another equity which we can analyse here is health equity of living being. It is observed that climate change does impact the health of individuals along with other living beings. The experts have noted rise in temperature, extreme precipitation, adverse weather conditions, rising sea level. These exposures can lead to food and water insecurity, negative health outcome such as heat related cardiopulmonary illnesses, vector-borne diseases and stress. The labour can lose working hours due to increase in high temperatures. After having a look into how equity in different dimensions is affected by climate change. Now let's have a glance at impact on livelihood.

Impact of Climate Change on Livelihood

Livelihood is an economic activity which gives a boost to the people and economy of the nation state. Every aspect has its impacts on the livelihood of people which could be negative and positive both. According to experts and surveys completed plus assessed earlier elucidate that extreme weather patterns can impact agriculture incomes. Increase in temperature, prolonged periods of droughts, floods and change in climate zones are going to affect the cropping system. The major impact will be on, natural resources, agriculture, water, temperature and change of seasons.

In a research paper by (Rautela and Karki, 2015) the impact of climate change on agricultural in mountainous region is going to depend on two factors. First direct effects from changes in temperature, precipitation, and carbon dioxide concentrations and secondly, indirect effects through changes in soil moisture, the distribution and frequency of infestation by pests and diseases. As the winter season span has reduced the plants and vegetation growing during this period has got affected too. For instance, plants are flowering at a time when conditions are not favourable for their growth and survival. This reduces the fruiting and productivity. Another reason for low productivity is use of chemical fertilizers. Chemical fertilizers make the formation of hard crust in the soil. Forest cover around their villages has become depleted and degraded which they attribute to

1. Road construction activities,
2. Increased fuel wood uses due to population pressure,
3. Loss of vegetation due to glacial action and other disasters,
4. Forest fire,
5. Overgrazing
6. Decreased regeneration rates of trees in the forest area.

Reduced rainfall and increased duration of dry spells are held responsible for low regeneration rates. These are reported to result in withering and drying of buds and flowers thereby adversely affecting growth and regeneration of forest. Degradation of forests in the mid-slopes, where concentration of population is high, has reduced the availability of fodder and leaf litter, with implications on the productivity of both livestock and agricultural lands. Impact on bird population due to climate change is reported in the form of shortened breeding period or failure to make nests and reproduce. Hence, the area is witnessing changes in temperature and precipitation regime. Both duration and amount of rainfall having changed significantly, most precipitation is received as rain rather than as snow. Changes in floral and faunal population and type together with changed animal behaviour are also observed.

According to the national conference on "climate change and its impact on livelihood", the poor and marginal farmers are often the most affected by climatic variability. It adversely impacts agriculture, fisheries and forestry thereby limiting production which affects availability of food. Declining production and diminishing resources also impact marketable surplus and access to market. Extreme weather events have caught attention of agrarian experts and scientists and practitioners alike and they are intensively focussing on natural farming, effective adaptation and coping strategies to arrest the impacts of climate change.

As per the Livelihood Security Climate Change, Migration and Conflict in the Sahel, the impacts of changing climatic conditions on the availability of natural resources, coupled with factors such as population growth, weak governance and land tenure challenges, have led to increased competition over scarce natural resources. These effects are going to increase the pressure of survival for human, other living beings and impact on livelihood is certain in the long run. After having view about impact, it's time we must take a look at government initiatives for climate change.

Government Initiatives for Climate Change

The major initiatives taken up by the world government are the seventeen sustainable development goals. Out of which the goal number 13 is to take urgent action to combat climate change and its impact.

As per the United Nations (2023), the goal thirteen take into account: -

1. To provide support and adaptive dimensions towards hazards and natural disasters in all the developed, developing and least developed countries.
2. Incorporate climate change actions into national and state policies, strategies and planning.
3. Inculcate information about climate change, adaptation, impact reduction and early warnings in education, awareness- raising and institutional capacity.
4. Promoting procedures for raising capacity for effective climate change along with planning and management in least developed countries and small island developing states, including focusing on women, youth, local and marginalized communities.

In this context various conferences, climate action summit and research-based reports are been made for studying, analysing the impact and solution of the challenges ahead. Also, creating a platform for all countries to participate and work individually and collaborate with other countries as well for achieving sustainability and balance in the climate.

As per the (Schroeder, 2023) the countries such as UK, Norway, France and New Zealand are some countries who are committed legally to reach net zero emissions by year 2050. Even other countries are taking several steps to combat climate change. They are framing policies and programs which promote less carbon foot prints by introducing electric vehicles, shifting to renewable sources of energy like solar, wind and hydro. Ban on single use plastic, changing the consumer behaviour towards consumption, transport, land use, forestry, sustainable habits, enhancing energy efficiency also promoting vegetable-based diet and biofuels.

All these steps have been promoted and launched by the governments of all the countries as per there availability of resources and infrastructure. But these steps are doesn't seems to be enough. As we have already entered the phase of climate change and its impact can be felt all over the places in reality.

On the contrary as per my reflection the significant steps are always taken in context of climate change either after a protocol, an agreement, or a summit. The beginning of the relevant steps taken earlier had been implemented but its journey from framing to the process of implementation is a tedious process for all countries. To strike a right balance and contribute a positive change is necessary to continue their production of activities. If we compare the steps taken earlier and now. One can state that the current actions taken into consideration are more fruitful to achieve equity and growth with the climate change than previous ones. Those steps were stepping stones which made the way to the real goals set to be achieved. Let's ponder over suggestions to preserve our environment.

Suggestions

To reverse climate change, we need to begin from oneself and adopt those measures which support climate and atmosphere around us. United Nation Environment Programme can help fight climate crisis in many ways. That are described below: -

1. Transport: It is a means which accounts for about a quarter of greenhouse gas emission. Many governments are functioning towards decarbonizing transport by introducing electric vehicles, emphasising on the utilization of public transport by the people. At the same time, it depends on citizens too. To make less carbon footprint and give their contribution in climate change. Sustainability should become the status symbol rather than the current scenario.
2. Power consumption: For zero carbon, option of renewable energy must be used by installing solar panels on roof which will automatically turn the heating down. Similarly, encouraging the utilization of electrical resources such as lights and other appliances at home must be as per one's requirement. This step will help in saving money and will add to sustainability.
3. Turning vegetarian or vegan: Eating plant-based food produces less carbon dioxide. If plant base diet is adopted it reduces chronic illnesses, such as heart disease, stroke, diabetes and cancer. This diet is not only healthy for humans but also for nature to produce. As it takes less virtual water to grow than animal-based food.

4. Shop local and buy sustainable products: Only seasonal and local food products must be bought. It will help minor trades and farms in the area and decreasing fossil fuel emissions related with transport and cold chain storage. Sustainable agriculture uses up to 56 per cent less energy, creates 64 per cent less emissions and permits for larger levels of biodiversity than conventional farming. If possible, one should try growing his or her own fruit, vegetables and herbs. One can plant them in a garden, on a balcony or even on a window sill. Set up a community garden in your neighbourhood to get others involved is another way to promote low carbon footprint.
5. Don't waste food: One-third of all food produced is either lost or wasted. According to UNEP's Food Waste Index Report 2021, people globally waste 1 billion tonnes of food each year, which accounts for around 8-10 per cent of global greenhouse gas emissions. Avoid waste by only buying what you need. Take advantage of every edible part of the foods you purchase. Measure portion sizes of rice and other staples before cooking them, store food correctly (use your freezer if you have one), be creative with leftovers, share extras with your friends and neighbours and contribute to a local food-sharing scheme. Make compost out of inedible remnants and use it to fertilize your garden. Composting is one of the best options for managing organic waste while also reducing environmental impacts.
6. Dress (climate) smart: The fashion industry accounts for about eight to ten percent of global carbon emission which is more than all international flights and maritime shipping combined. At the same time, 'fast fashion' has designed a throwaway culture that sees clothes quickly end up in landfills. But we can change this by buying fewer new clothes and wear them longer. Look for sustainable labels and use rental services for special occasions rather than buying new items that will only be worn once. Recycled pre-loved clothes and repair, when necessary, should be adopted.
7. Plant trees: Every year approximately 12 million hectares of forest are destroyed on pretext of development and this deforestation, together with agriculture and other land use changes, is responsible for roughly 25 per cent of global greenhouse gas emissions. We can all play a part in reversing this trend by planting trees, either individually or as part of a collective. For example, the Plant-for-the-Planet initiative allows people to sponsor tree-planting around the world.

8. Spread the word: Inspire your friends, family and co-workers to cut their carbon pollution. By taking small initiatives and join a global movement which aims to inspire people to take practical steps and challenge their leaders to act more boldly on climate. This is said by the experts that if 1 billion people took action, they could reduce as much as 20 per cent of global carbon emissions. Or one could sign up to the UN's Act Now Campaign on climate change and sustainability and add one's voice to this critical global debate.
9. Fly Less: Fly less to reduce carbon emission instead switch to virtual meetings, holidaying in local destinations or using trains instead of planes all are ways to cut down carbon emission.
10. Strong Implementation of goals by all nations: I would like to suggest that the process of framing to implementation must be at rapid pace so that necessary steps in this direction will make the world better well equipped to combat with the side effects of climate change.

Though there are more suggestions such no plastic, use products which are eco-friendly and many more which I leave up- to the readers to think and act. Now let's come to conclusion of this chapter.

CONCLUSION

To conclude, climate change is challenge which is difficult to meet until and unless all countries collectively work for the accomplishment of the sustainable goals and share technologies which can save environment and life of not only human but of those essential living being with whom we share this planet with. This does not mean that individually we must not try our bit to do our best to secure the atmosphere around us.

It is important that eco-friendly technology and education must become part of every human to preserve nature and work according to atmosphere congenial for survival of all. We have to develop ways in which human activities do not harm the environment. The amount of pollution our activities have created can be controlled by adopting methods and habits that keep our atmosphere clean and worthwhile for the welfare of the planet earth.

Also, how sustainable one is should become status symbol rather how many cars and money one have? Behavioural change among people is equally significant for bringing relevant changes in the society for the establishment of nontoxic climate which makes other follow the path of balanced life rather than imbalanced and unhealthy lifestyle which makes one hollow and fragile to survive the climate change. Finally, Awareness drive about environment should be made so simple and common to understand anybody can follow and its activities can add to the preservation of environment.

REFERENCES

Asian Development Bank (ADB). (2017). Impacts of sea level rise on economic growth in developing Asia. *ADB economics working paper series no. 507.* Asian Development Bank. https://www.adb.org/sites/default/files/publication/222066/ewp-507.pdf

Asuncion, R. C., & Lee, M. (2017). Impacts of sea level rise on economic growth in developing Asia. *Asian Development Bank Economics Working Paper Series*, (507).

Bates, B. C., Kundzewicz, Z. W., & Wu, S. (Eds). (2008). Climate change and water. Technical paper of the intergovernmental panel on climate change. IPCC Secretariat, Geneva.

Black, R., Bennett, S.R.G., Thomas, S.M., Beddington, J.R. (2011). *Migration as adaptation*. doi:. doi:10.1038/478477aCrossRef

Chartzoulakisa, K., & Bertaki, M. (2015). IRLA2014-the effects of irrigation and drainage on rural and urban landscapes, Patras, Greece sustainable water management in agriculture under climate change. *Agric Sci Procedia, 4*, 88–98.

EPA United States Environmental Protection Agency. (n.d.). Causes Of Climate Change. EPA. https://www.epa.gov/climatechange-science/causes-climate-change#5foot

FAO. (2008). Climate change and food security: a framework document. *Food and Agriculture Organization of the United Nations, 2.* (https://www.fao.org/forestry/15538-079b31d45081fe9c3dbc6ff34de4807e4.pdf)

FAO. (2009). *Fisheries and aquaculture in our changing climate: policy brief of the FAO for the UNFCCC COP-15 in Copenhagen*. Google Scholar

FAO. (2016). *2016-The State of Food and Agriculture Climate Change, agriculture and Food Security.* Food and Agriculture Organization of the United Nations. https://www.fao.org/3/a-i6030e.pdf

FAO. (2017). *Water for sustainable food and agriculture a report produced for the G20 presidency of Germany.* Food and Agriculture Organization of the United Nations. https://www.fao.org/3/a-i7959e.pdf

Fisher, M., Chaudhury, M., & McCusker, B. (2010). Do forests help rural households adapt to climate variability? Evidence from Southern Malawi. [Scholar]. *World Development, 38*(9), 1241–1250. doi:10.1016/j.worlddev.2010.03.005

IMF. (2017). *World economic outlook, October 2017 seeking sustainable growth: short-term recovery, long-term challenges.* International Monetary Fund. fromhttps://www.imf.org/en/Publications/WEO/Issues/2017/09/19/world-economicoutlook-october-2017

IOM. (2010). *The state of environmental migration 2010.* International Organization for Migration (IOM). https://publications.iom.int/books/state-environmental-migration-2010

IPCC. (2007). Climate Change 2007: Synthesis Report. Contribution of Working Groups I, II and III to the Fourth Assessment Report of the Intergovernmental Panel on Climate Change. IPCC.

IPCC. (2012). *Managing the risks of extreme events and disasters to advance climate change adaptation; A special report of working groups I and II of the intergovernmental panel on climate change.* Cambridge University Press.

IPCC. (2014). *Climate change 2014 synthesis report summary for policymakers.* IPCC. https://www.ipcc.ch/ipccreports/tar/wg1/index.php?idp=5

Levy, S. B., & Reolofs, C. (2019). Impact of Climate Change on Workers Health and Safety. *The Oxford Research Encyclopaedia of Global Public Health.* (https://oxfordre.com/publichealth/display/10.1093/acrefore/9780190632366.001.0001/acrefore9780190632366e39;jsessionid=408B3D2F2A2BD526474998930A1EADBE)

Maitre, N., Montt, G., Saget, C., Ernst, C., Gutiérrez, M. T., Kizu, T., & Karimova, T. -Kie-Song, M.L., & Tsukamoto, M. (2018). *The employment impact of climate change adaptation*, p 13-29. ILO. (https://www.ilo.org/wcmsp5/groups/public/ed_emp/documents/publication/wcms_645572.pdf)

McCarthy, J. (2022). How war impact climate change. *Global Citizen.* https://www.globalcitizen.org/en/content/how-war-impacts-the-environment-and-climatechange/#:~:text=Militaries%20consume%20enormous%20 amounts%20of,direct

National Academy of Sciences. (2020). Climate change: evidence and causes: Update 2020. The National Academies Press. doi:10.17226/25733EXITEXIT

Ortiz, A. D. (2018) BBC Future, ten simple ways to act on climate change. *BBC.* (https://www.bbc.com/future/article/20181102-what-can-i-do-about-climate-change)

Rautela, P., & Karki, B. (2015). Impact of Climate Change on Life and Livelihood of Indigenous People of Higher Himalaya in Uttarakhand, India [Science and Education Publishing.]. *American Journal of Environmental Protection*, *3*(4), 112–124.

UNFCC. (2020). *The Paris Agreement.* UNFCC. (https://unfccc.int/process-and-meetings/the-paris-agreement/the-paris-agreement)

United Nations. (2007). *From Stockholm to Kyoto: A Brief History of Climate Change.* UN. (https://www.un.org/en/chronicle/article/stockholm-kyoto-brief-history-climate-change#:~:text=Held%20in%20Stockholm%2C%20 Sweden%20from,recommendations%20)

United Nations Environment Programme. (2022). *10 ways you can help fight the climate crisis.* UNEP. (https://www.unep.org/news-and-stories/story/10-ways-you-can-help-fight-climate-crisis)

Compilation of References

Abbas, A. A. (2018). The bright future of Technopreneurship. *International Journal of Scientific and Engineering Research, 9*(12), 563–566.

Adhikari, J. (2006). Poverty, globalisation and gendered labour migration in Nepal. *Women and migration in Asia: Poverty, gender and migration, 2*, 87-106.

Afridi, F., Dinkelman, T., & Mahajan, K. (2018). Why are fewer married women joining the work force in rural India? A decomposition analysis over two decades. *Journal of Population Economics, 31*(3), 783–818. doi:10.100700148-017-0671-y

Agrawal, A., Gandhi, P., & Khare, P. (2021). Women empowerment through entrepreneurship: case study of a social entrepreneurial intervention in rural India. *International Journal of Organizational Analysis.*

Akkaşoğlu, S., Telbalkan, M., Yılmaz, E. Z., & Ulama, Ş. (2019). Yerel Halkın Kırsal Turizme Bakış Açısı: Samsun Kızılırmak Deltası Örneği. *Lnternational Journal Of Geography And Geography Education*, (40), 295–310. doi:10.32003/iggei.557902

Akşap, Y. (2018). Gastronomik Bir Değer Olarak Lavanta. *Uluslararası Global Turizm Araştırmaları Dergisi, 2*(1), 32–41.

Albayrak, A., and Tuzunkan, D. (2020). Kırsal Turizm Ve Türlerine Yönelik Hazırlanan Lisansüstü Tezlerin Bibliyometrik Analizi. *Turkish Studies- Social, 15*(1), 845-859.

Allais, S. (2011). What is a National Qualifications Framework?. *Journal of Contemporary Educational Studies/Sodobna Pedagogika, 62*(5).

Allais, S. (2012). Will skills save us? Rethinking the relationships between vocational education, skills development policies, and social policy in South Africa. *International Journal of Educational Development, 32*(5), 632–642. doi:10.1016/j.ijedudev.2012.01.001

Allais, S. (2019). TVET Reform and Qualifications Frameworks: What Is Known About What They Can and Can't Do? In S. McGrath, M. Mulder, J. Papier, & R. Suart (Eds.), *Handbook of Vocational Education and Training*. Springer., doi:10.1007/978-3-319-94532-3_43

Alnafrah, I., Bogdanova, E., & Maximova, T. (2019). Text Mining as a Facilitating Tool for Deploying Blockchain Technology in the Intellectual Property Rights System. *International Journal of Intellectual Property Management, 9*(2), 120–135. doi:10.1504/IJIPM.2019.100207

Altinay, L., Madanoglu, M., Daniele, R., & Lashley, C. (2012). The influence of family tradition and psychological traits on entrepreneurial intention. *International Journal of Hospitality Management, 31*(2), 489–499. doi:10.1016/j.ijhm.2011.07.007

Arslan, E., & Kendir, H. (2020). COVID-19 salgını sonrası yükselen trend kırsal turizm: Zile örneği. *Türk Turizm Araştırmaları Dergisi, 4*(4), 3668–3683. doi:10.26677/TR1010.2020.584

Ashifa, K. M. (2021). Analysis On The Determinants Of Health Status Among Tribal Communities. *Journal of Cardiovascular Disease Research, 12*(3), 531534.

Asian Development Bank (ADB). (2017). Impacts of sea level rise on economic growth in developing Asia. *ADB economics working paper series no. 507.* Asian Development Bank. https://www.adb.org/sites/default/files/publication/222066/ewp-507.pdf

Asuncion, R. C., & Lee, M. (2017). Impacts of sea level rise on economic growth in developing Asia. *Asian Development Bank Economics Working Paper Series*, (507).

Audretsch, D. B., & Belitski, M. (2017). Entrepreneurial ecosystems in cities: Establishing the framework conditions. *The Journal of Technology Transfer, 42*(5), 1030–1051. doi:10.100710961-016-9473-8

Autio, E. H., Keeley, R., Klofsten, M. G. C., Parker, G., & Hay, M. (2001). Entrepreneurial intent among students in Scandinavia and in the USA. *Enterprise and Innovation Management Studies, 2*(2), 145–160. doi:10.1080/14632440110094632

Aytuğar, S., & Aydoğdu, A. (2021). Kırsal Turizm Çekiciliği Olarak Lavanta ve Kastamonu İli Lavanta Turizmi Potansiyeli. *Uluslararası Türk Dünyası Turizm Araştırmaları Dergisi, 6*(1), 72–89.

Badulescu, D., Giurgiu, A., Istudor, N., & Badulescu, A. (2015). Rural tourism development and financing in Romania: A supply-side analysis. *Agricultural Economics, 61*(2), 72–82.

Bain, P. M. (2021). The Inherent Rights of Tribal Women. *Jus Corpus LJ, 2*, 773.

Bakar, R., Islam, M. A., & Lee, J. (2015). Entrepreneurship Education: Experiences in Selected Countries. *International Education Studies, 8*(1), 88–99. doi:10.5539/ies.v8n1p88

Bala, S. (2017). *ICT Imperatives to Bridge the Digital Divide: Gender Perspective*. VVGNLI. https://vvgnli.gov.in/en/nliresearchstudiesseries/nli-research-studies-series-no-1292017

Baporikar, N. (2015). Framework for social change through startups in India. [IJCESC]. *International Journal of Civic Engagement and Social Change, 2*(1), 30–42. doi:10.4018/IJCESC.2015010103

Barot, H. (2015). *Entrepreneurship - A Key to Success.*

Baruah, B. (2010, February). Women and globalosation: Challenges and opportunities facing construction workers in contemporary India. *Development in Practice, 20*(1), 31–44. doi:10.1080/09614520903436935

Bates, B. C., Kundzewicz, Z. W., & Wu, S. (Eds). (2008). Climate change and water. Technical paper of the intergovernmental panel on climate change. IPCC Secretariat, Geneva.

Baykal, F., & Ataberk, E. (2020). Kozbeyli'de (Foça/İzmir) Kırsal Turizmin Geliştirilmesi Hakkında Yerel Halkın Görüşleri. *Ege Coğrafya Dergisi*, *29*(1), 1–17.

Berger, E. S., & Kuckertz, A. (2016). Female entrepreneurship in startup ecosystems worldwide. *Journal of Business Research*, *69*(11), 5163–5168. doi:10.1016/j.jbusres.2016.04.098

Bertay, N., Carpio, M. A., & Klein, T. J. (2014). *The Effects of Access to Health Insurance for Informally Employed Individuals in Peru.* The Institute for the Study of Labor, Bonn- Germany, Working Paper no: 8709.

Bhagavatheeswaran, L., Nair, S., Stone, H., Isac, S., Hiremath, T., Raghavendra, T., & Beattie, T. S. (2016). The barriers and enablers to education among scheduled caste and scheduled tribe adolescent girls in northern Karnataka, South India: A qualitative study. *International Journal of Educational Development*, *49*, 262–270. doi:10.1016/j.ijedudev.2016.04.004

Bhagchandani, R. (2017). *How India can up its startup game by bolstering student entrepreneurship.* Your Story. https://yourstory.com/2017/01/india-startup-game-bolstering-student-entrepreneurship

Bharathi, N. S., Balaji, V., Christina, D., & Akash, A. (2021). *Vital Analysis of Women Empowerment in Marginalised Communities.*

Bhardwaj, B. R. (2021). Adoption, diffusion and consumer behaviour in technopreneurship. *International Journal of Emerging Markets*, *16*(2), 179–220. doi:10.1108/IJOEM-11-2018-0577

Bhattacharya, R., Bhattacharya, S., & Gill, K. (2017). The Adivasi land question in the neoliberal era. *The Land Question in India: State, Dispossession, and Capitalist Transition, 176.*

Birley, S. (1985). The role of networks in the entrepreneurial process. *Journal of Business Venturing*, *1*(1), 107–117. doi:10.1016/0883-9026(85)90010-2

Black, R., Bennett, S.R.G., Thomas, S.M., Beddington, J.R. (2011). *Migration as adaptation.* doi:. doi:10.1038/478477aCrossRef

Bocken, N., & Snihur, Y. (2020). Lean Startup and the business model: Experimenting for novelty and impact. *Long Range Planning*, *53*(4), 101953. doi:10.1016/j.lrp.2019.101953

Bortolini, R. F., Nogueira Cortimiglia, M., Danilevicz, A. D. M. F., & Ghezzi, A. (2021). Lean Startup: A comprehensive historical review. *Management Decision*, *59*(8), 1765–1783. doi:10.1108/MD-07-2017-0663

Bose, A. (1973). *Studies in India's Urbanistation: 1901-1971.* Tata-Mcgraw Hill.

Bozok, D., & Karaman, R. (2018). Isparta lavantasının kırsal turizm kapsamında swot analizi yöntemiyle değerlendirilmesi: Kuyucak köyü örneği. *International Journal of Social and Economic Sciences*, *8*(2), 27–33.

Brahmanandam, T., & BosuBabu, T. (2016). Educational status among the scheduled tribes: Issues and challenges. *Journal of Politics and Governance*, *5*(3), 57–66.

Brandt, W. (1998). Change and consensus in vocational education and training: The case of the German 'Dual System. In I. Finlay, N. Stuart, & S. Young (Eds.), *Changing vocational education and training. An International comparative perspective* (pp. 103–120). Routledge.

Bullough, A., Guelich, U., Manolova, T. S., & Schjoedt, L. (2022). Women's entrepreneurship and culture: Gender role expectations and identities, societal culture, and the entrepreneurial environment. *Small Business Economics*, *58*(2), 985–996. doi:10.100711187-020-00429-6

Cazes, S., & Verick, S. (2013). *Perspectives on Labour Economics for Development*. International Labour Organisation.

Çeken, H., Dalgın, T., & Çakır, N. (2012). Bir Alternatif Turizm Türü Olarak Kırsal Turizmin Gelişimini Etkileyen Faktörler Ve Kırsal Turizmin Etkileri. *International Journal Of Social And Economic Sciences*, *2*(2), 11–16.

Cengiz, G., & Akkuş, Ç. (2012). Kırsal Turizm Kapsamında Yöre Halkının Kalkındırılması: Erzurum Örneği. *Karamanoğlu Mehmetbey Üniversitesi Sosyal Ve Ekonomik Araştırmalar Dergisi*, *2012*(1), 61–74.

Cesaroni, F. M., Demartini, P., & Paoloni, P. (2017). Women in business and social media: Implications for female entrepreneurship in emerging countries. *African Journal of Business Management*, *11*(14), 316–326. doi:10.5897/AJBM2017.8281

Chakraborty, U. K. (2020). Opportunities for tribal entrepreneurship development in Jharkhand to combat post Covid-19 challenges. *Parikalpana: KIIT Journal of Management*, *16*(1and2), 150-163.

Chancel, S. (2022). Women, gender, and the informal economy: An assessment of ILO research and suggested ways forward. International Labour Organisation.

Chand, B., & Srivastav, R. (2014). *Industry Linked Technical Institutes Help Manual.* AICTE India. Www.Aicteindia.Org/Downloads/Aboutaicteciisurvey2015.Pdf?Msclkid=4ff9086fbc16 11ec83b8f1906b4b2661

Chartzoulakisa, K., & Bertaki, M. (2015). IRLA2014-the effects of irrigation and drainage on rural and urban landscapes, Patras, Greece sustainable water management in agriculture under climate change. *Agric Sci Procedia*, *4*, 88–98.

Chaudhari, S. L., & Sinha, M. (2021). A study on emerging trends in Indian startup ecosystem: Big data, crowd funding, shared economy. *International Journal of Innovation Science*, *13*(1), 1–16. doi:10.1108/IJIS-09-2020-0156

Chaudhary, A. (2018). *Why it is important to create and foster entrepreneurial mindset in India's high school students.* Your Story. https://yourstory.com/2018/02/entrepreneurship-mindset-high-school-students? utm _pageloadtype = scroll

Chaudhuri, K., Sasidharan, S., & Raj, R. S. N. (2020). Gender, small firm ownership, and credit access: Some insights from India. *Small Business Economics*, *54*(4), 1165–1181. doi:10.100711187-018-0124-3

Chawada, B., Bansal, R., & Kantharia, S. (2012). Plight of female construction workers of Surat city. *Indian Journal of Community Health*, *24*(1), 19–22.

Cheng, M. Y., Chan, W. S., & Mahmood, A. (2009). The effectiveness of entrepreneurship education in Malaysia. *Education + Training*, *51*(7), 555–566. doi:10.1108/00400910910992754

Chishty, S., & Singh, N. (2018). Nutritional status of tribal women (Saharia and Meena), Baran district of Rajasthan, India. *Nutrition & Food Science*, *48*(6), 922–939. doi:10.1108/NFS-01-2018-0018

Choudhury, S., & Kumar, S. (2022). Gender discrimination and marginalization of women in North-East India. *Journal of Public Affairs*, *22*(4), e2625. doi:10.1002/pa.2625

Creswell, J. W. (2018). *Nitel Araştırma Yöntemleri: Beş Yaklaşıma Göre Nitel Araştırma ve Araştırma Deseni, (Çeviri: Mesut Bütün ve Selçuk Beşir Demir)*. Siyasal Yayınevi.

Dabo, S. A. (2018). Critical Thinking in Entrepreneurship and Youth Attitudes towards Entrepreneurial Skill Acquisition in Plateau State, Nigeria. *International Journal of Scientific Research*. doi:10.21275/ART20203836

Dalgın, T., & And Yemenoğlu, E. (2020). Buldan İlçesi'nin Kırsal Turizm Potansiyelinin Belirlenmesine Yönelik Nitel Bir Araştırma. *Turar Turizm ve Araştırma Dergisi*, *9*(2), 121–143.

Dalmia, A. J. (2012, June). Strong women, weak bodies, muted voices. *Women construction workers in Delhi, 47*(26), pp. 249-255.

Damor, K. (2021). Gujarat ranks second in CSR funds received. *Times of India*. https://timesofindia.indiatimes.com/city/ahmedabad/gujarat-ranks-second-in-csr-funds-received/articleshow/87897669.cms

Dasgupta, S. (2018). Adivasi studies: From a historian's perspective. *History Compass*, *16*(10), e12486. doi:10.1111/hic3.12486

David, D., Gopalan, S., & Ramachandran, S. (2021). The startup environment and funding activity in India. In Investment in Startups and Small Business Financing (pp. 193-232). doi:10.1142/9789811235825_0007

Davis, A., & Ruddle, K. (2010). Constructing Confidence: Rational skepticism and systematic enquiry in local ecological knowledge research. *Ecological Applications*, *20*(3), 880–894. doi:10.1890/09-0422.1 PMID:20437971

De Vita, L., Mari, M., & Poggesi, S. (2014). Women entrepreneurs in and from developing countries: Evidences from the literature. *European Management Journal*, *32*(3), 451–460. doi:10.1016/j.emj.2013.07.009

Dearden, L., McIntosh, S., Myck, M., & Vignoles, A. (2002). The Returns to Academic and Vocational Qualifications in Britain. *Bulletin of Economic Research, 54*(3), 249–274. doi:10.1111/1467-8586.00152

Demir, C. (2019). Kokunun En Şifalı Hali: Lavanta. Göller Bölgesi Aylık Hakemli Ekonomi ve Kültür Dergisi. *Ayrıntı Dergisi, 7*(77), 7–10.

Demircioğlu, G. (1993). Kırsal Turizm Nedir? *Anatolia: Turizm Araştırmaları Dergisi, 4*(5), 8–10.

Devonish, D., Alleyne, P., Soverall, W. C., Marshall, A. Y., & Pounder, P. (2010). Explaining Entrepreneurial Intentions in the Caribbean. *International Journal of Entrepreneurial Behaviour & Research, 16*(2), 149–171. doi:10.1108/13552551011027020

Dev, S. M. (2013). Post-2015 Development Agenda: Employment and Growth with Special Reference to India. *IDS Bulletin, 44*(5-6), 63–71. doi:10.1111/1759-5436.12058

Dharni, K., & Goel, D. (2013). Startup operations and problems of honey bee entrepreneurs: Experience from India. *International Journal of Entrepreneurship and Small Business, 18*(3), 332–348. doi:10.1504/IJESB.2013.052520

Diandra, D., & Azmy, A. (2020). Understanding Definition of Entrepreneurship. *Journal of Management Accounting and Economics., 7*, 2020–2383.

Dinesh, K. K., & Sushil, N. A. (2019). Strategic innovation factors in startups: Results of a cross-case analysis of Indian startups. *Journal for Global Business Advancement, 12*(3), 449–470. doi:10.1504/JGBA.2019.10022956

Do Paco, A., Ferreira, J., Raposo, M., Rodrigues, R., & Dinis, A. (2011). Entrepreneurial intention among secondary students: Findings from Portugal. *International Journal of Entrepreneurship and Small Business, 13*(1), 92–106. doi:10.1504/IJESB.2011.040418

Drèze, J., & Sen, A. (2013). An uncertain glory. In *An uncertain glory*. Princeton University Press.

Dua, A., Ellingrud, K., Mahajan, D., & Silberg, J. (2020). Which small businesses are most vulnerable to COVID-19—and when. McKinsey & Company, 18.

Dubini, P., & Aldrich, H. (1991). Personal and extended networks are central to the entrepreneurial process. *Journal of Business Venturing, 6*(5), 305–313. doi:10.1016/0883-9026(91)90021-5

Durda, L., & Ključnikov, A. (2019). Social networks in entrepreneurial startups development. *Economia e Sociologia, 12*(3), 192–208.

Economic Times. (2013) 'Technopreneurs' take agriculture-related ventures to reap farm gain. *Economic Times*. https://economictimes.indiatimes.com/small-biz/startups/technopreneurs-take-agriculture-related-ventures-to-reap-farm-gain/articleshow/22620386.cms

Economic Times. (2022). Economic Survey 2022: At least 14,000 new startups recognised in India, up 20 times in five years. *Economic Times*. https://economictimes.indiatimes.com/tech/startups/economic-survey-2022-at-least-14000-new-startups-recognised-in-india/articleshow/89243366.cms

Eichhorst, W., Planas, N. R., Schmidl, R., & Zimmermann, K. F. (2012). *A Roadmap to Vocational Education and Training Systems Around the World*. Institute for the Study of Labour.

Emekli, G., Südaş, İ., & Soykan, F. (2007). Göç, kırsal kalkınma-kırsal turizm ve Türkiye. *Uluslararası Asya ve Kuzey Afrika Çalışmaları Kongresi, 38*, 10–15.

Engle, R. L., Dimitriadi, N., Gavidia, J. V., Schlaegel, C., Delanoe, S., Alvarado, I., He, X., Buame, S., & Wolff, B. (2010). Entrepreneurial intent. *International Journal of Entrepreneurial Behaviour & Research, 16*(1), 35–37. doi:10.1108/13552551011020063

EPA United States Environmental Protection Agency. (n.d.). Causes Of Climate Change. EPA. https://www.epa.gov/climatechange-science/causes-climate-change#5foot

Erdem, M. S., & Bozan, M. Türkiye'de Sürdürülebilir Kalkınma Çerçevesinde Ekolojik Turizmin Kalkınma Planları İçerisinde Değerlendirilmesi, *Sinop Üniversitesi Sosyal Bilimler Dergisi, 5*(1), 67-90.

Ertl, J. (2000). The transition of vocational education and training in Eastern Germany: Notes on the role of the European Union Programmes. *Comparative Education Review*, *44*(4), 464–492. doi:10.1086/447630

Escalfoni, R., Silva, M. F. D., & Oliveira, J. (2020, November). Analyzing social relations in startup ecosystems. In *XVI Brazilian Symposium on Information Systems* (pp. 1-7).

Eshun, G., & Tichaawa, T. M. (2020). Developing agro-tourism tours on the cocoa sector in africa: emerging issues from Ghana. *EuroEconomica, 39*(1).

Euler. (2013). *Achieving gender equality in education: Trends in research and USAID programming (1996-2006); A synthesis report*. MSI.

European Commission. (2007). Mediterranean water scarcity and drought report. Technical report on water scarcity and drought management in the Mediterranean and the Water Framework Directive. Mediterranean Water Scarcity and Drought Working Group, Brussels.

EY-FICCI. (2013). *Reaping India's promised demographic dividend- industry in driving seat*. EY- FICCI.

FAO. (2008). Climate change and food security: a framework document. *Food and Agriculture Organization of the United Nations, 2*. (https://www.fao.org/forestry/15538-079b31d45081fe9c3dbc6ff34de4807e4.pdf)

FAO. (2009). *Fisheries and aquaculture in our changing climate: policy brief of the FAO for the UNFCCC COP-15 in Copenhagen*. Google Scholar

FAO. (2016). *2016-The State of Food and Agriculture Climate Change, agriculture and Food Security*. Food and Agriculture Organization of the United Nations. https://www.fao.org/3/a-i6030e.pdf

FAO. (2017). *Water for sustainable food and agriculture a report produced for the G20 presidency of Germany.* Food and Agriculture Organization of the United Nations. https://www.fao.org/3/a-i7959e.pdf

Fersterer, J., & Winter-Ebmer, R. (2003a). Are Austrian Returns to Education Falling Over Time? *Labour Economics, 10*(1), 73–89. doi:10.1016/S0927-5371(02)00105-7

Fersterer, J., & Winter-Ebmer, R. (2003b). Smoking, Discount Rates and the Returns to Education. *Economics of Education Review, 22*(6), 561–566. doi:10.1016/S0272-7757(02)00072-9

FICCI. (2006). *Implementation of Apprenticeship in India: A Study by FICCI.* FICCI.

Fielden, S. L., Davidson, M. J., Gale, A. W., & Davey, C. L. (2000). Women in construction: The untapped resource. *Construction Management and Economics, 18*(1), 113–121. doi:10.1080/014461900371004

Fini, R., Grimaldi, R., Marzocchi, G. L., & Sobrero, M. (2009). The Foundation of Entrepreneurial Intention. *Conference proceedings in Summer Conference, 6,* 17-19.

Fisher, M., Chaudhury, M., & McCusker, B. (2010). Do forests help rural households adapt to climate variability? Evidence from Southern Malawi. [Scholar]. *World Development, 38*(9), 1241–1250. doi:10.1016/j.worlddev.2010.03.005

Fowosire, R. A. (2017). Technopreneurship: A view of technology, innovations and entrepreneurship. *Global Journals of Research in Engineering, 17*(F7), 41–46.

Franco, M., Haase, H., & Lautenschläger, A. (2010). Students' Entrepreneurial Intentions: An Inter-Regional Comparison. *Education + Training, 52*(4), 260–275. doi:10.1108/00400911011050945

Freeman, R. E. (1984). *Strategic management: A stakeholder approach.* Pitman Publishing Inc.

Gaidzanwa, F. (2008). *Skills and Skilled Work.* Oxford University Press.

Gangte, M. (2016). Gender and customary law: A case study of Mizo Tribe in North East India. *Indian Anthropologist*, 17-30.

Garg, D. (2019). The Agriculture Infrastructure in India– Connecting Dots to Paint a Bigger Picture. *Indian Folk.* https://www.indianfolk.com/agriculture-infrastructure-india-connecting-dots-paint-bigger-picture/

Gelaidan, H. M., & Abdullateef, A. O. (2017). Entrepreneurial intentions of business students in Malaysia: The role of self-confidence, educational and relation support. *Journal of Small Business and Enterprise Development, 24*(1), 54–67. doi:10.1108/JSBED-06-2016-0078

Giray, F. H., Kadakoğlu, B., Çetin, F., & Bamoi, A. G. A. (2019). Rural tourism marketing: Lavender tourism in Turkey. *Ciência Rural, 49*(2), 49. doi:10.1590/0103-8478cr20180651

Gluckman, M. (2017). *Politics, law and ritual in tribal society.* Routledge. doi:10.4324/9781315126913

Goldin, M., & Katz, J. (2002). *The Wiley Handbook of Vocational Education and Training.* Wiley Blackwell Publications.

Gorai, P., Dey, A., & Modak, B. K. (2022). Birhors of Purulia: marching toward mainstream of the society. In *Indigenous People and Nature* (pp. 29–60). Elsevier. doi:10.1016/B978-0-323-91603-5.00009-9

Government of India. (1968). *National Policy on Education.* Ministry of Human Resource and Development.

Government of India. (2020). National Education Policy. New Delhi: Ministry of Human Resource and Development. Government of India. (1986). National Policy on Education. New Delhi: Ministry of Human Resource and Development.

Government of India. (2023). *Economic Survey 2021-22.* Department of Economic Affairs.

Government of the Republic of Belarus. (2005*). State Program for the Revitalization and Development of Rural Areas, 2005-2010.* Government of the Republic of Belarus.

Greve, A., & Salaff, J. W. (2003). Social networks and entrepreneurship. *Entrepreneurship Theory and Practice*, *28*(1), 1–22. doi:10.1111/1540-8520.00029

Gupta, P. (2016). Status of tribal women in India: some observations. *Anudhyan: an international journal of social science*, *1*(1), 181-188.

Habeeb, S., Arya, V., & Ahmad, N. (2021). Home-based entrepreneuring for empowerment and sustainability of Muslim women: A study in the Indian context. *World Review of Science, Technology and Sustainable Development*, *17*(4), 334–347. doi:10.1504/WRSTSD.2021.117840

Harlanu, M., & Nugroho, A. (2015, February). The importance of technopreneurship management model for vocational school. In *3rd UPI International Conference on Technical and Vocational Education and Training* (pp. 147-150). Atlantis Press. 10.2991/ictvet-14.2015.33

Harris, M. L., Gibson, S. G., & Taylor, S. R. (2007). Examining the impact of small business institute participation on entrepreneurial attitudes. *Journal of Small Business Strategy*, *18*(2), 57–76.

Hazarika, B., & Goswami, K. (2018). Micro-entrepreneurship development in the handloom industry: An empirical analysis among the tribal women in Assam. *International Journal of Rural Management*, *14*(1), 22–38. doi:10.1177/0973005218754437

Hidayat, H., Herawati, S., Syahmaidi, E., Hidayati, A., & Ardi, Z. (2018). Designing of technopreneurship scientific learning framework in vocational-based higher education in Indonesia. [UAE]. *IACSIT International Journal of Engineering and Technology*, *7*(4), 123–127. doi:10.14419/ijet.v7i4.9.20632

Higgins, M. C. (2001). Changing careers: The effects of social context. *Journal of Organizational Behavior: The International Journal of Industrial. Occupational and Organizational Psychology and Behavior*, *22*(6), 595–618. doi:10.1002/job.104

Hirway, I. (2012). Missing labour force: An explanation. *Economic and Political Weekly*, 67–72.

Höflinger, P. J., Nagel, C., & Sandner, P. (2018). Reputation for Technological Innovation: Does It Actually Cohere with Innovative Activity? *Suma de Negocios*, *3*(1), 26–39. doi:10.1016/j.jik.2017.08.002

IAMR. (2013). *Low Female Employment in a Period of High Growth: Insights from a Primary Survey in Uttar Pradesh & Gujarat*. IAMR.

ILO. (n.d.). *Women and Men in the Informal Economy: A Statistical Picture*. Geneva: ILO& WEIGO.

IMF. (2017). *World economic outlook, October 2017 seeking sustainable growth: short-term recovery, long-term challenges*. International Monetary Fund. fromhttps://www.imf.org/en/Publications/WEO/Issues/2017/09/19/world-economicoutlook-october-2017

International Labour Organization (ILO). (2000). *ABC of women workers' rights and gender equality*. ILO.

IOM. (2010). *The state of environmental migration 2010*. International Organization for Migration (IOM). https://publications.iom.int/books/state-environmental-migration-2010

IPCC. (2007). Climate Change 2007: Synthesis Report. Contribution of Working Groups I, II and III to the Fourth Assessment Report of the Intergovernmental Panel on Climate Change. IPCC.

IPCC. (2012). *Managing the risks of extreme events and disasters to advance climate change adaptation; A special report of working groups I and II of the intergovernmental panel on climate change*. Cambridge University Press.

IPCC. (2014). *Climate change 2014 synthesis report summary for policymakers*. IPCC. https://www.ipcc.ch/ipccreports/tar/wg1/index.php?idp=5

Iqbal, B., & Yadav, A. (2021). Fourth Industrial Revolution. *Its Role and Contribution in Employment Generation and Skills Development.*, *1*, 85–96. doi:10.47509/JGETIB.1.1.2021.85-96

Islary, J. (2014). Health and health seeking behaviour among tribal communities in India: a socio-cultural perspective. *Journal of Tribal Intellectual Collective India*, 1-16.

Jacob, M. (2017). Entrepreneurships and Startup Programmes: Opportunities in Travel and Tourism. *Atna Journal of Tourism Studies*, *12*(2), 51–65. doi:10.12727/ajts.18.3

Jain, S. (2016). Growth of startup ecosystems in India. *International Journal of Applied Research*, *2*(12), 152–154.

Jha, S. N., Vishwakarma, R.K., Ahmad T.R.A., & Dixit, A.K. (2016). *Assessment of Quantitative Harvest and Post-Harvest Losses of Major Crops/Commodities in India*. Technical Report of Ministry of Food Processing Industries, Government of India and Indian Council of Agricultural Research (ICAR)/ ICAR-CIPHET, PAU, Ludhiyana.

Jin, F., Wu, A., & Hitt, L. (2017, February). Social is the new financial: How startup social media activity influences funding outcomes. In Academy of Management Proceedings (Vol. 1, p. 13329). Academy of Management.

Joshua, J. N., Swastika, I. P. A., & Primakara, S. T. M. I. K. (2020*). Competency Development of Computer and IT to Enhance the Innovative Human Resources through Technopreneurship Curriculum Implementation in Higher Education.*

Kalaiselvi, S. (2021). The Indian start up Ecosystem: Drivers, challenges and pillars of support. *GEDRAG & ORGANISATIE REVIEW*, *34*(4), 386–402.

Kamariotou, M., & Kitsios, F. (2022). Bringing Digital Innovation Strategies and Entrepreneurship: The Business Model Canvas in Open Data Ecosystem and Startups. *Future Internet*, *14*(5), 127. doi:10.3390/fi14050127

Kamdar, D., McAllister, D., & Turban, D. (2006). All in a Day's Work: How Follower Individual Differences and Justice Predict OCB Role Definitions and Behavior. *The Journal of Applied Psychology*, *7654*(4), 841–855. doi:10.1037/0021-9010.91.4.841 PMID:16834509

Kanan, R., & Raveendran, R. (2020). *Women's Economic Empowerment in India*. https://iwwage.org/wp-content/uploads/2020/10/Policy-Landscape-Sudy_Summary-report.pdf

Kane, E. (2004). *Girls' education in Africa: What do we know about strategies that work?* The World Bank.

Kannan, S. (2018). Excluded among the excluded: Status of Tribal women in Telangana. *International Journal of Innovative Studies in Sociology and Humanities*, *3*(12), 30–39.

Karali, A., Das, S., & Roy, H. (2021). Forty years of the rural tourism research: Reviewing the trend, pattern and future agenda. *Tourism Recreation Research*, 1–28. doi:10.1080/02508281.2021.1961065

Kasturi, S. V., & Bala Subrahmanya, M. H. (2014). Start-ups and small scale industry growth in India: Do institutional credit and start-ups make a difference? *International Journal of Entrepreneurial Venturing*, *6*(3), 277–298. doi:10.1504/IJEV.2014.064692

Kaur, P. (2011). Rural Technopreneurship: An Innovative Key To Development. [IJBMR]. *International Journal of Business Management & Research*, *1*, 8–16.

Kaya, M., & Erol, N. (2021). El sanatları ürünlerinin kırsal turizm kapsamında değerlendirilmesi: Espiye-Akkaya Köyü Örneği. *Journal of Humanities and Tourism Research*, *11*(1), 226–240. doi:10.14230/johut991

Khanday, Z. A., & Akram, M. (2012). Health status of marginalized groups in India. *International journal of applied sociology, 2*(6), 60-70.

Kickul, J., & D'Intino, R. S. (2005). *Measure for measure: modeling entrepreneurial self-efficacy onto instrumental tasks within the new venture creation process*. New England Journal of Entrepreneurship.

Kingdon, G. G. (1998). Does the labour market explain lower female schooling in India? *The Journal of Development Studies*, *35*(1), 39–65. doi:10.1080/00220389808422554

Kingdon, G. G., & Unni, J. (2001). Education and women's labour market outcomes in India. *Education Economics*, *9*(2), 173–195. doi:10.1080/09645290110056994

King, K. (2012). The geopolitics and meanings of India's massive skills development ambitions. *International Journal of Educational Development*, *98765*(5), 665–673. doi:10.1016/j.ijedudev.2012.02.001

King, K., & McGrath, S. (2002). Globalisation, Enterprise and Knowledge: Education, Training and Development in Africa. Oxford: *Symposium Books Ltd.* 10.15730/books.33

King, K., & Palmer, R. (2010). *Planning for Technical and Vocational Skills Development*. UNESCO.

Klasen, S., & Pieters, J. (2012). *Push or pull? Drivers of female labor force participation during India's economic boom.*

Klasen, S., & Pieters, J. (2015). What explains the stagnation of female labor force participation in urban India? *The World Bank Economic Review*, *29*(3), 449–478. doi:10.1093/wber/lhv003

Kodaş, D., & Sibel, S. Ü. (2012). Kırsal Turizm İle Kültürel Turizmin Bütünleşmesi. *Karamanoğlu Mehmetbey Üniversitesi Sosyal Ve Ekonomik Araştırmalar Dergisi*, *2012*(1), 169–174.

Koe, W. L., Mahphoth, M. H., Alias, N. E., Krishnan, R., & Arham, A. F. (2021). Factors influencing intention towards technopreneurship among university students. *Journal of Educational and Social Research*, *11*(1), 162–169. doi:10.36941/jesr-2021-0016

Kollmann, T., Kleine-Stegemann, L., de Cruppe, K., & Strauss, C. (2022). Eras of digital entrepreneurship: connecting the past, present, and future. In *Handbook of Digital Entrepreneurship* (pp. 49–73). Edward Elgar Publishing. doi:10.1007/978-3-658-37260-6

KoneruK. (2017). Women entrepreneurship in India-problems and prospects. *Available at* SSRN 3110340.

Kottegoda, S. (2006). *Bringing home the money: Migration and poverty in gender politics in Sri Lanka. Poverty, gender and migration*, 49-71.

Krishna, A., Agrawal, A., & Choudhary, A. (2016, December). Predicting the outcome of startups: less failure, more success. In 2016 *IEEE 16th International Conference on Data Mining Workshops* (ICDMW) (pp. 798-805). IEEE. 10.1109/ICDMW.2016.0118

Krishna, H. S. (2018). Entrepreneurial learning and Indian tech startup survival: An empirical investigation. *Asian Journal of Innovation and Policy*, *7*(1), 55–78.

Kristiansen, S., & Indarti, N. (2004). Entrepreneurial intention among Indonesian and Norwegian students. *Journal of Enterprising Culture*, *12*(01), 55–78. doi:10.1142/S021849580400004X

Kujur, R., & Minz, S. K. (2021). Proliferation of Tribal Migrants and Repercussion: Case Study from the Tribal Areas of Sundargarh District, Odisha (India). *Current Res. J. Soc. Sci. & Human.*, *4*(1), 27–44. doi:10.12944/CRJSSH.4.1.04

Kulkarni, G. (2007). Construction industry: More needs to be done. *Indian Journal of Occupational and Environmental Medicine*, *11*(1), 1. doi:10.4103/0019-5278.32455 PMID:21957363

Kumar, B. (2013). Gender discrimination among construction workers with reference to Vijaywada. *Journal of sociology ans social work, 1*(1), 42-53.

Kumar, B. R. (2013, June). Gender discrimination among construction workers with reference to Vijayawada. *Journal of Sociology and Social Work*, *1*(1), 42–53.

Kumar, M. (2021). Startups, Barriers and its Opportunities in India. [TURCOMAT]. *Turkish Journal of Computer and Mathematics Education*, *12*(9), 2200–2205.

Kumar, M. M., Pathak, V. K., & Ruikar, M. (2020). Tribal population in India: A public health challenge and road to future. *Journal of Family Medicine and Primary Care*, *9*(2), 508. doi:10.4103/jfmpc.jfmpc_992_19 PMID:32318373

Kumar, R. R., Singh, K. P., & Ete, L. (2021). Social innovation and entrepreneurship in Arunachal Pradesh: Opportunities and challenges. *Space and Culture, India*, *8*(4), 48–59. doi:10.20896aci.v8i4.924

Kumar, R., Kanaujiya, R., & Mishra, K. (2019). Resurgent India: An Exploratory Study to comprehend the Interplay of Public Expenditure and Governance. *Think India Journal*, *22*(14), 1840–1883.

Kunasekaran, P., Ramachandran, S., Yacob, M. R., & Shuib, A. (2011). Development of farmers' perception scale on agro tourism in Cameron Highlands, Malaysia. *World Applied Sciences Journal*, *12*, 10–18.

Lagarde, C. (2013). Dare the difference. *Finance & Development*, *50*(2).

Lal, T. (2021). Impact of financial inclusion on economic development of marginalized communities through the mediation of social and economic empowerment. *International Journal of Social Economics*, *48*(12), 1768–1793. doi:10.1108/IJSE-12-2020-0830

Lather, A. S., Garg, S., & Vikas, S. (2009). Entrepreneurship as a strategic development intervention to accelerate rural development: The case of Drishtee. *Asia Pacific Business Review*, *5*(1), 126–137. doi:10.1177/097324700900500115

Levy, S. B., & Reolofs, C. (2019). Impact of Climate Change on Workers Health and Safety. *The Oxford Research Encyclopaedia of Global Public Health.* (https://oxfordre.com/publichealth/display/10.1093/acrefore/9780190632366.001.0001/acrefore9780190632366e39;jsessionid=408B3D2F2A2BD526474998930A1EADBE)

Light, A. N., & Siegel, J. I. (2008). The social dimensions of entrepreneurship. In M. Casson, B. Yeing, A. Basu, & N. Wadeson (Eds.), *The Oxford Handbook of Entrepreneurship*. Oxford University Press.

Linan, F., & Chen, Y. W. (2009). Development and cross–cultural application of a specific instrument to measure entrepreneurial intentions. *Entrepreneurship Theory and Practice*, *33*(3), 593–617. doi:10.1111/j.1540-6520.2009.00318.x

Lin, F.-J., & Lai, C. (2021). Key Factors Affecting Technological Capabilities in Small and Medium-Sized Enterprises in Taiwan. *The International Entrepreneurship and Management Journal*, *17*(1), 131–143. doi:10.100711365-019-00632-2

Loscocco, K., & Bird, S. R. (2012). Gendered paths: Why women lag behind men in small business success. *Work and Occupations*, *39*(2), 183–219. doi:10.1177/0730888412444282

Luthje, C., & Franke, N. (2003). The 'making' of an entrepreneur: Testing a model of entrepreneurial intent among engineering students at MIT. *Research Management*, *33*(2), 135–147.

Mahalakshmi, J. (2015). Protection to women in India: A judicial Perspective. *Labour Law Journal*, 29-33.

Maitre, N., Montt, G., Saget, C., Ernst, C., Gutiérrez, M. T., Kizu, T., & Karimova, T. -Kie-Song, M.L., & Tsukamoto, M. (2018). *The employment impact of climate change adaptation*, p 13-29. ILO. (https://www.ilo.org/wcmsp5/groups/public/ed_emp/documents/publication/wcms_645572.pdf)

Malamud, O., & Eleches, C. (2010). General Education versus Vocational Training: Evidence from an Economy in Transition. *The Review of Economics and Statistics*, *92*(1), 43–60. doi:10.1162/rest.2009.11339

Malhotra, R. K., Bohra, N. S., & Upadhyay, R. (2021). An Investigation Of Sustainable Development Within CSR For Rural Development In India, *Ilkogretim Online Elementary Education. Online (Bergheim)*, *20*(01).

Malpani, R., & Ghosh, A. (2020). Business Sustainability Measures in Tribal Jharkhand. *Drishtikon: A Management Journal, 11*(1), 66.

Mammen, K., & Paxson, C. (2000). Women's work and economic development. *The Journal of Economic Perspectives*, *14*(4), 141–164. doi:10.1257/jep.14.4.141

Maniktala, J., & Punjabi, L.C. (2016). Corporate Social Responsibility: Perspectives and Challenges in Rural India. *IOSR Journal of Business and Management* (IOSR-JBM) pp. 41-46.

Manjunatha, B. R., & Gangadhar, M. R. (2018). Socio-Economic Status of the Bettakuruba Tribal Women: a Case Study from the Chamarajanagara District, Karnataka. *Antrocom: Online Journal of Anthropology, 14*(1).

Manshani, S., & Dubey, A. (2017). Startup women in startup India: A study of women entrepreneurs in India. [IJBGM]. *International Journal of Business and Management*, *6*(4), 91–100.

Maranda, M.F., & Comeau, Y. (2000). Some contributions of sociology to the understanding of career. *The future of career*, 37-52.

Masenya, T. M. (2021). Technopreneurship development: digital strategy for youth self-employment in the digital economy. In *Handbook of Research on Management and Strategies for Digital Enterprise Transformation* (pp. 196–218). IGI Global. doi:10.4018/978-1-7998-5015-1.ch010

Mason, C., & Brown, R. (2014). Entrepreneurial ecosystems and growth oriented entrepreneurship. *Final report to OECD, Paris, 30*(1), 77-102.

Mathur, A., Sharma, S. K., & Saha, P. (2014). The Vocational Training System: A Learner's Perspective. In S. Mehrotra (Ed.), *India's Skills Challenge: Reforming Vocational Education and Training to Harness the Demographic Dividend* (pp. 177–200). Oxford University Press. doi:10.1093/acprof:oso/9780199452774.003.0005

Matlay, H., Packham, G., Jones, P., Miller, C., Pickernell, D., & Thomas, B. (2010). Attitudes towards entrepreneurship education: A comparative analysis. *Education + Training*, *52*(8/9), 568–586. doi:10.1108/00400911011088926

MCA. (2013). *The Companies Act, 2013.* Ministry of Corporate Affairs. https://www.mca.gov.in/Ministry/pdf/CompaniesAct2013.pdf

MCA. (2014). *General Circular No 21/2014.* Ministry of Corporate Affairs. https://www.mca.gov.in/Ministry/pdf/General_Circular_21_2014.pdf

McCarthy, J. (2022). How war impact climate change. *Global Citizen.* https://www.globalcitizen.org/en/content/how-war-impacts-the-environment-and-climatechange/#:~:text=Militaries%20consume%20enormous%20amounts%20of,direct

McGrath, S. (2012). Vocational learning for development: A policy in need of a theory? *International Journal of Educational Development*, *32*(5), 623–632. doi:10.1016/j.ijedudev.2011.12.001

Mehrotra, S., & Ghosh, D. (2012). *The International Experience with National Training Funds: Lessons for India, IAMR Policy Brief No. 1.*

Mehrotra, S. (2014). *India's Skill Challenge: Reforming Vocational Education and Training to Harness the Demographic Dividend.* Oxford University Press. doi:10.1093/acprof:oso/9780199452774.001.0001

Mehrotra, S., Gandhi, A., & Sahoo, B. K. (2013). Estimating India's Skill Gap: On a Realistic Basis for 2022. *Economic and Political Weekly*, 102–111.

Mehrotra, S., & Parida, J. K. (2017). Why is the labour force participation of women declining in India? *World Development*, *98*, 360–380. doi:10.1016/j.worlddev.2017.05.003

Middleton, J., Ziderman, A., & Adams, A. V. (1993). *Skills for Productivity: vocational education and training in developing countries*. Oxford University Press.

Ministry of Agriculture and Food of the Republic of Belarus. (2008): Agropromyshlenny complex (Agro-Industrial sector). Minsk.

Ministry of Rural Development. (2019). *Development of Rural Areas is one of the Priorities of the Modi Government.* Rural NIC. https://rural.nic.in/en/press-release/development-rural-areas-one-priorities-modi-government-narendra-singh-tomar

Minsk. (2021). *National Statistical Committee of the Republic of Belarus.* Statistical book, Agriculture of the Republic of Belarus, Minsk

Mishra, M. (2014). Vertically integrated skill development and vocational training for socio-economically marginalized youth: The experience at Gram Tarang and Centurion University, India. *Prospects, 44*, 297–316. doi:10.100711125-014-9308-z

MoLE. (2009). *National Skill Development Policy*. Government of India.

Moriano, J. A., Gorgievski, M., Laguna, M., Stephan, U., & Zarafshani, K. (2012). A cross-cultural approach to understanding entrepreneurial intention. *Journal of Career Development, 39*(2), 162–185. doi:10.1177/0894845310384481

Moyce, S. C., & Schenker, M. (2018). Migrant workers and their occupational health and safety. *Annual Review of Public Health, 39*(1), 351–365. doi:10.1146/annurev-publhealth-040617-013714 PMID:29400993

Munshi, K., & Rosenzweig, M. (2006). Traditional institutions meet the modern world: Caste, gender, and schooling choice in a globalizing economy. *The American Economic Review, 96*(4), 1225–1252. doi:10.1257/aer.96.4.1225

Mustafa, M. J., Hernandez, E., Mahon, C., & Chee, L. K. (2016). Entrepreneurial intentions of university students in an emerging economy: The influence of university support and proactive personality on students' entrepreneurial intention. *Journal of Entrepreneurship in Emerging Economies.*

Nabi, G., Holden, R., & Birdthistle, N. (2008). An examination of tertiary students' desire to found an enterprise. *Education + Training, 50*(7), 552–567. doi:10.1108/00400910810909027

Naik, A., & Patel, P. (2022). Government Schemes for Entrepreneurship Programs. In *Agricultural Microbiology Based Entrepreneurship: Making Money from Microbes* (pp. 25–40). Springer Nature Singapore.

Nanda, R., & Sorensen, J. (2009). Workplace Peers and Entrepreneurship. *Harvard Business School Entrepreneurial Management* (08-051).

Narain, J. P. (2019). Health of tribal populations in India: How long can we afford to neglect? *The Indian Journal of Medical Research, 149*(3), 313. doi:10.4103/ijmr.IJMR_2079_18 PMID:31249192

Nath, P., Verma, A., Dhusia, N., & More, N. (2006). Study on Impact of Natural Disasters And Its Relationship With Rainfall Distribution in The State of Uttar Pradesh During, 2006-2010. *Conference Paper.*

National Academy of Sciences. (2020). Climate change: evidence and causes: Update 2020. The National Academies Press. doi:10.17226/25733EXITEXIT

National Skill Development Corporation (NSDC). (2018). *'Skilling Today for a Brighter Tomorrow' Annual Report 2017-18.* New Delhi.

National Skill Development Corporation (NSDC). (2019). Estimating the Skill Stock In Uttar Pradesh, State Report 2019. New Delhi.

Neff, D. F., Sen, K., & Kling, V. (2012). *The puzzling decline in rural women's labor force participation in India: A reexamination.*

Neff, G. (2012). *Venture labor: Work and the burden of risk in innovative industries.* MIT press. doi:10.7551/mitpress/9780262017480.001.0001

Nguyen, N. T. H., Suwanno, S., Thongma, W., & Visuthismajarn, P. (2018). The attitudes of residents towards agro-tourism impacts and its effects on participation in agro-tourism development: The case study of Vietnam. *African Journal of Hospitality, Tourism and Leisure*, *7*(4), 1–18.

Nuthalapati, C. S., Srinivas, K., Pandey, N., & Sharma, R. (2020). Startups with open innovation: Accelerating technological change and food value chain flows in India. *Indian Journal of Agricultural Economics*, *75*(4), 415–437.

O'Connor, A., Stam, E., Sussan, F., & Audretsch, D. B. (2018). Entrepreneurial ecosystems: The foundations of place-based renewal. *Entrepreneurial ecosystems: Place-based transformations and transitions,* 1-21.

OECD. (2010). *A Family Affair: Inter-generational Social Mobility across OECD Countries.* OECD.

Oishi, N. (2005). *Women in motion: Globalization, state policies, and labor migration in Asia.* Stanford University Press. doi:10.1515/9780804766906

Okada, A. (2012). Skills Development for Youth in India: Challenges and Opportunities. *Kokusai Kyoiku Kyoryoku Ronshu*, *879*, 169–193.

Olarewaju, T., & Fernando, J. (2020). Gender Inequality and Female Entrepreneurship in Developing Countries. In W. Leal Filho, A. Azul, L. Brandli, A. Lange Salvia, & T. Wall (Eds.), *Decent Work and Economic Growth. Encyclopedia of the UN Sustainable Development Goals.* Springer., doi:10.1007/978-3-319-71058-7_92-1

Olsen, W., & Mehta, S. (2006). *Female Labour Participation in Rural and Urban India: Does Housewives' Work Count?* Research Gate. https://www.researchgate.net/publication/228461844

Ongun, U., & Erbaş, E. (2020). Sosyal Medyanın Destinasyon Gelişimindeki Rolü: Lavanta Kokulu Kuyucak Köyü Örneği. *Journal of Tourism and Gastronomy Studies*, *8*(4), 3129–3154. doi:10.21325/jotags.2020.755

Ongun, U., Gövder, B., & Kösekahyaoğlu, L. (2018). Kırsal turizm kapsamında yerel halkın beklentileri: Isparta Kuyucak Lavanta Vadisi örneği. *Turar Turizm ve Araştırma Dergisi*, *7*(2), 43–58.

Oosterbeek, H., & Webbink, D. (2007). Wage effects of an extra year of basic vocational education. *Economics of Education Review*, *7689*(4), 408–411. doi:10.1016/j.econedurev.2006.07.013

Ortiz, A. D. (2018) BBC Future, ten simple ways to act on climate change. *BBC.* (https://www.bbc.com/future/article/20181102-what-can-i-do-about-climate-change)

Oxfam. (2005). Beyond access for girls and boys: How to achieve good-quality, gender-equitable education. *Education and Gender Equality Series, Programme Insights*. OXFAM.

Ozen Kutanis, R., Bayraktaroglu, S., & Bozkurt, O. (2006). Is the personality features important in entrepreneurial orientation and experience? In *14th National Management and Organization Congress Proceedings*. Ataturk University.

Ozkazanc-Pan, B., & Clark Muntean, S. (2018). Networking towards (in) equality: Women entrepreneurs in technology. *Gender, Work and Organization*, *25*(4), 379–400. doi:10.1111/gwao.12225

Pages, C., & Stampini, M. (2007). *No Education, No Good Jobs? Evidence on the Relationship between Education and Labour Market Segmentation*. Institute for Study of Labour.

Pandey, K. (2019). India's Unemployment Rate Doubled in Two Years: SoE in Figures. *Down to Earth.* https://www.downtoearth.org.in/news/economy/india-s-unemployment-ratedoubled-in-two-years-soe-in-figures-64953

Pandey, D. (1998). Migrant labour, employment and gender dimensions. *The Indian Journal of Social Work*, *62*(1), 743–765.

Pandlier, R. (2017). *Get the Policies Right First: How to get India's Women into the Workforce.* Business Standard. https://www.businessstandard.com/article/opinion/rohini-pande-getting-india-s-women-into-theworkforce-117031601398_1.html

Paramasivan, C., & Muthusamy, S. (2017). Technopreneurship and development of IT and ITeS industry in India. *Imperial Journal of Interdisciplinary Research, 3*(11).

Paramasivan, C., & Muthusamy, S. (2016). Emerging trends in new start-up technopreneurs. *Journal of Business and Management*, *2*(7).

Paray, M. R. (2019). Status Of Tribal Women In India With Special Reference To The Socio-Economic And Educational Condition. *Ilkogretim Online*, *18*(4), 2284–2292.

Parmar, R. B. (2016*). A Study of the Problems of Girl Child Education in the Narmada District of Gujarat* [Doctoral dissertation, Maharaja Sayajirao University of Baroda (India)].

Patel, J., Matharu, S., Changle, R., & Pachori, C. D. S. (2022). Indofills Industries–A Venture seeking Turnaround. *Journal of Positive School Psychology*, 6590-6593.

Patel, J.R. (2014). Role of corporate social responsibility in rural development. *Research Hub-International Multidisciplinary Research Journal*, *1*(2).

Patel, H. C., Moitra, M., Momin, M. I., & Kantharia, S. L. (2012). Working conditions of male construction worker and it's impact on their life: A cross sectional study in Surat city. *National Journal of Community Medicine*, *3*(4), 652–656.

Pischke, J., & Wachter, T. (2008). Zero Returns to Compulsory Schooling in Germany: Evidence and Interpretation. *The Review of Economics and Statistics*, *90*(3), 592–598. doi:10.1162/rest.90.3.592

Planning Commission. (1964). Report of the Joint Study Team on Eastern Districts. Planning Commission.

Planning Commission. (2007). *Scenario of the Village*. Planning Commission. http://planningcommission.nic.in/plans/stateplan/.../sdr_orich16.doc

Poonam. (2016), Corporate Social Responsibility in Rural Development Sector: An Introduction, *International Journal of Scientific and Research Publications*, *5*(10).

Postigo, S., Iacobucci, D., & Tamborini, M. F. (2006). Undergraduate students as a source of potential entrepreneurs: a comparative study between Italy and Argentina. *International entrepreneurship education: Issues and Newness*, 218-240.

Poulomi, P., Nanda, S., Anand, S., Sharma, S., & Nandi, S. (2020). *Skilling and Non-Traditional Livelihoods*. International Centre for Research on Women. https://assets.ey.com/content/dam/ey-sites/ey-com/en_in/topics/corporate-social-responsibility/icrw-vikalp-policy-report-on-skilling-and-non traditional-livelihoods.pd

Powell, M. (2019). Trends and forecasting of employment intensity of growth in India. *Journal of the Asia Pacific Economy*, *765*, 438–459.

Prabhakar, S., & Nimesh, A. (2022). Skill development programmes for women in India: Current status and future perspectives. *World Journal of Advanced Engineering Technology and Sciences*, *7*(1), 128–136. doi:10.30574/wjaets.2022.7.1.0105

Pradhan, B. K., Singh, S. K., & Mitra, A. (2015). Female labour supply in a developing economy: A tale from a primary survey. *Journal of International Development*, *27*(1), 99–111. doi:10.1002/jid.2994

Prakash, S., & Singh, B. (2013). Economics and Constraints Analysis of Rice Production in Jhansi District Of Uttar Pradesh, India. *Plant Archives*, *13*(2), 865–869.

Prasad, R. N. (2015). Theoretical Counter on CSR, Trusteeship, Corporate Social Responsibility & Peace.

Premi, M. K. (2001). Who Migrates to Delhi? *Demography India*, *30*(1), 49–59.

Prohorovs, A., Bistrova, J., & Ten, D. (2019). Startup success factors in the capital attraction stage: Founders' perspective. *Journal of East-West Business*, *25*(1), 26–51. doi:10.1080/10669868.2018.1503211

Psacharopoulos, G. (1994). Returns to investment in education: A global update. *World Development*, *22*(9), 1325–1343. doi:10.1016/0305-750X(94)90007-8

Psacharopoulos, G., & Tzannatos, Z. (1992). Women's employment and pay in Latin America. *Finance & Development*, *29*, 14–14.

Punnaiah, A. (2018). Issues and Challenges of Tribal Education: A Study of Telangana State. *International Education and Research Journal*, *4*(1), 49–51.

Qasim, Y., & Mahmood, Z. (2022). Technopreneurship Education: The Way to Rebuild COVID-19 Affected Economy. *Journal of Management Research*, *9*(1).

Quintini, G., & Martin, S. (2006). *Starting Well or Losing their Way?: The Position of Youth in the Labour Market. OECD SOCIAL*. Employment And Migration Working Papers.

Rangarajan, C., Seema, & Vibeesh, E. M. (2014). Developments in the Workforce between 2009-10 and 2011-12. *Economic and Political Weekly*, 117–121.

Rao, V. (2017). *Can Student Entrepreneurship be the answer to India's Jobless-growth problem?* Your Story. https://yourstory.com/2017/07/student-entrepreneurship-sv-co

Rao, K., Joshi, S., Mathur, A. K., & Sahoo, B. K. (2014). The Vocational Training System: An Employer's Perspective. In S. Mehrotra (Ed.), *India's Skill Challenge: Reforming Vocational Education and Training to Harness the Demographic Dividend* (pp. 200–223). Oxford University Press. doi:10.1093/acprof:oso/9780199452774.003.0006

Rao, M. (2015). Step by step to soft-skills training: How to enhance employability skills in students. *Human Resource Management International Digest*, *76*(6), 34–36. doi:10.1108/HRMID-06-2015-0099

Rautela, P., & Karki, B. (2015). Impact of Climate Change on Life and Livelihood of Indigenous People of Higher Himalaya in Uttarakhand, India [Science and Education Publishing.]. *American Journal of Environmental Protection*, *3*(4), 112–124.

Rele, J. R. (1969). Trends and Significance of Internal Migration in India. *Sankhya Series B*, *31*(3-4), 501–508.

Report, F. A. O. (2016). *India at a glance*. Food and Agricultural Organisation of the UN. Retrieved from https://www.fao.org/india/fao-in-india/india-at-a-glance/en/

Report, I. (2022). *National Family Health Survey 2019-21 (NFHS-5)*. International Institute of Population Studies. https://ruralindiaonline.org/en/library/resource/national-family-health-survey-nfhs-5-2019-21-india/

Reserve Bank of India. (1984). *Agricultural Productivity in Eastern India*. RBI.

Roberts, K. D. (1997). China's Tidal Wave of Migrant Labour: What can we learn from Mexican Undocumented Migration to United States. *The International Migration Review*, *31*(2), 249–293. PMID:12292872

Roberts, L. P., & Robinson, P. B. (2010). Home-based entrepreneurs, commercial entrepreneurs and white-collar workers: A comparative study of attitudes toward self-esteem, personal control and business growth. *Journal of Small Business and Entrepreneurship*, *23*(3), 333–353. doi:10.1080/08276331.2010.10593489

Roemer, J. (1998). *Equality of opportunity*. Harvard University Press. doi:10.4159/9780674042872

Rosalina, P. D., Dupre, K., & Wang, Y. (2021). Rural tourism: A systematic literature review on definitions and challenges. *Journal of Hospitality and Tourism Management*, *47*, 134–149. doi:10.1016/j.jhtm.2021.03.001

Rural Communities. (n.d.). Ministry of Economy of Belarus.https://economy.gov.by/en/selo-en/

Ryan, P. (2001). The School-to-Work Transition: A Cross-National Perspective. *Journal of Economic Literature*, 2345–2365.

Saha, P., & Verick, S. (2017). Casualization and shift of rural workers to non-farm activities. *Rural Labour Mobility in Times of Structural Transformation: Dynamics and Perspectives from Asian Economies*, 127-150.

Sahira, S., & Surangi, H. A. K. N. S. (2022). *Is there any Digital Gender Divide? Exploring challenges faced by Female Technopreneurs in Sri Lanka*.

Sahoo, M., & Pradhan, J. (2021). Reproductive health care status of the displaced tribal women in India: An analysis using Nussbaum Central human capabilities. *Health Care for Women International*, *42*(4-6), 390–419. doi:10.1080/07399332.2020.1743994 PMID:32223700

Sahoo, S. R. (2015). Technopreneurship: A Synthesis Based on Case Studies of Rural Innovators in India. In *Eleventh Biennial Conference on Entrepreneurship* (pp. 410-417).

Sahu, T. N., Agarwala, V., & Maity, S. (2021). Effectiveness of microcredit in employment generation and livelihood transformation of tribal women entrepreneurs: Evidence from PMMY. *Journal of Small Business and Entrepreneurship*, 1–22. doi:10.1080/08276331.2021.1928847

Salamzadeh, A., & Kawamorita Kesim, H. (2017). The enterprising communities and startup ecosystem in Iran. *Journal of Enterprising Communities: People and Places in the Global Economy*, *11*(4), 456–479. doi:10.1108/JEC-07-2015-0036

Sampene, A. K., Li, C., Agyeman, F. O., Robert, B., Nicholas, L., Moses, S., & Salomon, A. A. (2021). A Critical Assessment of The Role of Entrepreneurship Development in the 21st Century. *European Journal of Business and Innovation Research*, *9*(5), 1–26.

Sang, K., & Powell, A. (2012). Gender inequality in the construction industry: Lessons from Pierre Bourdieu. *In Proceedings of the 28th Annual ARCOM Conference* (pp. 237-247). Edinburgh, UK: Association of Researchers in Construction Management.

Sarma, G. (2014). An analytical study on entrepreneurial activity as a tool for socio-economic development of tribal women in BTAD area of Assam. *IOSR Journal of Economics and Finance*, *3*(2), 49–52. doi:10.9790/5933-03214952

Savickas, M. (2002). Career construction. A developmental theory of vocational behaviour. In *Career choice and development* (pp. 149–285). Jossey-Bass.

Saxena, P., & Gandhi, A. (2014). Reforming Apprenticeship Training. In S. Mehrotra (Ed.), *India's Skills Challenge: Reforming Vocational Education and Training to Harness the Demographic Dividend* (pp. 129–177). Oxford University Press. doi:10.1093/acprof:oso/9780199452774.003.0004

Scarlat, C. (2014). Technopreneurship-An emerging concept. *FAIMA Business & Management Journal*, *2*(3), 5.

Schwarz, E. J., Wdowiak, M. A., Almer-Jarz, D. A., & Breitenecker, R. J. (2009). The effects of attitudes and perceived environment conditions on students' entrepreneurial intent An Austrian perspective. *Education + Training*, *51*(4), 272–291. doi:10.1108/00400910910964566

Sequeira, J., Mueller, S. L., & McGee, J. E. (2007). The influence of social ties and self-efficacy in forming entrepreneurial intentions and motivating nascent behavior. *Journal of Developmental Entrepreneurship*, *12*(03), 275–293. doi:10.1142/S108494670700068X

Sergeant, J., & Crawford, J. (2001). *National youth entrepreneurship attitude survey*. Department of Industry, Science and Resources.

Sesen, H. (2013). Personality or environment? A comprehensive study on the entrepreneurial intentions of university students. *Education + Training*, *55*(7), 624–640. doi:10.1108/ET-05-2012-0059

Seth, S. (2021). *Why Entrepreneurship Is Important to the Economy*. Investiopedia. (https://www.investopedia.com/articles/personal-finance/101414/why-entrepreneursare-important-economy.asp)

Sezen, B., & Boz, İ. (2021). Ziyaretçilerin Kırsal Turizm Faaliyetlerinden Memnuniyet Düzeyi: Cumalıkızık Köyü Örneği. *Black Sea Journal of Public and Social Science*, *4*(1), 24–33. doi:10.52704/bssocialscience.779509

Shanmugham, M., & Kishore, S. (2012). Integration of prior learning and assessment in the IGNOU community college system for Skill Development. *Turkish Online Journal of Distance Education*, *765*, 311–321.

Shanti, K (1991). Issues relating to economic migration of females. *The Indian journal of labour Economics, 34* (4), 335-46.

Sharma, D., Tiwari, B. K., Chaturvedi, S. S., & Diengdoh, E. (2015). Status, utilization and economic valuation of Non-timber Forest Products of Arunachal Pradesh, India. *Journal of Forest and Environmental Science*, *31*(1), 24–37. doi:10.7747/JFES.2015.31.1.24

Sharma, S., Mehra, D., Akhtar, F., & Mehra, S. (2020). Evaluation of a community-based intervention for health and economic empowerment of marginalized women in India. *BMC Public Health, 20*(1), 1–16. doi:10.118612889-020-09884-y PMID:33228667

Sharma, U. (1986). *Women's work, Class and the Urban Household: A study of Shimla, North India*. Tavistock Publications.

Sharma, Y. (2013). Women entrepreneur in India. *IOSR Journal of Business and Management, 15*(3), 9–14. doi:10.9790/487X-1530914

Sheoran, M., & Kumar, D. (2020). Role of environmental concerns on the startups networking: A study of Indian startups. *International Journal of Mathematical. Engineering and Management Sciences, 5*(6), 1300–1311.

Shook, C. L., & Bratianu, C. (2010). Entrepreneurial intent in a transitional economy: An application of the theory of planned behavior to Romanian students. *The International Entrepreneurship and Management Journal, 6*(3), 231–247. doi:10.100711365-008-0091-2

Siddiqui, A. B. (2012). Problems encountered by women entrepreneurs in India. *International Journal of Applied Research & Studies, 1*(2), 01-11.

Silva, L. (2022). The impact of the COVID-19 pandemic on rural tourism: A case study from Portugal. *Anatolia, 33*(1), 157–159. doi:10.1080/13032917.2021.1875015

Singh, A. M. (1984). Rural to Urban migration of women in India: Patterns and Implications. In J T Fawcett et al (eds), Women in the Cities of South Asia: Migration and Urban Adaptation. Boulder, Colorado: West view press

Singh, S. (2019). Determinants of Agriculture Production in Uttar Pradesh, India: A regional analysis. *Research Review International journal of Multidisciplinary, 4*(1).

Singh, V. K. (2021). Policy and regulatory changes for a successful startup revolution: Experiences from the startup action plan in India. In Investment in Startups and Small Business Financing (pp. 33-67).

Singh, A. K. (1981). *Patterns of Regional Development: A Comparative Study*. Sterling Publishers.

Singh, C. K. (2003). Skill, Education and Employment: A Dissenting Essay. *Economic and Political Weekly, 458*, 3271–3276.

Singh, S. (2010). Digital divide in India: Measurement, determinants and policy for addressing the challenges in bridging the digital divide. [IJIDE]. *International Journal of Innovation in the Digital Economy, 1*(2), 1–24. doi:10.4018/jide.2010040101

Sinha, A., & Dorschner, J. P. (2010). India: Rising Power or a Mere Revolution of Rising Expectation? *Northeastern Political Science Association, 2345*(1), 345–367. doi:10.1057/pol.2009.19

Sommer, L., & Haug, M. (2011). Intention as a Cognitive Antecedent to International Entrepreneurship: Understanding the Moderating Roles of Knowledge and Experience. *The International Entrepreneurship and Management Journal*, *7*(1), 111–142. doi:10.100711365-010-0162-z

Sonam (2022). Customary Laws: Cultural Identity of Indigenous People, *National Seminar on Tribal Culture and Philosophy in Oral Narratives*, *1*(1), 39.

Sonam, Kala, S., Prabhakar, P., & Banerjee, M. (2021). Post-training Knowledge and Attitude Assessment of the Women Entrepreneurs towards Mushroom Cultivation. *International Journal of Agriculture Environment and Biotechnology*, *14*(2), 229–234.

Sonne, L. (2012). Innovative initiatives supporting inclusive innovation in India: Social business incubation and micro venture capital. *Technological Forecasting and Social Change*, *79*(4), 638–647. doi:10.1016/j.techfore.2011.06.008

Soriano, D. R., & Huarng, K. H. (2013). Innovation and entrepreneurship in knowledge industries. *Journal of Business Research*, *66*(10), 1964–1969. doi:10.1016/j.jbusres.2013.02.019

Souitaris, V., Zerbinati, S., & Al-Laham, A. (2007). Do entrepreneurship programmes raise entrepreneurial intention of science and engineering students? The effect of learning, inspiration and resources. *Journal of Business Venturing*, *22*(4), 566–591. doi:10.1016/j.jbusvent.2006.05.002

Soykan, F. (2003). Kirsal Turizm Ve Türkiye Turizmi İçin Önemi. *Ege Coğrafya Dergisi*, *12*(1), 1–11.

Spender, J. C., Corvello, V., Grimaldi, M., & Rippa, P. (2017). Startups and open innovation: A review of the literature. *European Journal of Innovation Management*, *20*(1), 4–30. doi:10.1108/EJIM-12-2015-0131

Spilerman, A. (2009). Student learning outcomes from a gender perspective: What do international assessments tell us? *Paper presented at the World Bank's Global Symposium - Education: A Critical Path to Gender Equality and Women's Empowerment*, Washington, DC.

Srivastava, M. Z. (2014). Reconsidering women's work in rural India: Analysis of NSSO data, 2004–05 and 2011–12. *Economic and Political Weekly*, *52*(1), 45–52.

Stam, E., & Van de Ven, A. (2021). Entrepreneurial ecosystem elements. *Small Business Economics*, *56*(2), 809–832. doi:10.100711187-019-00270-6

Subas, R. (1984). Dynamics of Agrarian Relations in Sultanpur East Uttar Pradesh. *Social Scientist, 12*(7), 57-63.

Subrahmanian, R. (2005). *Scaling Up" Good Practices in Girls' Education. United Nations Educational, Scientific and Cultural Organization*. UNESCO.

Subrahmanya, M. B. (2017). Comparing the entrepreneurial ecosystems for technology startups in Bangalore and Hyderabad, India. *Technology Innovation Management Review*, *7*(7), 47–62. doi:10.22215/timreview/1090

Sudarshan, R. M. (2014). *Enabling women's work.* ILO.

Sundari, S. (2004). *Migrant Women and Urban labour Market: Concepts and Case studies of problems, gains and losses*. Deep and Deep.

Suseno, Y., & Abbott, L. (2021). Women entrepreneurs' digital social innovation: Linking gender, entrepreneurship, social innovation and information systems. *Information Systems Journal, 31*(5), 717–744. doi:10.1111/isj.12327

Tansel, A. (1996). Urban male wage earners and moonlighting in Turkey. In *Working paper series/Economic Research Forum; 9601*. Economic Research Forum, Cairo, EG.

Tanwar, N., Tripathi, R. K., Hooda, E., Khan, M., & Godara, P. (2017). Assessment of Agricultural Development in Eastern Uttar Pradesh. *Annals of Biology, 33*(1), 139–144.

Tarhan, Y., Açıksöz, S., & Çelik, D. (2019). Lavanta Tarımı Ve Sürdürülebilir Kalkınma: Isparta/ Keçiborlu-Kuyucak Köyü Örneği. *Bartın University International Journal of Natural and Applied Sciences, 2*(2), 216–227.

Thapar-Björkert, S., Maiorano, D., & Blomkvist, H. (2019). Empowerment mechanisms-employment guarantee, women and Dalits in India. *Contemporary South Asia, 27*(4), 486–501. doi:10.1080/09584935.2019.1686750

Tirth, R., Badal, P. S., Singh, O. P., & Singh, R. (2015). Constraints to agricultural Diversification in Mirzapur District of Uttar Pradesh. *Economic affairs, 60*(2), 273-276.

Tiwari, A., Hogan, T., & O'Gorman, C. (2021). The good, the bad, and the ugly of 'Startup India'-a review of India's entrepreneurship policy. [EPW]. *Economic and Political Weekly, 56*(50), 45–52.

Tiwari, N. (2017). Women entrepreneurship in India: A literature review. *American Journal of Entrepreneurship, 2*(1), 47–60.

Tiwary, G., & Gangopadhyay, P. (2011). A review on the occupational health and social security of unorganized workers in the construction industry. *Indian Journal of Occupational and Environmental Medicine, 15*(1), 18. doi:10.4103/0019-5278.83003 PMID:21808496

Todeschini, B. V., Boelter, A. S., de Souza, J. S., & Cortimiglia, M. N. (2017). Risk management from the perspective of startups. *European Journal of Applied Business and Management, 3*(3).

Tomar, S. (2023). Unicorn Start-ups in India: A Brief Study. *IJFMR-International Journal For Multidisciplinary Research, 5*(1), 1–17.

Tonder, A. H., & Aspoy, T. M. (2017). When Work Comes First: Young Adults in Vocational Education and Training in Norway. *International Journal for Research in Vocational Education and Training, 543*(3), 270–288. doi:10.13152/IJRVET.4.3.5

Torun, E. (2013). Kırsal Turizmin Bölge İnsanına Katkıları. *Karamanoğlu Mehmetbey Üniversitesi Sosyal Ve Ekonomik Araştırmalar Dergisi, 2013*(1), 31–37.

Tripathi, N., Seppänen, P., Boominathan, G., Oivo, M., & Liukkunen, K. (2019). Insights into startup ecosystems through exploration of multi-vocal literature. *Information and Software Technology, 105*, 56–77. doi:10.1016/j.infsof.2018.08.005

Tripathy, S. N. (2017). Microfinance in empowering tribal women: Evidence from the villages of KBK Districts (Odisha). *Journal of Land and Rural Studies, 5*(2), 97–109. doi:10.1177/2321024917700938

Tuncer, B., & Bakırcı, M. (2021). Ekolojik Çiftliklerin Entegre Kırsal Turizm Bağlamında Analizi: Muğla İli Örneği. *Coğrafya Dergisi, 0*(42), 85–100. doi:10.26650/JGEOG2020-824039

UN. (2019). *Women's Country Gender Equality Brief (CGEB)*. UN.

UNFCC. (2020). *The Paris Agreement*. UNFCC. (https://unfccc.int/process-and-meetings/the-paris-agreement/the-paris-agreement)

United Nations Economic and Social Council. (2006). *"Economic, social and cultural rights: Girls' right to education." n.p.* United Nations.

United Nations Educational, Scientific and Cultural Organization (UNESCO). (2003). *Gender and education for all: The leap to equality*. UNESCO.

United Nations Environment Programme. (2022). *10 ways you can help fight the climate crisis*. UNEP. (https://www.unep.org/news-and-stories/story/10-ways-you-can-help-fight-climate-crisis)

United Nations. (2007). *From Stockholm to Kyoto: A Brief History of Climate Change*. UN. (https://www.un.org/en/chronicle/article/stockholm-kyoto-brief-history-climate-change#:~:text=Held%20in%20Stockholm%2C%20Sweden%20from,recommendations%20)

United States Agency for International Development (USAID). (2005). *Education strategy: Improving lives through learning*. USAID.

United States Department of State. (2004). *Advancing the rights of women: An overview of significant progress made by the U.S. in the 10 years since the Beijing conference on women*. State Government. https://www.state.gov/p/io/rls/othr/35882.htm

Urban, B. (2006). Entrepreneurship in the rainbow nation: Effect of cultural values and ESE on intentions. *Journal of Developmental Entrepreneurship, 11*(03), 171–186. doi:10.1142/S1084946706000386

Uzun, B., Dalgın, T., Çeken, H., & Özer, Ç. 82022). Arı Turizminin Kırsal Kalkınma Üzerindeki Etkisi: Marmaris Örneği. *Asya Studies, 6*(22), 179-192.

Vaidyanathan, A. (1987). Agricultural Development in Eastern India. *Economic and Political Weekly, 22*(52), 2259–2263. https://www.jstor.org/stable/4377916

Vaishar, A., & Šťastná, M. (2022). Impact of the COVID-19 pandemic on rural tourism in Czechia Preliminary considerations. *Current Issues in Tourism, 25*(2), 187–191. doi:10.1080/13683500.2020.1839027

Vastradmath, N. (2015). The Role of Corporate Social Responsibility for an Inclusive Growth in the Society. *International Journal of Scientific and Research Publications*, *5*(10).

Vondracek, F.W. (1990). A developmental-contextual approach to career development research. *Methodological approaches to the study of career*, 37-56.

Wibawa, T., Widjanarko, H., Utomo, H. S., Suratna, S., & Wahyurini, E. (2020, October). Technopreneurship Based Product Innovation: a Case Study on Small Entrepreneur. In *Proceeding of LPPM UPN "Veteran" Yogyakarta Conference Series 2020–Engineering and Science Series* (*Vol. 1,* pp. 439-444).

World Bank Report. (2018). Rural population (% of total population)- India. World Bank. https://data.worldbank.org/indicator/SP.RUR.TOTL.ZS?locations=IN

World Bank. (2007). *Skill Development in India: The Vocational Education and Training System.* Human Development Unit, South Asia Region.

World Bank. (2019). *World Development Report 2019: The Changing Nature of Work. Washington: World Bank. World Bank. (2019). World Development Report 2019: The Changing Nature of Work.* World Bank.

Yavuz, E., & Zığındere, Y. Ö. (2000). Sürdürülebilir Kalkınmanın Turizme Etkisi. *Balıkesir Üniversitesi Sosyal Bilimler Enstitüsü Dergisi*, *3*(4), 322–336.

Yazgan, Ş., & Kadanalı, E. (2012). Ağrı İlinin Kırsal Turizm Potansiyelinin Değerlendirilmesi. *Karamanoğlu Mehmetbey Üniversitesi Sosyal Ve Ekonomik Araştırmalar Dergisi*, *2012*(1), 5–10.

Yılmaz, G. Ö., & Gürol, N. K. (2012). Balıkesir ilinin kırsal turizm potansiyelinin değerlendirilmesi. *Karamanoğlu Mehmetbey Üniversitesi Sosyal ve Ekonomik Araştırmalar Dergisi*, *2012*(2), 23–32.

Young, R.A., Valach, L., & Collin, A. (2002). A contextualist explanation of career. *Career choice and development, 4*, 206-252.

Yurtkoru, E. S., Kuşcu, Z. K., & Doğanay, A. (2014). Exploring the antecedents of entrepreneurial intention on Turkish university students. *Procedia: Social and Behavioral Sciences*, *150*, 841–850. doi:10.1016/j.sbspro.2014.09.093

Zampetakis, L. A., Kafetsios, K., Bouranta, N., Dewett, T., & Moustakis, V. S. (2009). On the relationship between emotional intelligence and entrepreneurial attitudes and intentions. *International Journal of Entrepreneurial Behaviour & Research*, *15*(6), 595–618. doi:10.1108/13552550910995452

Zapkau, F. B., Schwens, C., Steinmetz, H., & Kabst, R. (2015). Disentangling the effect of prior entrepreneurial exposure on entrepreneurial intention. *Journal of Business Research*, *68*(3), 639–653. doi:10.1016/j.jbusres.2014.08.007

Related References

To continue our tradition of advancing information science and technology research, we have compiled a list of recommended IGI Global readings. These references will provide additional information and guidance to further enrich your knowledge and assist you with your own research and future publications.

Abdul Razak, R., & Mansor, N. A. (2021). Instagram Influencers in Social Media-Induced Tourism: Rethinking Tourist Trust Towards Tourism Destination. In M. Dinis, L. Bonixe, S. Lamy, & Z. Breda (Eds.), *Impact of New Media in Tourism* (pp. 135-144). IGI Global. https://doi.org/10.4018/978-1-7998-7095-1.ch009

Abir, T., & Khan, M. Y. (2022). Importance of ICT Advancement and Culture of Adaptation in the Tourism and Hospitality Industry for Developing Countries. In C. Ramos, S. Quinteiro, & A. Gonçalves (Eds.), *ICT as Innovator Between Tourism and Culture* (pp. 30–41). IGI Global. https://doi.org/10.4018/978-1-7998-8165-0.ch003

Abtahi, M. S., Behboudi, L., & Hasanabad, H. M. (2017). Factors Affecting Internet Advertising Adoption in Ad Agencies. *International Journal of Innovation in the Digital Economy*, *8*(4), 18–29. doi:10.4018/IJIDE.2017100102

Afenyo-Agbe, E., & Mensah, I. (2022). Principles, Benefits, and Barriers to Community-Based Tourism: Implications for Management. In I. Mensah & E. Afenyo-Agbe (Eds.), *Prospects and Challenges of Community-Based Tourism and Changing Demographics* (pp. 1–29). IGI Global. doi:10.4018/978-1-7998-7335-8.ch001

Agbo, V. M. (2022). Distributive Justice Issues in Community-Based Tourism. In I. Mensah & E. Afenyo-Agbe (Eds.), *Prospects and Challenges of Community-Based Tourism and Changing Demographics* (pp. 107–129). IGI Global. https://doi.org/10.4018/978-1-7998-7335-8.ch005

Agrawal, S. (2017). The Impact of Emerging Technologies and Social Media on Different Business(es): Marketing and Management. In O. Rishi & A. Sharma (Eds.), *Maximizing Business Performance and Efficiency Through Intelligent Systems* (pp. 37–49). Hershey, PA: IGI Global. doi:10.4018/978-1-5225-2234-8.ch002

Ahmad, A., & Johari, S. (2022). Georgetown as a Gastronomy Tourism Destination: Visitor Awareness Towards Revisit Intention of Nasi Kandar Restaurant. In M. Valeri (Ed.), *New Governance and Management in Touristic Destinations* (pp. 71–83). IGI Global. https://doi.org/10.4018/978-1-6684-3889-3.ch005

Alkhatib, G., & Bayouq, S. T. (2021). A TAM-Based Model of Technological Factors Affecting Use of E-Tourism. *International Journal of Tourism and Hospitality Management in the Digital Age*, *5*(2), 50–67. https://doi.org/10.4018/IJTHMDA.20210701.oa1

Altinay Ozdemir, M. (2021). Virtual Reality (VR) and Augmented Reality (AR) Technologies for Accessibility and Marketing in the Tourism Industry. In C. Eusébio, L. Teixeira, & M. Carneiro (Eds.), *ICT Tools and Applications for Accessible Tourism* (pp. 277-301). IGI Global. https://doi.org/10.4018/978-1-7998-6428-8.ch013

Anantharaman, R. N., Rajeswari, K. S., Angusamy, A., & Kuppusamy, J. (2017). Role of Self-Efficacy and Collective Efficacy as Moderators of Occupational Stress Among Software Development Professionals. *International Journal of Human Capital and Information Technology Professionals*, *8*(2), 45–58. doi:10.4018/IJHCITP.2017040103

Aninze, F., El-Gohary, H., & Hussain, J. (2018). The Role of Microfinance to Empower Women: The Case of Developing Countries. *International Journal of Customer Relationship Marketing and Management*, *9*(1), 54–78. doi:10.4018/IJCRMM.2018010104

Antosova, G., Sabogal-Salamanca, M., & Krizova, E. (2021). Human Capital in Tourism: A Practical Model of Endogenous and Exogenous Territorial Tourism Planning in Bahía Solano, Colombia. In V. Costa, A. Moura, & M. Mira (Eds.), *Handbook of Research on Human Capital and People Management in the Tourism Industry* (pp. 282–302). IGI Global. https://doi.org/10.4018/978-1-7998-4318-4.ch014

Arsenijević, O. M., Orčić, D., & Kastratović, E. (2017). Development of an Optimization Tool for Intangibles in SMEs: A Case Study from Serbia with a Pilot Research in the Prestige by Milka Company. In M. Vemić (Ed.), *Optimal Management Strategies in Small and Medium Enterprises* (pp. 320–347). Hershey, PA: IGI Global. doi:10.4018/978-1-5225-1949-2.ch015

Aryanto, V. D., Wismantoro, Y., & Widyatmoko, K. (2018). Implementing Eco-Innovation by Utilizing the Internet to Enhance Firm's Marketing Performance: Study of Green Batik Small and Medium Enterprises in Indonesia. *International Journal of E-Business Research, 14*(1), 21–36. doi:10.4018/IJEBR.2018010102

Asero, V., & Billi, S. (2022). New Perspective of Networking in the DMO Model. In M. Valeri (Ed.), *New Governance and Management in Touristic Destinations* (pp. 105–118). IGI Global. https://doi.org/10.4018/978-1-6684-3889-3.ch007

Atiku, S. O., & Fields, Z. (2017). Multicultural Orientations for 21st Century Global Leadership. In N. Baporikar (Ed.), *Management Education for Global Leadership* (pp. 28–51). Hershey, PA: IGI Global. doi:10.4018/978-1-5225-1013-0.ch002

Atiku, S. O., & Fields, Z. (2018). Organisational Learning Dimensions and Talent Retention Strategies for the Service Industries. In N. Baporikar (Ed.), *Global Practices in Knowledge Management for Societal and Organizational Development* (pp. 358–381). Hershey, PA: IGI Global. doi:10.4018/978-1-5225-3009-1.ch017

Atsa'am, D. D., & Kuset Bodur, E. (2021). Pattern Mining on How Organizational Tenure Affects the Psychological Capital of Employees Within the Hospitality and Tourism Industry: Linking Employees' Organizational Tenure With PsyCap. *International Journal of Tourism and Hospitality Management in the Digital Age, 5*(2), 17–28. https://doi.org/10.4018/IJTHMDA.2021070102

Ávila, L., & Teixeira, L. (2018). The Main Concepts Behind the Dematerialization of Business Processes. In M. Khosrow-Pour, D.B.A. (Ed.), Encyclopedia of Information Science and Technology, Fourth Edition (pp. 888-898). Hershey, PA: IGI Global. https://doi.org/ doi:10.4018/978-1-5225-2255-3.ch076

Ayorekire, J., Mugizi, F., Obua, J., & Ampaire, G. (2022). Community-Based Tourism and Local People's Perceptions Towards Conservation: The Case of Queen Elizabeth Conservation Area, Uganda. In I. Mensah & E. Afenyo-Agbe (Eds.), *Prospects and Challenges of Community-Based Tourism and Changing Demographics* (pp. 56–82). IGI Global. https://doi.org/10.4018/978-1-7998-7335-8.ch003

Baleiro, R. (2022). Tourist Literature and the Architecture of Travel in Olga Tokarczuk and Patti Smith. In R. Baleiro & R. Pereira (Eds.), *Global Perspectives on Literary Tourism and Film-Induced Tourism* (pp. 202-216). IGI Global. https://doi.org/10.4018/978-1-7998-8262-6.ch011

Barat, S. (2021). Looking at the Future of Medical Tourism in Asia. *International Journal of Tourism and Hospitality Management in the Digital Age, 5*(1), 19–33. https://doi.org/10.4018/IJTHMDA.2021010102

Barbosa, C. A., Magalhães, M., & Nunes, M. R. (2021). Travel Instagramability: A Way of Choosing a Destination? In M. Dinis, L. Bonixe, S. Lamy, & Z. Breda (Eds.), *Impact of New Media in Tourism* (pp. 173-190). IGI Global. https://doi.org/10.4018/978-1-7998-7095-1.ch011

Bari, M. W., & Khan, Q. (2021). Pakistan as a Destination of Religious Tourism. In E. Alaverdov & M. Bari (Eds.), *Global Development of Religious Tourism* (pp. 1-10). IGI Global. https://doi.org/10.4018/978-1-7998-5792-1.ch001

Bartens, Y., Chunpir, H. I., Schulte, F., & Voß, S. (2017). Business/IT Alignment in Two-Sided Markets: A COBIT 5 Analysis for Media Streaming Business Models. In S. De Haes & W. Van Grembergen (Eds.), *Strategic IT Governance and Alignment in Business Settings* (pp. 82–111). Hershey, PA: IGI Global. doi:10.4018/978-1-5225-0861-8.ch004

Bashayreh, A. M. (2018). Organizational Culture and Organizational Performance. In W. Lee & F. Sabetzadeh (Eds.), *Contemporary Knowledge and Systems Science* (pp. 50–69). Hershey, PA: IGI Global. doi:10.4018/978-1-5225-5655-8.ch003

Bechthold, L., Lude, M., & Prügl, R. (2021). Crisis Favors the Prepared Firm: How Organizational Ambidexterity Relates to Perceptions of Organizational Resilience. In A. Zehrer, G. Glowka, K. Schwaiger, & V. Ranacher-Lackner (Eds.), *Resiliency Models and Addressing Future Risks for Family Firms in the Tourism Industry* (pp. 178–205). IGI Global. https://doi.org/10.4018/978-1-7998-7352-5.ch008

Bedford, D. A. (2018). Sustainable Knowledge Management Strategies: Aligning Business Capabilities and Knowledge Management Goals. In N. Baporikar (Ed.), *Global Practices in Knowledge Management for Societal and Organizational Development* (pp. 46–73). Hershey, PA: IGI Global. doi:10.4018/978-1-5225-3009-1.ch003

Bekjanov, D., & Matyusupov, B. (2021). Influence of Innovative Processes in the Competitiveness of Tourist Destination. In J. Soares (Ed.), *Innovation and Entrepreneurial Opportunities in Community Tourism* (pp. 243–263). IGI Global. https://doi.org/10.4018/978-1-7998-4855-4.ch014

Bharwani, S., & Musunuri, D. (2018). Reflection as a Process From Theory to Practice. In M. Khosrow-Pour, D.B.A. (Ed.), Encyclopedia of Information Science and Technology, Fourth Edition (pp. 1529-1539). Hershey, PA: IGI Global. doi:10.4018/978-1-5225-2255-3.ch132

Bhatt, G. D., Wang, Z., & Rodger, J. A. (2017). Information Systems Capabilities and Their Effects on Competitive Advantages: A Study of Chinese Companies. *Information Resources Management Journal*, *30*(3), 41–57. doi:10.4018/IRMJ.2017070103

Bhushan, M., & Yadav, A. (2017). Concept of Cloud Computing in ESB. In R. Bhadoria, N. Chaudhari, G. Tomar, & S. Singh (Eds.), *Exploring Enterprise Service Bus in the Service-Oriented Architecture Paradigm* (pp. 116–127). Hershey, PA: IGI Global. doi:10.4018/978-1-5225-2157-0.ch008

Bhushan, S. (2017). System Dynamics Base-Model of Humanitarian Supply Chain (HSCM) in Disaster Prone Eco-Communities of India: A Discussion on Simulation and Scenario Results. *International Journal of System Dynamics Applications*, *6*(3), 20–37. doi:10.4018/IJSDA.2017070102

Binder, D., & Miller, J. W. (2021). A Generations' Perspective on Employer Branding in Tourism. In V. Costa, A. Moura, & M. Mira (Eds.), *Handbook of Research on Human Capital and People Management in the Tourism Industry* (pp. 152–174). IGI Global. https://doi.org/10.4018/978-1-7998-4318-4.ch008

Birch Freeman, A. A., Mensah, I., & Antwi, K. B. (2022). Smiling vs. Frowning Faces: Community Participation for Sustainable Tourism in Ghanaian Communities. In I. Mensah & E. Afenyo-Agbe (Eds.), *Prospects and Challenges of Community-Based Tourism and Changing Demographics* (pp. 83–106). IGI Global. https://doi.org/10.4018/978-1-7998-7335-8.ch004

Biswas, A., & De, A. K. (2017). On Development of a Fuzzy Stochastic Programming Model with Its Application to Business Management. In S. Trivedi, S. Dey, A. Kumar, & T. Panda (Eds.), *Handbook of Research on Advanced Data Mining Techniques and Applications for Business Intelligence* (pp. 353–378). Hershey, PA: IGI Global. doi:10.4018/978-1-5225-2031-3.ch021

Boragnio, A., & Faracce Macia, C. (2021). "Taking Care of Yourself at Home": Use of E-Commerce About Food and Care During the COVID-19 Pandemic in the City of Buenos Aires. In M. Korstanje (Ed.), *Socio-Economic Effects and Recovery Efforts for the Rental Industry: Post-COVID-19 Strategies* (pp. 45–71). IGI Global. https://doi.org/10.4018/978-1-7998-7287-0.ch003

Borges, V. D. (2021). Happiness: The Basis for Public Policy in Tourism. In A. Perinotto, V. Mayer, & J. Soares (Eds.), *Rebuilding and Restructuring the Tourism Industry: Infusion of Happiness and Quality of Life* (pp. 1–25). IGI Global. https://doi.org/10.4018/978-1-7998-7239-9.ch001

Bücker, J., & Ernste, K. (2018). Use of Brand Heroes in Strategic Reputation Management: The Case of Bacardi, Adidas, and Daimler. In A. Erdemir (Ed.), *Reputation Management Techniques in Public Relations* (pp. 126–150). Hershey, PA: IGI Global. doi:10.4018/978-1-5225-3619-2.ch007

Buluk Eşitti, B. (2021). COVID-19 and Alternative Tourism: New Destinations and New Tourism Products. In M. Demir, A. Dalgıç, & F. Ergen (Eds.), *Handbook of Research on the Impacts and Implications of COVID-19 on the Tourism Industry* (pp. 786–805). IGI Global. https://doi.org/10.4018/978-1-7998-8231-2.ch038

Bureš, V. (2018). Industry 4.0 From the Systems Engineering Perspective: Alternative Holistic Framework Development. In R. Brunet-Thornton & F. Martinez (Eds.), *Analyzing the Impacts of Industry 4.0 in Modern Business Environments* (pp. 199–223). Hershey, PA: IGI Global. doi:10.4018/978-1-5225-3468-6.ch011

Buzady, Z. (2017). Resolving the Magic Cube of Effective Case Teaching: Benchmarking Case Teaching Practices in Emerging Markets – Insights from the Central European University Business School, Hungary. In D. Latusek (Ed.), *Case Studies as a Teaching Tool in Management Education* (pp. 79–103). Hershey, PA: IGI Global. doi:10.4018/978-1-5225-0770-3.ch005

Camillo, A. (2021). *Legal Matters, Risk Management, and Risk Prevention: From Forming a Business to Legal Representation*. IGI Global. doi:10.4018/978-1-7998-4342-9.ch004

Căpusneanu, S., & Topor, D. I. (2018). Business Ethics and Cost Management in SMEs: Theories of Business Ethics and Cost Management Ethos. In I. Oncioiu (Ed.), *Ethics and Decision-Making for Sustainable Business Practices* (pp. 109–127). Hershey, PA: IGI Global. doi:10.4018/978-1-5225-3773-1.ch007

Chan, R. L., Mo, P. L., & Moon, K. K. (2018). Strategic and Tactical Measures in Managing Enterprise Risks: A Study of the Textile and Apparel Industry. In K. Strang, M. Korstanje, & N. Vajjhala (Eds.), *Research, Practices, and Innovations in Global Risk and Contingency Management* (pp. 1–19). Hershey, PA: IGI Global. doi:10.4018/978-1-5225-4754-9.ch001

Charlier, S. D., Burke-Smalley, L. A., & Fisher, S. L. (2018). Undergraduate Programs in the U.S: A Contextual and Content-Based Analysis. In J. Mendy (Ed.), *Teaching Human Resources and Organizational Behavior at the College Level* (pp. 26–57). Hershey, PA: IGI Global. doi:10.4018/978-1-5225-2820-3.ch002

Chumillas, J., Güell, M., & Quer, P. (2022). The Use of ICT in Tourist and Educational Literary Routes: The Role of the Guide. In C. Ramos, S. Quinteiro, & A. Gonçalves (Eds.), *ICT as Innovator Between Tourism and Culture* (pp. 15–29). IGI Global. https://doi.org/10.4018/978-1-7998-8165-0.ch002

Dahlberg, T., Kivijärvi, H., & Saarinen, T. (2017). IT Investment Consistency and Other Factors Influencing the Success of IT Performance. In S. De Haes & W. Van Grembergen (Eds.), *Strategic IT Governance and Alignment in Business Settings* (pp. 176–208). Hershey, PA: IGI Global. doi:10.4018/978-1-5225-0861-8.ch007

Damnjanović, A. M. (2017). Knowledge Management Optimization through IT and E-Business Utilization: A Qualitative Study on Serbian SMEs. In M. Vemić (Ed.), *Optimal Management Strategies in Small and Medium Enterprises* (pp. 249–267). Hershey, PA: IGI Global. doi:10.4018/978-1-5225-1949-2.ch012

Daneshpour, H. (2017). Integrating Sustainable Development into Project Portfolio Management through Application of Open Innovation. In M. Vemić (Ed.), *Optimal Management Strategies in Small and Medium Enterprises* (pp. 370–387). Hershey, PA: IGI Global. doi:10.4018/978-1-5225-1949-2.ch017

Daniel, A. D., & Reis de Castro, V. (2018). Entrepreneurship Education: How to Measure the Impact on Nascent Entrepreneurs. In A. Carrizo Moreira, J. Guilherme Leitão Dantas, & F. Manuel Valente (Eds.), *Nascent Entrepreneurship and Successful New Venture Creation* (pp. 85–110). Hershey, PA: IGI Global. doi:10.4018/978-1-5225-2936-1.ch004

David, R., Swami, B. N., & Tangirala, S. (2018). Ethics Impact on Knowledge Management in Organizational Development: A Case Study. In N. Baporikar (Ed.), *Global Practices in Knowledge Management for Societal and Organizational Development* (pp. 19–45). Hershey, PA: IGI Global. doi:10.4018/978-1-5225-3009-1.ch002

De Uña-Álvarez, E., & Villarino-Pérez, M. (2022). Fostering Ecocultural Resources, Identity, and Tourism in Inland Territories (Galicia, NW Spain). In G. Fernandes (Ed.), *Challenges and New Opportunities for Tourism in Inland Territories: Ecocultural Resources and Sustainable Initiatives* (pp. 1-16). IGI Global. https://doi.org/10.4018/978-1-7998-7339-6.ch001

Delias, P., & Lakiotaki, K. (2018). Discovering Process Horizontal Boundaries to Facilitate Process Comprehension. *International Journal of Operations Research and Information Systems, 9*(2), 1–31. doi:10.4018/IJORIS.2018040101

Denholm, J., & Lee-Davies, L. (2018). Success Factors for Games in Business and Project Management. In *Enhancing Education and Training Initiatives Through Serious Games* (pp. 34–68). Hershey, PA: IGI Global. doi:10.4018/978-1-5225-3689-5.ch002

Deshpande, M. (2017). Best Practices in Management Institutions for Global Leadership: Policy Aspects. In N. Baporikar (Ed.), *Management Education for Global Leadership* (pp. 1–27). Hershey, PA: IGI Global. doi:10.4018/978-1-5225-1013-0.ch001

Deshpande, M. (2018). Policy Perspectives for SMEs Knowledge Management. In N. Baporikar (Ed.), *Knowledge Integration Strategies for Entrepreneurship and Sustainability* (pp. 23–46). Hershey, PA: IGI Global. doi:10.4018/978-1-5225-5115-7.ch002

Dezdar, S. (2017). ERP Implementation Projects in Asian Countries: A Comparative Study on Iran and China. *International Journal of Information Technology Project Management*, *8*(3), 52–68. doi:10.4018/IJITPM.2017070104

Domingos, D., Respício, A., & Martinho, R. (2017). Reliability of IoT-Aware BPMN Healthcare Processes. In C. Reis & M. Maximiano (Eds.), *Internet of Things and Advanced Application in Healthcare* (pp. 214–248). Hershey, PA: IGI Global. doi:10.4018/978-1-5225-1820-4.ch008

Dosumu, O., Hussain, J., & El-Gohary, H. (2017). An Exploratory Study of the Impact of Government Policies on the Development of Small and Medium Enterprises in Developing Countries: The Case of Nigeria. *International Journal of Customer Relationship Marketing and Management*, *8*(4), 51–62. doi:10.4018/IJCRMM.2017100104

Durst, S., Bruns, G., & Edvardsson, I. R. (2017). Retaining Knowledge in Smaller Building and Construction Firms. *International Journal of Knowledge and Systems Science*, *8*(3), 1–12. doi:10.4018/IJKSS.2017070101

Edvardsson, I. R., & Durst, S. (2017). Outsourcing, Knowledge, and Learning: A Critical Review. *International Journal of Knowledge-Based Organizations*, *7*(2), 13–26. doi:10.4018/IJKBO.2017040102

Edwards, J. S. (2018). Integrating Knowledge Management and Business Processes. In M. Khosrow-Pour, D.B.A. (Ed.), Encyclopedia of Information Science and Technology, Fourth Edition (pp. 5046-5055). Hershey, PA: IGI Global. doi:10.4018/978-1-5225-2255-3.ch437

Eichelberger, S., & Peters, M. (2021). Family Firm Management in Turbulent Times: Opportunities for Responsible Tourism. In A. Zehrer, G. Glowka, K. Schwaiger, & V. Ranacher-Lackner (Eds.), *Resiliency Models and Addressing Future Risks for Family Firms in the Tourism Industry* (pp. 103–124). IGI Global. https://doi.org/10.4018/978-1-7998-7352-5.ch005

Eide, D., Hjalager, A., & Hansen, M. (2022). Innovative Certifications in Adventure Tourism: Attributes and Diffusion. In R. Augusto Costa, F. Brandão, Z. Breda, & C. Costa (Eds.), *Planning and Managing the Experience Economy in Tourism* (pp. 161-175). IGI Global. https://doi.org/10.4018/978-1-7998-8775-1.ch009

Ejiogu, A. O. (2018). Economics of Farm Management. In *Agricultural Finance and Opportunities for Investment and Expansion* (pp. 56–72). Hershey, PA: IGI Global. doi:10.4018/978-1-5225-3059-6.ch003

Ekanem, I., & Abiade, G. E. (2018). Factors Influencing the Use of E-Commerce by Small Enterprises in Nigeria. *International Journal of ICT Research in Africa and the Middle East*, *7*(1), 37–53. doi:10.4018/IJICTRAME.2018010103

Ekanem, I., & Alrossais, L. A. (2017). Succession Challenges Facing Family Businesses in Saudi Arabia. In P. Zgheib (Ed.), *Entrepreneurship and Business Innovation in the Middle East* (pp. 122–146). Hershey, PA: IGI Global. doi:10.4018/978-1-5225-2066-5.ch007

El Faquih, L., & Fredj, M. (2017). Ontology-Based Framework for Quality in Configurable Process Models. *Journal of Electronic Commerce in Organizations*, *15*(2), 48–60. doi:10.4018/JECO.2017040104

Faisal, M. N., & Talib, F. (2017). Building Ambidextrous Supply Chains in SMEs: How to Tackle the Barriers? *International Journal of Information Systems and Supply Chain Management*, *10*(4), 80–100. doi:10.4018/IJISSCM.2017100105

Fernandes, T. M., Gomes, J., & Romão, M. (2017). Investments in E-Government: A Benefit Management Case Study. *International Journal of Electronic Government Research*, *13*(3), 1–17. doi:10.4018/IJEGR.2017070101

Figueira, L. M., Honrado, G. R., & Dionísio, M. S. (2021). Human Capital Management in the Tourism Industry in Portugal. In V. Costa, A. Moura, & M. Mira (Eds.), *Handbook of Research on Human Capital and People Management in the Tourism Industry* (pp. 1–19). IGI Global. doi:10.4018/978-1-7998-4318-4.ch001

Gao, S. S., Oreal, S., & Zhang, J. (2018). Contemporary Financial Risk Management Perceptions and Practices of Small-Sized Chinese Businesses. In I. Management Association (Ed.), Global Business Expansion: Concepts, Methodologies, Tools, and Applications (pp. 917-931). Hershey, PA: IGI Global. doi:10.4018/978-1-5225-5481-3.ch041

Garg, R., & Berning, S. C. (2017). Indigenous Chinese Management Philosophies: Key Concepts and Relevance for Modern Chinese Firms. In B. Christiansen & G. Koc (Eds.), *Transcontinental Strategies for Industrial Development and Economic Growth* (pp. 43–57). Hershey, PA: IGI Global. doi:10.4018/978-1-5225-2160-0.ch003

Gencer, Y. G. (2017). Supply Chain Management in Retailing Business. In U. Akkucuk (Ed.), *Ethics and Sustainability in Global Supply Chain Management* (pp. 197–210). Hershey, PA: IGI Global. doi:10.4018/978-1-5225-2036-8.ch011

Gera, R., Arora, S., & Malik, S. (2021). Emotional Labor in the Tourism Industry: Strategies, Antecedents, and Outcomes. In V. Costa, A. Moura, & M. Mira (Eds.), *Handbook of Research on Human Capital and People Management in the Tourism Industry* (pp. 73–91). IGI Global. https://doi.org/10.4018/978-1-7998-4318-4.ch004

Giacosa, E. (2018). The Increasing of the Regional Development Thanks to the Luxury Business Innovation. In L. Carvalho (Ed.), *Handbook of Research on Entrepreneurial Ecosystems and Social Dynamics in a Globalized World* (pp. 260–273). Hershey, PA: IGI Global. doi:10.4018/978-1-5225-3525-6.ch011

Glowka, G., Tusch, M., & Zehrer, A. (2021). The Risk Perception of Family Business Owner-Manager in the Tourism Industry: A Qualitative Comparison of the Intra-Firm Senior and Junior Generation. In A. Zehrer, G. Glowka, K. Schwaiger, & V. Ranacher-Lackner (Eds.), *Resiliency Models and Addressing Future Risks for Family Firms in the Tourism Industry* (pp. 126–153). IGI Global. https://doi.org/10.4018/978-1-7998-7352-5.ch006

Glykas, M., & George, J. (2017). Quality and Process Management Systems in the UAE Maritime Industry. *International Journal of Productivity Management and Assessment Technologies*, *5*(1), 20–39. doi:10.4018/IJPMAT.2017010102

Glykas, M., Valiris, G., Kokkinaki, A., & Koutsoukou, Z. (2018). Banking Business Process Management Implementation. *International Journal of Productivity Management and Assessment Technologies*, *6*(1), 50–69. doi:10.4018/IJPMAT.2018010104

Gomes, J., & Romão, M. (2017). The Balanced Scorecard: Keeping Updated and Aligned with Today's Business Trends. *International Journal of Productivity Management and Assessment Technologies*, *5*(2), 1–15. doi:10.4018/IJPMAT.2017070101

Gomes, J., & Romão, M. (2017). Aligning Information Systems and Technology with Benefit Management and Balanced Scorecard. In S. De Haes & W. Van Grembergen (Eds.), *Strategic IT Governance and Alignment in Business Settings* (pp. 112–131). Hershey, PA: IGI Global. doi:10.4018/978-1-5225-0861-8.ch005

Goyal, A. (2021). Communicating and Building Destination Brands With New Media. In M. Dinis, L. Bonixe, S. Lamy, & Z. Breda (Eds.), *Impact of New Media in Tourism* (pp. 1-20). IGI Global. https://doi.org/10.4018/978-1-7998-7095-1.ch001

Grefen, P., & Turetken, O. (2017). Advanced Business Process Management in Networked E-Business Scenarios. *International Journal of E-Business Research, 13*(4), 70–104. doi:10.4018/IJEBR.2017100105

Guasca, M., Van Broeck, A. M., & Vanneste, D. (2021). Tourism and the Social Reintegration of Colombian Ex-Combatants. In J. da Silva, Z. Breda, & F. Carbone (Eds.), *Role and Impact of Tourism in Peacebuilding and Conflict Transformation* (pp. 66-86). IGI Global. https://doi.org/10.4018/978-1-7998-5053-3.ch005

Haider, A., & Saetang, S. (2017). Strategic IT Alignment in Service Sector. In S. Rozenes & Y. Cohen (Eds.), *Handbook of Research on Strategic Alliances and Value Co-Creation in the Service Industry* (pp. 231–258). Hershey, PA: IGI Global. doi:10.4018/978-1-5225-2084-9.ch012

Hajilari, A. B., Ghadaksaz, M., & Fasghandis, G. S. (2017). Assessing Organizational Readiness for Implementing ERP System Using Fuzzy Expert System Approach. *International Journal of Enterprise Information Systems, 13*(1), 67–85. doi:10.4018/IJEIS.2017010105

Haldorai, A., Ramu, A., & Murugan, S. (2018). Social Aware Cognitive Radio Networks: Effectiveness of Social Networks as a Strategic Tool for Organizational Business Management. In H. Bansal, G. Shrivastava, G. Nguyen, & L. Stanciu (Eds.), *Social Network Analytics for Contemporary Business Organizations* (pp. 188–202). Hershey, PA: IGI Global. doi:10.4018/978-1-5225-5097-6.ch010

Hall, O. P. Jr. (2017). Social Media Driven Management Education. *International Journal of Knowledge-Based Organizations, 7*(2), 43–59. doi:10.4018/IJKBO.2017040104

Hanifah, H., Halim, H. A., Ahmad, N. H., & Vafaei-Zadeh, A. (2017). Innovation Culture as a Mediator Between Specific Human Capital and Innovation Performance Among Bumiputera SMEs in Malaysia. In N. Ahmad, T. Ramayah, H. Halim, & S. Rahman (Eds.), *Handbook of Research on Small and Medium Enterprises in Developing Countries* (pp. 261–279). Hershey, PA: IGI Global. doi:10.4018/978-1-5225-2165-5.ch012

Hartlieb, S., & Silvius, G. (2017). Handling Uncertainty in Project Management and Business Development: Similarities and Differences. In Y. Raydugin (Ed.), *Handbook of Research on Leveraging Risk and Uncertainties for Effective Project Management* (pp. 337–362). Hershey, PA: IGI Global. doi:10.4018/978-1-5225-1790-0.ch016

Hass, K. B. (2017). Living on the Edge: Managing Project Complexity. In Y. Raydugin (Ed.), *Handbook of Research on Leveraging Risk and Uncertainties for Effective Project Management* (pp. 177–201). Hershey, PA: IGI Global. doi:10.4018/978-1-5225-1790-0.ch009

Hawking, P., & Carmine Sellitto, C. (2017). Developing an Effective Strategy for Organizational Business Intelligence. In M. Tavana (Ed.), *Enterprise Information Systems and the Digitalization of Business Functions* (pp. 222–237). Hershey, PA: IGI Global. doi:10.4018/978-1-5225-2382-6.ch010

Hawking, P., & Sellitto, C. (2017). A Fast-Moving Consumer Goods Company and Business Intelligence Strategy Development. *International Journal of Enterprise Information Systems, 13*(2), 22–33. doi:10.4018/IJEIS.2017040102

Hawking, P., & Sellitto, C. (2017). Business Intelligence Strategy: Two Case Studies. *International Journal of Business Intelligence Research, 8*(2), 17–30. doi:10.4018/IJBIR.2017070102

Hee, W. J., Jalleh, G., Lai, H., & Lin, C. (2017). E-Commerce and IT Projects: Evaluation and Management Issues in Australian and Taiwanese Hospitals. *International Journal of Public Health Management and Ethics, 2*(1), 69–90. doi:10.4018/IJPHME.2017010104

Hernandez, A. A. (2018). Exploring the Factors to Green IT Adoption of SMEs in the Philippines. *Journal of Cases on Information Technology, 20*(2), 49–66. doi:10.4018/JCIT.2018040104

Hollman, A., Bickford, S., & Hollman, T. (2017). Cyber InSecurity: A Post-Mortem Attempt to Assess Cyber Problems from IT and Business Management Perspectives. *Journal of Cases on Information Technology, 19*(3), 42–70. doi:10.4018/JCIT.2017070104

Ibrahim, F., & Zainin, N. M. (2021). Exploring the Technological Impacts: The Case of Museums in Brunei Darussalam. *International Journal of Tourism and Hospitality Management in the Digital Age, 5*(1), 1–18. https://doi.org/10.4018/IJTHMDA.2021010101

Igbinakhase, I. (2017). Responsible and Sustainable Management Practices in Developing and Developed Business Environments. In Z. Fields (Ed.), *Collective Creativity for Responsible and Sustainable Business Practice* (pp. 180–207). Hershey, PA: IGI Global. doi:10.4018/978-1-5225-1823-5.ch010

Iwata, J. J., & Hoskins, R. G. (2017). Managing Indigenous Knowledge in Tanzania: A Business Perspective. In P. Jain & N. Mnjama (Eds.), *Managing Knowledge Resources and Records in Modern Organizations* (pp. 198–214). Hershey, PA: IGI Global. doi:10.4018/978-1-5225-1965-2.ch012

Jain, P. (2017). Ethical and Legal Issues in Knowledge Management Life-Cycle in Business. In P. Jain & N. Mnjama (Eds.), *Managing Knowledge Resources and Records in Modern Organizations* (pp. 82–101). Hershey, PA: IGI Global. doi:10.4018/978-1-5225-1965-2.ch006

James, S., & Hauli, E. (2017). Holistic Management Education at Tanzanian Rural Development Planning Institute. In N. Baporikar (Ed.), *Management Education for Global Leadership* (pp. 112–136). Hershey, PA: IGI Global. doi:10.4018/978-1-5225-1013-0.ch006

Janošková, M., Csikósová, A., & Čulková, K. (2018). Measurement of Company Performance as Part of Its Strategic Management. In R. Leon (Ed.), *Managerial Strategies for Business Sustainability During Turbulent Times* (pp. 309–335). Hershey, PA: IGI Global. doi:10.4018/978-1-5225-2716-9.ch017

Jean-Vasile, A., & Alecu, A. (2017). Theoretical and Practical Approaches in Understanding the Influences of Cost-Productivity-Profit Trinomial in Contemporary Enterprises. In A. Jean Vasile & D. Nicolò (Eds.), *Sustainable Entrepreneurship and Investments in the Green Economy* (pp. 28–62). Hershey, PA: IGI Global. doi:10.4018/978-1-5225-2075-7.ch002

Joia, L. A., & Correia, J. C. (2018). CIO Competencies From the IT Professional Perspective: Insights From Brazil. *Journal of Global Information Management, 26*(2), 74–103. doi:10.4018/JGIM.2018040104

Juma, A., & Mzera, N. (2017). Knowledge Management and Records Management and Competitive Advantage in Business. In P. Jain & N. Mnjama (Eds.), *Managing Knowledge Resources and Records in Modern Organizations* (pp. 15–28). Hershey, PA: IGI Global. doi:10.4018/978-1-5225-1965-2.ch002

K., I., & A, V. (2018). Monitoring and Auditing in the Cloud. In K. Munir (Ed.), *Cloud Computing Technologies for Green Enterprises* (pp. 318-350). Hershey, PA: IGI Global. https://doi.org/ doi:10.4018/978-1-5225-3038-1.ch013

Kabra, G., Ghosh, V., & Ramesh, A. (2018). Enterprise Integrated Business Process Management and Business Intelligence Framework for Business Process Sustainability. In A. Paul, D. Bhattacharyya, & S. Anand (Eds.), *Green Initiatives for Business Sustainability and Value Creation* (pp. 228–238). Hershey, PA: IGI Global. doi:10.4018/978-1-5225-2662-9.ch010

Kaoud, M. (2017). Investigation of Customer Knowledge Management: A Case Study Research. *International Journal of Service Science, Management, Engineering, and Technology, 8*(2), 12–22. doi:10.4018/IJSSMET.2017040102

Katuu, S. (2018). A Comparative Assessment of Enterprise Content Management Maturity Models. In N. Gwangwava & M. Mutingi (Eds.), *E-Manufacturing and E-Service Strategies in Contemporary Organizations* (pp. 93–118). Hershey, PA: IGI Global. doi:10.4018/978-1-5225-3628-4.ch005

Khan, M. Y., & Abir, T. (2022). The Role of Social Media Marketing in the Tourism and Hospitality Industry: A Conceptual Study on Bangladesh. In C. Ramos, S. Quinteiro, & A. Gonçalves (Eds.), *ICT as Innovator Between Tourism and Culture* (pp. 213–229). IGI Global. https://doi.org/10.4018/978-1-7998-8165-0.ch013

Kinnunen, S., Ylä-Kujala, A., Marttonen-Arola, S., Kärri, T., & Baglee, D. (2018). Internet of Things in Asset Management: Insights from Industrial Professionals and Academia. *International Journal of Service Science, Management, Engineering, and Technology, 9*(2), 104–119. doi:10.4018/IJSSMET.2018040105

Klein, A. Z., Sabino de Freitas, A., Machado, L., Freitas, J. C. Jr, Graziola, P. G. Jr, & Schlemmer, E. (2017). Virtual Worlds Applications for Management Education. In L. Tomei (Ed.), *Exploring the New Era of Technology-Infused Education* (pp. 279–299). Hershey, PA: IGI Global. doi:10.4018/978-1-5225-1709-2.ch017

Kővári, E., Saleh, M., & Steinbachné Hajmásy, G. (2022). The Impact of Corporate Digital Responsibility (CDR) on Internal Stakeholders' Satisfaction in Hungarian Upscale Hotels. In M. Valeri (Ed.), *New Governance and Management in Touristic Destinations* (pp. 35–51). IGI Global. https://doi.org/10.4018/978-1-6684-3889-3.ch003

Kożuch, B., & Jabłoński, A. (2017). Adopting the Concept of Business Models in Public Management. In M. Lewandowski & B. Kożuch (Eds.), *Public Sector Entrepreneurship and the Integration of Innovative Business Models* (pp. 10–46). Hershey, PA: IGI Global. doi:10.4018/978-1-5225-2215-7.ch002

Kumar, J., Adhikary, A., & Jha, A. (2017). Small Active Investors' Perceptions and Preferences Towards Tax Saving Mutual Fund Schemes in Eastern India: An Empirical Note. *International Journal of Asian Business and Information Management, 8*(2), 35–45. doi:10.4018/IJABIM.2017040103

Latusi, S., & Fissore, M. (2021). Pilgrimage Routes to Happiness: Comparing the Camino de Santiago and Via Francigena. In A. Perinotto, V. Mayer, & J. Soares (Eds.), *Rebuilding and Restructuring the Tourism Industry: Infusion of Happiness and Quality of Life* (pp. 157–182). IGI Global. https://doi.org/10.4018/978-1-7998-7239-9.ch008

Lavassani, K. M., & Movahedi, B. (2017). Applications Driven Information Systems: Beyond Networks toward Business Ecosystems. *International Journal of Innovation in the Digital Economy*, *8*(1), 61–75. doi:10.4018/IJIDE.2017010104

Lazzareschi, V. H., & Brito, M. S. (2017). Strategic Information Management: Proposal of Business Project Model. In G. Jamil, A. Soares, & C. Pessoa (Eds.), *Handbook of Research on Information Management for Effective Logistics and Supply Chains* (pp. 59–88). Hershey, PA: IGI Global. doi:10.4018/978-1-5225-0973-8.ch004

Lechuga Sancho, M. P., & Martín Navarro, A. (2022). Evolution of the Literature on Social Responsibility in the Tourism Sector: A Systematic Literature Review. In G. Fernandes (Ed.), *Challenges and New Opportunities for Tourism in Inland Territories: Ecocultural Resources and Sustainable Initiatives* (pp. 169–186). IGI Global. https://doi.org/10.4018/978-1-7998-7339-6.ch010

Lederer, M., Kurz, M., & Lazarov, P. (2017). Usage and Suitability of Methods for Strategic Business Process Initiatives: A Multi Case Study Research. *International Journal of Productivity Management and Assessment Technologies*, *5*(1), 40–51. doi:10.4018/IJPMAT.2017010103

Lee, I. (2017). A Social Enterprise Business Model and a Case Study of Pacific Community Ventures (PCV). In V. Potocan, M. Üngan, & Z. Nedelko (Eds.), *Handbook of Research on Managerial Solutions in Non-Profit Organizations* (pp. 182–204). Hershey, PA: IGI Global. doi:10.4018/978-1-5225-0731-4.ch009

Leon, L. A., Seal, K. C., Przasnyski, Z. H., & Wiedenman, I. (2017). Skills and Competencies Required for Jobs in Business Analytics: A Content Analysis of Job Advertisements Using Text Mining. *International Journal of Business Intelligence Research*, *8*(1), 1–25. doi:10.4018/IJBIR.2017010101

Levy, C. L., & Elias, N. I. (2017). SOHO Users' Perceptions of Reliability and Continuity of Cloud-Based Services. In M. Moore (Ed.), *Cybersecurity Breaches and Issues Surrounding Online Threat Protection* (pp. 248–287). Hershey, PA: IGI Global. doi:10.4018/978-1-5225-1941-6.ch011

Levy, M. (2018). Change Management Serving Knowledge Management and Organizational Development: Reflections and Review. In N. Baporikar (Ed.), *Global Practices in Knowledge Management for Societal and Organizational Development* (pp. 256–270). Hershey, PA: IGI Global. doi:10.4018/978-1-5225-3009-1.ch012

Lewandowski, M. (2017). Public Organizations and Business Model Innovation: The Role of Public Service Design. In M. Lewandowski & B. Kożuch (Eds.), *Public Sector Entrepreneurship and the Integration of Innovative Business Models* (pp. 47–72). Hershey, PA: IGI Global. doi:10.4018/978-1-5225-2215-7.ch003

Lhannaoui, H., Kabbaj, M. I., & Bakkoury, Z. (2017). A Survey of Risk-Aware Business Process Modelling. *International Journal of Risk and Contingency Management*, *6*(3), 14–26. doi:10.4018/IJRCM.2017070102

Li, J., Sun, W., Jiang, W., Yang, H., & Zhang, L. (2017). How the Nature of Exogenous Shocks and Crises Impact Company Performance?: The Effects of Industry Characteristics. *International Journal of Risk and Contingency Management*, *6*(4), 40–55. doi:10.4018/IJRCM.2017100103

Lopez-Fernandez, M., Perez-Perez, M., Serrano-Bedia, A., & Cobo-Gonzalez, A. (2021). Small and Medium Tourism Enterprise Survival in Times of Crisis: "El Capricho de Gaudí. In D. Toubes & N. Araújo-Vila (Eds.), *Risk, Crisis, and Disaster Management in Small and Medium-Sized Tourism Enterprises* (pp. 103–129). IGI Global. doi:10.4018/978-1-7998-6996-2.ch005

Mahajan, A., Maidullah, S., & Hossain, M. R. (2022). Experience Toward Smart Tour Guide Apps in Travelling: An Analysis of Users' Reviews on Audio Odigos and Trip My Way. In R. Augusto Costa, F. Brandão, Z. Breda, & C. Costa (Eds.), *Planning and Managing the Experience Economy in Tourism* (pp. 255-273). IGI Global. https://doi.org/10.4018/978-1-7998-8775-1.ch014

Malega, P. (2017). Small and Medium Enterprises in the Slovak Republic: Status and Competitiveness of SMEs in the Global Markets and Possibilities of Optimization. In M. Vemić (Ed.), *Optimal Management Strategies in Small and Medium Enterprises* (pp. 102–124). Hershey, PA: IGI Global. doi:10.4018/978-1-5225-1949-2.ch006

Malewska, K. M. (2017). Intuition in Decision-Making on the Example of a Non-Profit Organization. In V. Potocan, M. Üngan, & Z. Nedelko (Eds.), *Handbook of Research on Managerial Solutions in Non-Profit Organizations* (pp. 378–399). Hershey, PA: IGI Global. doi:10.4018/978-1-5225-0731-4.ch018

Maroofi, F. (2017). Entrepreneurial Orientation and Organizational Learning Ability Analysis for Innovation and Firm Performance. In N. Baporikar (Ed.), *Innovation and Shifting Perspectives in Management Education* (pp. 144–165). Hershey, PA: IGI Global. doi:10.4018/978-1-5225-1019-2.ch007

Marques, M., Moleiro, D., Brito, T. M., & Marques, T. (2021). Customer Relationship Management as an Important Relationship Marketing Tool: The Case of the Hospitality Industry in Estoril Coast. In M. Dinis, L. Bonixe, S. Lamy, & Z. Breda (Eds.), Impact of New Media in Tourism (pp. 39-56). IGI Global. https://doi.org/doi:10.4018/978-1-7998-7095-1.ch003

Martins, P. V., & Zacarias, M. (2017). A Web-based Tool for Business Process Improvement. *International Journal of Web Portals*, *9*(2), 68–84. doi:10.4018/IJWP.2017070104

Matthies, B., & Coners, A. (2017). Exploring the Conceptual Nature of e-Business Projects. *Journal of Electronic Commerce in Organizations*, *15*(3), 33–63. doi:10.4018/JECO.2017070103

Mayer, V. F., Fraga, C. C., & Silva, L. C. (2021). Contributions of Neurosciences to Studies of Well-Being in Tourism. In A. Perinotto, V. Mayer, & J. Soares (Eds.), *Rebuilding and Restructuring the Tourism Industry: Infusion of Happiness and Quality of Life* (pp. 108–128). IGI Global. https://doi.org/10.4018/978-1-7998-7239-9.ch006

McKee, J. (2018). Architecture as a Tool to Solve Business Planning Problems. In M. Khosrow-Pour, D.B.A. (Ed.), Encyclopedia of Information Science and Technology, Fourth Edition (pp. 573-586). Hershey, PA: IGI Global. doi:10.4018/978-1-5225-2255-3.ch050

McMurray, A. J., Cross, J., & Caponecchia, C. (2018). The Risk Management Profession in Australia: Business Continuity Plan Practices. In N. Bajgoric (Ed.), *Always-On Enterprise Information Systems for Modern Organizations* (pp. 112–129). Hershey, PA: IGI Global. doi:10.4018/978-1-5225-3704-5.ch006

Meddah, I. H., & Belkadi, K. (2018). Mining Patterns Using Business Process Management. In R. Hamou (Ed.), *Handbook of Research on Biomimicry in Information Retrieval and Knowledge Management* (pp. 78–89). Hershey, PA: IGI Global. doi:10.4018/978-1-5225-3004-6.ch005

Melian, A. G., & Camprubí, R. (2021). The Accessibility of Museum Websites: The Case of Barcelona. In C. Eusébio, L. Teixeira, & M. Carneiro (Eds.), *ICT Tools and Applications for Accessible Tourism* (pp. 234–255). IGI Global. https://doi.org/10.4018/978-1-7998-6428-8.ch011

Mendes, L. (2017). TQM and Knowledge Management: An Integrated Approach Towards Tacit Knowledge Management. In D. Jaziri-Bouagina & G. Jamil (Eds.), *Handbook of Research on Tacit Knowledge Management for Organizational Success* (pp. 236–263). Hershey, PA: IGI Global. doi:10.4018/978-1-5225-2394-9.ch009

Menezes, V. D., & Cavagnaro, E. (2021). Communicating Sustainable Initiatives in the Hotel Industry: The Case of the Hotel Jakarta Amsterdam. In F. Brandão, Z. Breda, R. Costa, & C. Costa (Eds.), *Handbook of Research on the Role of Tourism in Achieving Sustainable Development Goals* (pp. 224-234). IGI Global. https://doi.org/10.4018/978-1-7998-5691-7.ch013

Menezes, V. D., & Cavagnaro, E. (2021). Communicating Sustainable Initiatives in the Hotel Industry: The Case of the Hotel Jakarta Amsterdam. In F. Brandão, Z. Breda, R. Costa, & C. Costa (Eds.), *Handbook of Research on the Role of Tourism in Achieving Sustainable Development Goals* (pp. 224-234). IGI Global. https://doi.org/10.4018/978-1-7998-5691-7.ch013

Mitas, O., Bastiaansen, M., & Boode, W. (2022). If You're Happy, I'm Happy: Emotion Contagion at a Tourist Information Center. In R. Augusto Costa, F. Brandão, Z. Breda, & C. Costa (Eds.), *Planning and Managing the Experience Economy in Tourism* (pp. 122-140). IGI Global. https://doi.org/10.4018/978-1-7998-8775-1.ch007

Mnjama, N. M. (2017). Preservation of Recorded Information in Public and Private Sector Organizations. In P. Jain & N. Mnjama (Eds.), *Managing Knowledge Resources and Records in Modern Organizations* (pp. 149–167). Hershey, PA: IGI Global. doi:10.4018/978-1-5225-1965-2.ch009

Mokoqama, M., & Fields, Z. (2017). Principles of Responsible Management Education (PRME): Call for Responsible Management Education. In Z. Fields (Ed.), *Collective Creativity for Responsible and Sustainable Business Practice* (pp. 229–241). Hershey, PA: IGI Global. doi:10.4018/978-1-5225-1823-5.ch012

Monteiro, A., Lopes, S., & Carbone, F. (2021). Academic Mobility: Bridging Tourism and Peace Education. In J. da Silva, Z. Breda, & F. Carbone (Eds.), *Role and Impact of Tourism in Peacebuilding and Conflict Transformation* (pp. 275-301). IGI Global. https://doi.org/10.4018/978-1-7998-5053-3.ch016

Muniapan, B. (2017). Philosophy and Management: The Relevance of Vedanta in Management. In P. Ordóñez de Pablos (Ed.), *Managerial Strategies and Solutions for Business Success in Asia* (pp. 124–139). Hershey, PA: IGI Global. doi:10.4018/978-1-5225-1886-0.ch007

Murad, S. E., & Dowaji, S. (2017). Using Value-Based Approach for Managing Cloud-Based Services. In A. Turuk, B. Sahoo, & S. Addya (Eds.), *Resource Management and Efficiency in Cloud Computing Environments* (pp. 33–60). Hershey, PA: IGI Global. doi:10.4018/978-1-5225-1721-4.ch002

Mutahar, A. M., Daud, N. M., Thurasamy, R., Isaac, O., & Abdulsalam, R. (2018). The Mediating of Perceived Usefulness and Perceived Ease of Use: The Case of Mobile Banking in Yemen. *International Journal of Technology Diffusion*, *9*(2), 21–40. doi:10.4018/IJTD.2018040102

Naidoo, V. (2017). E-Learning and Management Education at African Universities. In N. Baporikar (Ed.), *Management Education for Global Leadership* (pp. 181–201). Hershey, PA: IGI Global. doi:10.4018/978-1-5225-1013-0.ch009

Naidoo, V., & Igbinakhase, I. (2018). Opportunities and Challenges of Knowledge Retention in SMEs. In N. Baporikar (Ed.), *Knowledge Integration Strategies for Entrepreneurship and Sustainability* (pp. 70–94). Hershey, PA: IGI Global. doi:10.4018/978-1-5225-5115-7.ch004

Naumov, N., & Costandachi, G. (2021). Creativity and Entrepreneurship: Gastronomic Tourism in Mexico. In J. Soares (Ed.), *Innovation and Entrepreneurial Opportunities in Community Tourism* (pp. 90–108). IGI Global. https://doi.org/10.4018/978-1-7998-4855-4.ch006

Nayak, S., & Prabhu, N. (2017). Paradigm Shift in Management Education: Need for a Cross Functional Perspective. In N. Baporikar (Ed.), *Management Education for Global Leadership* (pp. 241–255). Hershey, PA: IGI Global. doi:10.4018/978-1-5225-1013-0.ch012

Nedelko, Z., & Potocan, V. (2017). Management Solutions in Non-Profit Organizations: Case of Slovenia. In V. Potocan, M. Üngan, & Z. Nedelko (Eds.), *Handbook of Research on Managerial Solutions in Non-Profit Organizations* (pp. 1–22). Hershey, PA: IGI Global. doi:10.4018/978-1-5225-0731-4.ch001

Nedelko, Z., & Potocan, V. (2017). Priority of Management Tools Utilization among Managers: International Comparison. In V. Wang (Ed.), *Encyclopedia of Strategic Leadership and Management* (pp. 1083–1094). Hershey, PA: IGI Global. doi:10.4018/978-1-5225-1049-9.ch075

Nedelko, Z., Raudeliūnienė, J., & Črešnar, R. (2018). Knowledge Dynamics in Supply Chain Management. In N. Baporikar (Ed.), *Knowledge Integration Strategies for Entrepreneurship and Sustainability* (pp. 150–166). Hershey, PA: IGI Global. doi:10.4018/978-1-5225-5115-7.ch008

Nguyen, H. T., & Hipsher, S. A. (2018). Innovation and Creativity Used by Private Sector Firms in a Resources-Constrained Environment. In S. Hipsher (Ed.), *Examining the Private Sector's Role in Wealth Creation and Poverty Reduction* (pp. 219–238). Hershey, PA: IGI Global. doi:10.4018/978-1-5225-3117-3.ch010

Obicci, P. A. (2017). Risk Sharing in a Partnership. In *Risk Management Strategies in Public-Private Partnerships* (pp. 115–152). Hershey, PA: IGI Global. doi:10.4018/978-1-5225-2503-5.ch004

Obidallah, W. J., & Raahemi, B. (2017). Managing Changes in Service Oriented Virtual Organizations: A Structural and Procedural Framework to Facilitate the Process of Change. *Journal of Electronic Commerce in Organizations*, *15*(1), 59–83. doi:10.4018/JECO.2017010104

Ojo, O. (2017). Impact of Innovation on the Entrepreneurial Success in Selected Business Enterprises in South-West Nigeria. *International Journal of Innovation in the Digital Economy*, *8*(2), 29–38. doi:10.4018/IJIDE.2017040103

Okdinawati, L., Simatupang, T. M., & Sunitiyoso, Y. (2017). Multi-Agent Reinforcement Learning for Value Co-Creation of Collaborative Transportation Management (CTM). *International Journal of Information Systems and Supply Chain Management*, *10*(3), 84–95. doi:10.4018/IJISSCM.2017070105

Olivera, V. A., & Carrillo, I. M. (2021). Organizational Culture: A Key Element for the Development of Mexican Micro and Small Tourist Companies. In J. Soares (Ed.), *Innovation and Entrepreneurial Opportunities in Community Tourism* (pp. 227–242). IGI Global. doi:10.4018/978-1-7998-4855-4.ch013

Ossorio, M. (2022). Corporate Museum Experiences in Enogastronomic Tourism. In R. Augusto Costa, F. Brandão, Z. Breda, & C. Costa (Eds.), Planning and Managing the Experience Economy in Tourism (pp. 107-121). IGI Global. https://doi.org/doi:10.4018/978-1-7998-8775-1.ch006

Ossorio, M. (2022). Enogastronomic Tourism in Times of Pandemic. In G. Fernandes (Ed.), *Challenges and New Opportunities for Tourism in Inland Territories: Ecocultural Resources and Sustainable Initiatives* (pp. 241–255). IGI Global. https://doi.org/10.4018/978-1-7998-7339-6.ch014

Özekici, Y. K. (2022). ICT as an Acculturative Agent and Its Role in the Tourism Context: Introduction, Acculturation Theory, Progress of the Acculturation Theory in Extant Literature. In C. Ramos, S. Quinteiro, & A. Gonçalves (Eds.), *ICT as Innovator Between Tourism and Culture* (pp. 42–66). IGI Global. https://doi.org/10.4018/978-1-7998-8165-0.ch004

Pal, K. (2018). Building High Quality Big Data-Based Applications in Supply Chains. In A. Kumar & S. Saurav (Eds.), *Supply Chain Management Strategies and Risk Assessment in Retail Environments* (pp. 1–24). Hershey, PA: IGI Global. doi:10.4018/978-1-5225-3056-5.ch001

Palos-Sanchez, P. R., & Correia, M. B. (2018). Perspectives of the Adoption of Cloud Computing in the Tourism Sector. In J. Rodrigues, C. Ramos, P. Cardoso, & C. Henriques (Eds.), *Handbook of Research on Technological Developments for Cultural Heritage and eTourism Applications* (pp. 377–400). Hershey, PA: IGI Global. doi:10.4018/978-1-5225-2927-9.ch018

Papadopoulou, G. (2021). Promoting Gender Equality and Women Empowerment in the Tourism Sector. In F. Brandão, Z. Breda, R. Costa, & C. Costa (Eds.), Handbook of Research on the Role of Tourism in Achieving Sustainable Development Goals (pp. 152-174). IGI Global. https://doi.org/ doi:10.4018/978-1-7998-5691-7.ch009

Papp-Váry, Á. F., & Tóth, T. Z. (2022). Analysis of Budapest as a Film Tourism Destination. In R. Baleiro & R. Pereira (Eds.), *Global Perspectives on Literary Tourism and Film-Induced Tourism* (pp. 257-279). IGI Global. https://doi.org/10.4018/978-1-7998-8262-6.ch014

Patiño, B. E. (2017). New Generation Management by Convergence and Individual Identity: A Systemic and Human-Oriented Approach. In N. Baporikar (Ed.), *Innovation and Shifting Perspectives in Management Education* (pp. 119–143). Hershey, PA: IGI Global. doi:10.4018/978-1-5225-1019-2.ch006

Patro, C. S. (2021). Digital Tourism: Influence of E-Marketing Technology. In M. Dinis, L. Bonixe, S. Lamy, & Z. Breda (Eds.), *Impact of New Media in Tourism* (pp. 234-254). IGI Global. https://doi.org/10.4018/978-1-7998-7095-1.ch014

Pawliczek, A., & Rössler, M. (2017). Knowledge of Management Tools and Systems in SMEs: Knowledge Transfer in Management. In A. Bencsik (Ed.), *Knowledge Management Initiatives and Strategies in Small and Medium Enterprises* (pp. 180–203). Hershey, PA: IGI Global. doi:10.4018/978-1-5225-1642-2.ch009

Pejic-Bach, M., Omazic, M. A., Aleksic, A., & Zoroja, J. (2018). Knowledge-Based Decision Making: A Multi-Case Analysis. In R. Leon (Ed.), *Managerial Strategies for Business Sustainability During Turbulent Times* (pp. 160–184). Hershey, PA: IGI Global. doi:10.4018/978-1-5225-2716-9.ch009

Perano, M., Hysa, X., & Calabrese, M. (2018). Strategic Planning, Cultural Context, and Business Continuity Management: Business Cases in the City of Shkoder. In A. Presenza & L. Sheehan (Eds.), *Geopolitics and Strategic Management in the Global Economy* (pp. 57–77). Hershey, PA: IGI Global. doi:10.4018/978-1-5225-2673-5.ch004

Pereira, R., Mira da Silva, M., & Lapão, L. V. (2017). IT Governance Maturity Patterns in Portuguese Healthcare. In S. De Haes & W. Van Grembergen (Eds.), *Strategic IT Governance and Alignment in Business Settings* (pp. 24–52). Hershey, PA: IGI Global. doi:10.4018/978-1-5225-0861-8.ch002

Pérez-Uribe, R. I., Torres, D. A., Jurado, S. P., & Prada, D. M. (2018). Cloud Tools for the Development of Project Management in SMEs. In R. Perez-Uribe, C. Salcedo-Perez, & D. Ocampo-Guzman (Eds.), *Handbook of Research on Intrapreneurship and Organizational Sustainability in SMEs* (pp. 95–120). Hershey, PA: IGI Global. doi:10.4018/978-1-5225-3543-0.ch005

Petrisor, I., & Cozmiuc, D. (2017). Global Supply Chain Management Organization at Siemens in the Advent of Industry 4.0. In L. Saglietto & C. Cezanne (Eds.), *Global Intermediation and Logistics Service Providers* (pp. 123–142). Hershey, PA: IGI Global. doi:10.4018/978-1-5225-2133-4.ch007

Pierce, J. M., Velliaris, D. M., & Edwards, J. (2017). A Living Case Study: A Journey Not a Destination. In N. Silton (Ed.), *Exploring the Benefits of Creativity in Education, Media, and the Arts* (pp. 158–178). Hershey, PA: IGI Global. doi:10.4018/978-1-5225-0504-4.ch008

Pipia, S., & Pipia, S. (2021). Challenges of Religious Tourism in the Conflict Region: An Example of Jerusalem. In E. Alaverdov & M. Bari (Eds.), *Global Development of Religious Tourism* (pp. 135-148). IGI Global. https://doi.org/10.4018/978-1-7998-5792-1.ch009

Poulaki, P., Kritikos, A., Vasilakis, N., & Valeri, M. (2022). The Contribution of Female Creativity to the Development of Gastronomic Tourism in Greece: The Case of the Island of Naxos in the South Aegean Region. In M. Valeri (Ed.), *New Governance and Management in Touristic Destinations* (pp. 246–258). IGI Global. https://doi.org/10.4018/978-1-6684-3889-3.ch015

Radosavljevic, M., & Andjelkovic, A. (2017). Multi-Criteria Decision Making Approach for Choosing Business Process for the Improvement: Upgrading of the Six Sigma Methodology. In J. Stanković, P. Delias, S. Marinković, & S. Rochhia (Eds.), *Tools and Techniques for Economic Decision Analysis* (pp. 225–247). Hershey, PA: IGI Global. doi:10.4018/978-1-5225-0959-2.ch011

Radovic, V. M. (2017). Corporate Sustainability and Responsibility and Disaster Risk Reduction: A Serbian Overview. In M. Camilleri (Ed.), *CSR 2.0 and the New Era of Corporate Citizenship* (pp. 147–164). Hershey, PA: IGI Global. doi:10.4018/978-1-5225-1842-6.ch008

Raghunath, K. M., Devi, S. L., & Patro, C. S. (2018). Impact of Risk Assessment Models on Risk Factors: A Holistic Outlook. In K. Strang, M. Korstanje, & N. Vajjhala (Eds.), *Research, Practices, and Innovations in Global Risk and Contingency Management* (pp. 134–153). Hershey, PA: IGI Global. doi:10.4018/978-1-5225-4754-9.ch008

Raman, A., & Goyal, D. P. (2017). Extending IMPLEMENT Framework for Enterprise Information Systems Implementation to Information System Innovation. In M. Tavana (Ed.), *Enterprise Information Systems and the Digitalization of Business Functions* (pp. 137–177). Hershey, PA: IGI Global. doi:10.4018/978-1-5225-2382-6.ch007

Rao, Y., & Zhang, Y. (2017). The Construction and Development of Academic Library Digital Special Subject Databases. In L. Ruan, Q. Zhu, & Y. Ye (Eds.), *Academic Library Development and Administration in China* (pp. 163–183). Hershey, PA: IGI Global. doi:10.4018/978-1-5225-0550-1.ch010

Ravasan, A. Z., Mohammadi, M. M., & Hamidi, H. (2018). An Investigation Into the Critical Success Factors of Implementing Information Technology Service Management Frameworks. In K. Jakobs (Ed.), *Corporate and Global Standardization Initiatives in Contemporary Society* (pp. 200–218). Hershey, PA: IGI Global. doi:10.4018/978-1-5225-5320-5.ch009

Rezaie, S., Mirabedini, S. J., & Abtahi, A. (2018). Designing a Model for Implementation of Business Intelligence in the Banking Industry. *International Journal of Enterprise Information Systems*, *14*(1), 77–103. doi:10.4018/IJEIS.2018010105

Richards, V., Matthews, N., Williams, O. J., & Khan, Z. (2021). The Challenges of Accessible Tourism Information Systems for Tourists With Vision Impairment: Sensory Communications Beyond the Screen. In C. Eusébio, L. Teixeira, & M. Carneiro (Eds.), *ICT Tools and Applications for Accessible Tourism* (pp. 26–54). IGI Global. https://doi.org/10.4018/978-1-7998-6428-8.ch002

Rodrigues de Souza Neto, V., & Marques, O. (2021). Rural Tourism Fostering Welfare Through Sustainable Development: A Conceptual Approach. In A. Perinotto, V. Mayer, & J. Soares (Eds.), *Rebuilding and Restructuring the Tourism Industry: Infusion of Happiness and Quality of Life* (pp. 38–57). IGI Global. https://doi.org/10.4018/978-1-7998-7239-9.ch003

Romano, L., Grimaldi, R., & Colasuonno, F. S. (2017). Demand Management as a Success Factor in Project Portfolio Management. In L. Romano (Ed.), *Project Portfolio Management Strategies for Effective Organizational Operations* (pp. 202–219). Hershey, PA: IGI Global. doi:10.4018/978-1-5225-2151-8.ch008

Rubio-Escuderos, L., & García-Andreu, H. (2021). Competitiveness Factors of Accessible Tourism E-Travel Agencies. In C. Eusébio, L. Teixeira, & M. Carneiro (Eds.), *ICT Tools and Applications for Accessible Tourism* (pp. 196–217). IGI Global. https://doi.org/10.4018/978-1-7998-6428-8.ch009

Rucci, A. C., Porto, N., Darcy, S., & Becka, L. (2021). Smart and Accessible Cities?: Not Always – The Case for Accessible Tourism Initiatives in Buenos Aries and Sydney. In C. Eusébio, L. Teixeira, & M. Carneiro (Eds.), *ICT Tools and Applications for Accessible Tourism* (pp. 115–145). IGI Global. https://doi.org/10.4018/978-1-7998-6428-8.ch006

Ruhi, U. (2018). Towards an Interdisciplinary Socio-Technical Definition of Virtual Communities. In M. Khosrow-Pour, D.B.A. (Ed.), Encyclopedia of Information Science and Technology, Fourth Edition (pp. 4278-4295). Hershey, PA: IGI Global. doi:10.4018/978-1-5225-2255-3.ch371

Ryan, L., Catena, M., Ros, P., & Stephens, S. (2021). Designing Entrepreneurial Ecosystems to Support Resource Management in the Tourism Industry. In V. Costa, A. Moura, & M. Mira (Eds.), *Handbook of Research on Human Capital and People Management in the Tourism Industry* (pp. 265–281). IGI Global. https://doi.org/10.4018/978-1-7998-4318-4.ch013

Sabuncu, I. (2021). Understanding Tourist Perceptions and Expectations During Pandemic Through Social Media Big Data. In M. Demir, A. Dalgıç, & F. Ergen (Eds.), *Handbook of Research on the Impacts and Implications of COVID-19 on the Tourism Industry* (pp. 330–350). IGI Global. https://doi.org/10.4018/978-1-7998-8231-2.ch016

Safari, M. R., & Jiang, Q. (2018). The Theory and Practice of IT Governance Maturity and Strategies Alignment: Evidence From Banking Industry. *Journal of Global Information Management*, *26*(2), 127–146. doi:10.4018/JGIM.2018040106

Sahoo, J., Pati, B., & Mohanty, B. (2017). Knowledge Management as an Academic Discipline: An Assessment. In B. Gunjal (Ed.), *Managing Knowledge and Scholarly Assets in Academic Libraries* (pp. 99–126). Hershey, PA: IGI Global. doi:10.4018/978-1-5225-1741-2.ch005

Saini, D. (2017). Relevance of Teaching Values and Ethics in Management Education. In N. Baporikar (Ed.), *Management Education for Global Leadership* (pp. 90–111). Hershey, PA: IGI Global. doi:10.4018/978-1-5225-1013-0.ch005

Sambhanthan, A. (2017). Assessing and Benchmarking Sustainability in Organisations: An Integrated Conceptual Model. *International Journal of Systems and Service-Oriented Engineering*, *7*(4), 22–43. doi:10.4018/IJSSOE.2017100102

Sambhanthan, A., & Potdar, V. (2017). A Study of the Parameters Impacting Sustainability in Information Technology Organizations. *International Journal of Knowledge-Based Organizations*, *7*(3), 27–39. doi:10.4018/IJKBO.2017070103

Sánchez-Fernández, M. D., & Manríquez, M. R. (2018). The Entrepreneurial Spirit Based on Social Values: The Digital Generation. In P. Isaias & L. Carvalho (Eds.), *User Innovation and the Entrepreneurship Phenomenon in the Digital Economy* (pp. 173–193). Hershey, PA: IGI Global. doi:10.4018/978-1-5225-2826-5.ch009

Sanchez-Ruiz, L., & Blanco, B. (2017). Process Management for SMEs: Barriers, Enablers, and Benefits. In M. Vemić (Ed.), *Optimal Management Strategies in Small and Medium Enterprises* (pp. 293–319). Hershey, PA: IGI Global. doi:10.4018/978-1-5225-1949-2.ch014

Sanz, L. F., Gómez-Pérez, J., & Castillo-Martinez, A. (2018). Analysis of the European ICT Competence Frameworks. In V. Ahuja & S. Rathore (Eds.), *Multidisciplinary Perspectives on Human Capital and Information Technology Professionals* (pp. 225–245). Hershey, PA: IGI Global. doi:10.4018/978-1-5225-5297-0.ch012

Sarvepalli, A., & Godin, J. (2017). Business Process Management in the Classroom. *Journal of Cases on Information Technology*, *19*(2), 17–28. doi:10.4018/JCIT.2017040102

Saxena, G. G., & Saxena, A. (2021). Host Community Role in Medical Tourism Development. In M. Singh & S. Kumaran (Eds.), *Growth of the Medical Tourism Industry and Its Impact on Society: Emerging Research and Opportunities* (pp. 105–127). IGI Global. https://doi.org/10.4018/978-1-7998-3427-4.ch006

Saygili, E. E., Ozturkoglu, Y., & Kocakulah, M. C. (2017). End Users' Perceptions of Critical Success Factors in ERP Applications. *International Journal of Enterprise Information Systems*, *13*(4), 58–75. doi:10.4018/IJEIS.2017100104

Saygili, E. E., & Saygili, A. T. (2017). Contemporary Issues in Enterprise Information Systems: A Critical Review of CSFs in ERP Implementations. In M. Tavana (Ed.), *Enterprise Information Systems and the Digitalization of Business Functions* (pp. 120–136). Hershey, PA: IGI Global. doi:10.4018/978-1-5225-2382-6.ch006

Schwaiger, K. M., & Zehrer, A. (2021). The COVID-19 Pandemic and Organizational Resilience in Hospitality Family Firms: A Qualitative Approach. In A. Zehrer, G. Glowka, K. Schwaiger, & V. Ranacher-Lackner (Eds.), *Resiliency Models and Addressing Future Risks for Family Firms in the Tourism Industry* (pp. 32–49). IGI Global. https://doi.org/10.4018/978-1-7998-7352-5.ch002

Scott, N., & Campos, A. C. (2022). Cognitive Science of Tourism Experiences. In R. Augusto Costa, F. Brandão, Z. Breda, & C. Costa (Eds.), Planning and Managing the Experience Economy in Tourism (pp. 1-21). IGI Global. https://doi.org/ doi:10.4018/978-1-7998-8775-1.ch001

Seidenstricker, S., & Antonino, A. (2018). Business Model Innovation-Oriented Technology Management for Emergent Technologies. In M. Khosrow-Pour, D.B.A. (Ed.), Encyclopedia of Information Science and Technology, Fourth Edition (pp. 4560-4569). Hershey, PA: IGI Global. doi:10.4018/978-1-5225-2255-3.ch396

Selvi, M. S. (2021). Changes in Tourism Sales and Marketing Post COVID-19. In M. Demir, A. Dalgıç, & F. Ergen (Eds.), *Handbook of Research on the Impacts and Implications of COVID-19 on the Tourism Industry* (pp. 437–460). IGI Global. doi:10.4018/978-1-7998-8231-2.ch021

Senaratne, S., & Gunarathne, A. D. (2017). Excellence Perspective for Management Education from a Global Accountants' Hub in Asia. In N. Baporikar (Ed.), *Management Education for Global Leadership* (pp. 158–180). Hershey, PA: IGI Global. doi:10.4018/978-1-5225-1013-0.ch008

Sensuse, D. I., & Cahyaningsih, E. (2018). Knowledge Management Models: A Summative Review. *International Journal of Information Systems in the Service Sector, 10*(1), 71–100. doi:10.4018/IJISSS.2018010105

Seth, M., Goyal, D., & Kiran, R. (2017). Diminution of Impediments in Implementation of Supply Chain Management Information System for Enhancing its Effectiveness in Indian Automobile Industry. *Journal of Global Information Management, 25*(3), 1–20. doi:10.4018/JGIM.2017070101

Seyal, A. H., & Rahman, M. N. (2017). Investigating Impact of Inter-Organizational Factors in Measuring ERP Systems Success: Bruneian Perspectives. In M. Tavana (Ed.), *Enterprise Information Systems and the Digitalization of Business Functions* (pp. 178–204). Hershey, PA: IGI Global. doi:10.4018/978-1-5225-2382-6.ch008

Shaqrah, A. A. (2018). Analyzing Business Intelligence Systems Based on 7s Model of McKinsey. *International Journal of Business Intelligence Research, 9*(1), 53–63. doi:10.4018/IJBIR.2018010104

Sharma, A. J. (2017). Enhancing Sustainability through Experiential Learning in Management Education. In N. Baporikar (Ed.), *Management Education for Global Leadership* (pp. 256–274). Hershey, PA: IGI Global. doi:10.4018/978-1-5225-1013-0.ch013

Shetty, K. P. (2017). Responsible Global Leadership: Ethical Challenges in Management Education. In N. Baporikar (Ed.), *Innovation and Shifting Perspectives in Management Education* (pp. 194–223). Hershey, PA: IGI Global. doi:10.4018/978-1-5225-1019-2.ch009

Sinthupundaja, J., & Kohda, Y. (2017). Effects of Corporate Social Responsibility and Creating Shared Value on Sustainability. *International Journal of Sustainable Entrepreneurship and Corporate Social Responsibility*, *2*(1), 27–38. doi:10.4018/IJSECSR.2017010103

Škarica, I., & Hrgović, A. V. (2018). Implementation of Total Quality Management Principles in Public Health Institutes in the Republic of Croatia. *International Journal of Productivity Management and Assessment Technologies*, *6*(1), 1–16. doi:10.4018/IJPMAT.2018010101

Skokic, V. (2021). How Small Hotel Owners Practice Resilience: Longitudinal Study Among Small Family Hotels in Croatia. In A. Zehrer, G. Glowka, K. Schwaiger, & V. Ranacher-Lackner (Eds.), *Resiliency Models and Addressing Future Risks for Family Firms in the Tourism Industry* (pp. 50–73). IGI Global. doi:10.4018/978-1-7998-7352-5.ch003

Smuts, H., Kotzé, P., Van der Merwe, A., & Loock, M. (2017). Framework for Managing Shared Knowledge in an Information Systems Outsourcing Context. *International Journal of Knowledge Management*, *13*(4), 1–30. doi:10.4018/IJKM.2017100101

Sousa, M. J., Cruz, R., Dias, I., & Caracol, C. (2017). Information Management Systems in the Supply Chain. In G. Jamil, A. Soares, & C. Pessoa (Eds.), *Handbook of Research on Information Management for Effective Logistics and Supply Chains* (pp. 469–485). Hershey, PA: IGI Global. doi:10.4018/978-1-5225-0973-8.ch025

Spremic, M., Turulja, L., & Bajgoric, N. (2018). Two Approaches in Assessing Business Continuity Management Attitudes in the Organizational Context. In N. Bajgoric (Ed.), *Always-On Enterprise Information Systems for Modern Organizations* (pp. 159–183). Hershey, PA: IGI Global. doi:10.4018/978-1-5225-3704-5.ch008

Steenkamp, A. L. (2018). Some Insights in Computer Science and Information Technology. In *Examining the Changing Role of Supervision in Doctoral Research Projects: Emerging Research and Opportunities* (pp. 113–133). Hershey, PA: IGI Global. doi:10.4018/978-1-5225-2610-0.ch005

Stipanović, C., Rudan, E., & Zubović, V. (2022). Reaching the New Tourist Through Creativity: Sustainable Development Challenges in Croatian Coastal Towns. In M. Valeri (Ed.), *New Governance and Management in Touristic Destinations* (pp. 231–245). IGI Global. https://doi.org/10.4018/978-1-6684-3889-3.ch014

Tabach, A., & Croteau, A. (2017). Configurations of Information Technology Governance Practices and Business Unit Performance. *International Journal of IT/ Business Alignment and Governance*, *8*(2), 1–27. doi:10.4018/IJITBAG.2017070101

Talaue, G. M., & Iqbal, T. (2017). Assessment of e-Business Mode of Selected Private Universities in the Philippines and Pakistan. *International Journal of Online Marketing*, *7*(4), 63–77. doi:10.4018/IJOM.2017100105

Tam, G. C. (2017). Project Manager Sustainability Competence. In *Managerial Strategies and Green Solutions for Project Sustainability* (pp. 178–207). Hershey, PA: IGI Global. doi:10.4018/978-1-5225-2371-0.ch008

Tambo, T. (2018). Fashion Retail Innovation: About Context, Antecedents, and Outcome in Technological Change Projects. In I. Management Association (Ed.), Fashion and Textiles: Breakthroughs in Research and Practice (pp. 233-260). Hershey, PA: IGI Global. https://doi.org/ doi:10.4018/978-1-5225-3432-7.ch010

Tantau, A. D., & Frăţilă, L. C. (2018). Information and Management System for Renewable Energy Business. In *Entrepreneurship and Business Development in the Renewable Energy Sector* (pp. 200–244). Hershey, PA: IGI Global. doi:10.4018/978-1-5225-3625-3.ch006

Teixeira, N., Pardal, P. N., & Rafael, B. G. (2018). Internationalization, Financial Performance, and Organizational Challenges: A Success Case in Portugal. In L. Carvalho (Ed.), *Handbook of Research on Entrepreneurial Ecosystems and Social Dynamics in a Globalized World* (pp. 379–423). Hershey, PA: IGI Global. doi:10.4018/978-1-5225-3525-6.ch017

Teixeira, P., Teixeira, L., Eusébio, C., Silva, S., & Teixeira, A. (2021). The Impact of ICTs on Accessible Tourism: Evidence Based on a Systematic Literature Review. In C. Eusébio, L. Teixeira, & M. Carneiro (Eds.), *ICT Tools and Applications for Accessible Tourism* (pp. 1–25). IGI Global. doi:10.4018/978-1-7998-6428-8.ch001

Trad, A., & Kalpić, D. (2018). The Business Transformation Framework, Agile Project and Change Management. In M. Khosrow-Pour, D.B.A. (Ed.), Encyclopedia of Information Science and Technology, Fourth Edition (pp. 620-635). Hershey, PA: IGI Global. https://doi.org/ doi:10.4018/978-1-5225-2255-3.ch054

Trad, A., & Kalpić, D. (2018). The Business Transformation and Enterprise Architecture Framework: The Financial Engineering E-Risk Management and E-Law Integration. In B. Sergi, F. Fidanoski, M. Ziolo, & V. Naumovski (Eds.), *Regaining Global Stability After the Financial Crisis* (pp. 46–65). Hershey, PA: IGI Global. doi:10.4018/978-1-5225-4026-7.ch003

Trengereid, V. (2022). Conditions of Network Engagement: The Quest for a Common Good. In R. Augusto Costa, F. Brandão, Z. Breda, & C. Costa (Eds.), *Planning and Managing the Experience Economy in Tourism* (pp. 69-84). IGI Global. https://doi.org/10.4018/978-1-7998-8775-1.ch004

Turulja, L., & Bajgoric, N. (2018). Business Continuity and Information Systems: A Systematic Literature Review. In N. Bajgoric (Ed.), *Always-On Enterprise Information Systems for Modern Organizations* (pp. 60–87). Hershey, PA: IGI Global. doi:10.4018/978-1-5225-3704-5.ch004

Vargas-Hernández, J. G. (2017). Professional Integrity in Business Management Education. In N. Baporikar (Ed.), *Management Education for Global Leadership* (pp. 70–89). Hershey, PA: IGI Global. doi:10.4018/978-1-5225-1013-0.ch004

Varnacı Uzun, F. (2021). The Destination Preferences of Foreign Tourists During the COVID-19 Pandemic and Attitudes Towards: Marmaris, Turkey. In M. Demir, A. Dalgıç, & F. Ergen (Eds.), *Handbook of Research on the Impacts and Implications of COVID-19 on the Tourism Industry* (pp. 285–306). IGI Global. https://doi.org/10.4018/978-1-7998-8231-2.ch014

Vasista, T. G., & AlAbdullatif, A. M. (2017). Role of Electronic Customer Relationship Management in Demand Chain Management: A Predictive Analytic Approach. *International Journal of Information Systems and Supply Chain Management, 10*(1), 53–67. doi:10.4018/IJISSCM.2017010104

Vieru, D., & Bourdeau, S. (2017). Survival in the Digital Era: A Digital Competence-Based Multi-Case Study in the Canadian SME Clothing Industry. *International Journal of Social and Organizational Dynamics in IT, 6*(1), 17–34. doi:10.4018/IJSODIT.2017010102

Vijayan, G., & Kamarulzaman, N. H. (2017). An Introduction to Sustainable Supply Chain Management and Business Implications. In M. Khan, M. Hussain, & M. Ajmal (Eds.), *Green Supply Chain Management for Sustainable Business Practice* (pp. 27–50). Hershey, PA: IGI Global. doi:10.4018/978-1-5225-0635-5.ch002

Vlachvei, A., & Notta, O. (2017). Firm Competitiveness: Theories, Evidence, and Measurement. In A. Vlachvei, O. Notta, K. Karantininis, & N. Tsounis (Eds.), *Factors Affecting Firm Competitiveness and Performance in the Modern Business World* (pp. 1–42). Hershey, PA: IGI Global. doi:10.4018/978-1-5225-0843-4.ch001

Wang, C., Schofield, M., Li, X., & Ou, X. (2017). Do Chinese Students in Public and Private Higher Education Institutes Perform at Different Level in One of the Leadership Skills: Critical Thinking?: An Exploratory Comparison. In V. Wang (Ed.), *Encyclopedia of Strategic Leadership and Management* (pp. 160–181). Hershey, PA: IGI Global. doi:10.4018/978-1-5225-1049-9.ch013

Wang, J. (2017). Multi-Agent based Production Management Decision System Modelling for the Textile Enterprise. *Journal of Global Information Management, 25*(4), 1–15. doi:10.4018/JGIM.2017100101

Wiedemann, A., & Gewald, H. (2017). Examining Cross-Domain Alignment: The Correlation of Business Strategy, IT Management, and IT Business Value. *International Journal of IT/Business Alignment and Governance, 8*(1), 17–31. doi:10.4018/IJITBAG.2017010102

Wolf, R., & Thiel, M. (2018). Advancing Global Business Ethics in China: Reducing Poverty Through Human and Social Welfare. In S. Hipsher (Ed.), *Examining the Private Sector's Role in Wealth Creation and Poverty Reduction* (pp. 67–84). Hershey, PA: IGI Global. doi:10.4018/978-1-5225-3117-3.ch004

Yablonsky, S. (2018). Innovation Platforms: Data and Analytics Platforms. In *Multi-Sided Platforms (MSPs) and Sharing Strategies in the Digital Economy: Emerging Research and Opportunities* (pp. 72–95). Hershey, PA: IGI Global. doi:10.4018/978-1-5225-5457-8.ch003

Yaşar, B. (2021). The Impact of COVID-19 on Volatility of Tourism Stocks: Evidence From BIST Tourism Index. In M. Demir, A. Dalgıç, & F. Ergen (Eds.), *Handbook of Research on the Impacts and Implications of COVID-19 on the Tourism Industry* (pp. 23–44). IGI Global. https://doi.org/10.4018/978-1-7998-8231-2.ch002

Yusoff, A., Ahmad, N. H., & Halim, H. A. (2017). Agropreneurship among Gen Y in Malaysia: The Role of Academic Institutions. In N. Ahmad, T. Ramayah, H. Halim, & S. Rahman (Eds.), *Handbook of Research on Small and Medium Enterprises in Developing Countries* (pp. 23–47). Hershey, PA: IGI Global. doi:10.4018/978-1-5225-2165-5.ch002

Zacher, D., & Pechlaner, H. (2021). Resilience as an Opportunity Approach: Challenges and Perspectives for Private Sector Participation on a Community Level. In A. Zehrer, G. Glowka, K. Schwaiger, & V. Ranacher-Lackner (Eds.), *Resiliency Models and Addressing Future Risks for Family Firms in the Tourism Industry* (pp. 75–102). IGI Global. https://doi.org/10.4018/978-1-7998-7352-5.ch004

Zanin, F., Comuzzi, E., & Costantini, A. (2018). The Effect of Business Strategy and Stock Market Listing on the Use of Risk Assessment Tools. In *Management Control Systems in Complex Settings: Emerging Research and Opportunities* (pp. 145–168). Hershey, PA: IGI Global. doi:10.4018/978-1-5225-3987-2.ch007

Zgheib, P. W. (2017). Corporate Innovation and Intrapreneurship in the Middle East. In P. Zgheib (Ed.), *Entrepreneurship and Business Innovation in the Middle East* (pp. 37–56). Hershey, PA: IGI Global. doi:10.4018/978-1-5225-2066-5.ch003

About the Contributors

Shashi Bala, Senior Fellow, V.V. Giri National Labour Institute, Noida, India was awarded Ph.D from the Centre of Study for Diplomacy, International law and Economics/School of International Studies/Jawaharlal Nehru University, New Delhi. She is coordinating the activities of the Centre for Gender & Labour Studies and the Centre for Agrarian Relations, Rural and Behavioral Studies at the Institute. She has been trained on various themes like Gender Budgeting by the Ministry of Women and Child Development, New Delhi; National Service Scheme (NSS) by the University of Delhi; Gender Sensitivity & Prevention and Redressal of Sexual Harassment of Women at Workplace by Integrated Training & Policy Research; Mainstreaming Gender Equality: Concepts and Instruments by ILO/ITC Turin, Italy; Leadership for Employment Promotion in Fragile Settings organised by ILO/ITC Turin, Italy); Global E-coaching Forum: Effective Project Implementation in Emergency Situations by ILO/ITC Turin, Italy); ILO's South Asian Regional Training Course on "Evidence-based Policy Making for Decent Work" by ILO/ITC Turin, Italy. She is the presiding officer and Founder Convener of Preventing Sexual Harassment Committee at the Institute. Her research areas majorly focus on Labour Economics; Skill Development; Social Security; Gender Budgeting; Gender Issues; & Behavioral Skills. She has been a Visiting Researcher 2008 at Korean Labour Institute, Seoul, South Korea, where she conducted a study on Gender Issues in the Korean Labour Market. In addition to her contribution towards research activities, she also coordinates various training programmes. As a trainer, she coordinates training programmes on various themes with a specific focus on Gender, rural development and behavioural skills .

Puja Singhal is an Assistant Professor at National Centre for School Leadership (NCSL), NIEPA, New Delhi. She is a gold medalist in Economics and has a Doctorate from the Jai Narain Vyas University, Jodhpur (Rajasthan). She also worked with V.V.Giri National Labor Institute (Ministry of Labor and Employment) and was involved in policy-oriented projects. Now she organizes workshops, capacity development programs on gender and leadership at NCSL and works as a National

Coordinator of five states of India. In 2015, she presented her paper at 4th European and International Conference for Learning Innovations and Quality (LINQ), in Brussels (Belgium) and in 2018 at London in 12th International Conference on Gender studies, and Education. She has published extensively in the form of books, research papers, and articles in peer-reviewed and reputed academic journals, like Emerald, IGI Global, Inderscience, etc., and also received the best paper award twice. Her areas of special interest are Vocational Education, Gender issues, E-Learning and Innovation in education, Skill Development, School Leadership. She can be accessed at pujasinghal@niepa.ac.in

* * *

Rinki Arora is working as a Research Associate with VV Giri National Labour Institute. She has over 3 years of experience working as a Researcher in multiple business domains for both Government and corporate sector . She is an MBA with dual specialisation in Finance and Human Resource. She completed her Diploma in Training and Development from Indian Society of Training and Development.

Kavita Baliyan is working as Assistant Professor (Fellow), in Giri Institute of Development Studies (GIDS), Lucknow from 26th November 2013 to till date. Dr. Kavita Baliyan was born in a farmer's family in the Baghpat district of Uttar Pradesh. She has a brilliant academic career and obtained her M.A. and M. Phil degrees in economics from Ch. Charan Singh University, Meerut. She was awarded the ICSSR Doctoral Fellowship to work on the topic "Participation and Economic Contribution of Women in Agriculture with Special Reference to Western Uttar Pradesh "at the Giri Institute of Development Studies, Lucknow. She obtained her Ph.D. Degree from the Chhatrapati Shahu Ji Maharaj University, Kanpur. She has worked as a Senior Research Fellow in NCAP, Pusa, New Delhi and as a Research Associate in the National Mission for Empowerment of Women, Ministry of Women and Child Development, GOI, New Delhi. In 2013 she joined the Giri Institute of Development Studies, Lucknow as an Assistant Professor. Dr. Baliyan has published more than 30 research papers in various reputed journals and two books. She has also presented many papers in national and international conferences and seminars. She has completed many research projects related to agriculture, rural development, migration, and gender studies. Major areas of her research interest are agricultural development and gender studies.

Serkan Bertan worked as a Research Assistant at the Pamukkale University before he attended the PhD Program at Dokuz Eylul University in 2002 and completed his PhD studies within four years. After his PhD degree he joined to Pamukkale University at Department of Tourism and Hotel Management. In 2009 Dr. Serkan was invited as a fellow researcher to Department of Hotel, Restaurant and Tourism Management University of South Carolina for his Post PhD Studies. Assoc. Prof. Dr., Faculty of Tourism, Pamukkale University at Denizli, Turkey.

Litty Denis is an Assistant Professor in the Centre for Studies in Social Management, School of Social Sciences at Central University of Gujarat. She has been teaching in both doctoral and graduate programs in the area of Management for the last 20 years. Her areas of interest include financial inclusion, corporate social responsibility and sustainable development. She has published a number of research papers in national and international journals and also edited books in the area of management. She has completed her M.Phil. & Ph.D. degree in Management from Gujarat University and is a qualified Company Secretary, ICSI, dealing with compliances of the Company Laws in India. She has completed a couple of projects recently, one with Government of Gujarat for preparation of District Human Development Report and another project on Impact of Microfinance on Tribal Areas of Gujarat funded by the Central University of Gujarat. She can be reached at litty.denis@cug.ac.in; littydenis@yahoo.com

Parul Dubey is currently working as an Assistant Professor in AI Department, G H Raisoni College of Engineering,Nagpur, India . Authors highest degree is the degree of Masters in Computer Engineering. She is also a PhD. Research scholar at C.V.Raman University, Bilaspur, Chattishgarh, India. She is indulged in research activities too. She has 7 Indian published patents and 1 Indian Granted patent. She holds around 10 publications which are part of conferences, journals and book chapters . Author is an AWS Certified Cloud Practitioner badge holder, which is a proof for the expertise in AWS. Currently guiding many Engineering students to learn the AWS platform and complete their projects.

Pushkar Dubey presently works at Department of Management, Pandit Sundarlal Sharma (Open) University Chhattisgarh as an Assistant Professor & Head. Dr. Dubey's key area of interest is Human Resource, Service Quality, ICT, Workplace Spirituality, OCB. His current research project is "A Study on Characteristics, Attitude and Intention of Engineering Undergraduates towards Entrepreneurship in Chhattisgarh State".

Neema Gnanadey is working as an Associate Professor, Centre for Rural Development Studies, Bangalore University, Bengaluru. the area of interest is women and child development, rural development, NGO management, Development and Research Methodology. published 24 articles, produced 6 Ph.D scholars.9 M.Phil, trained for low cost education for the anganawadi workers.

Gaganpreet Kaur is a former Assistant Professor in Amity University, Uttar Pradesh. She has an academic experience and expertise of teaching human resource and company law. She has also worked in Amity University, Uttar Pradesh and S.D.College and led many group training sessions. She also possess research experience and have many research papers published in National and International Journals like serial publications, transstellar publication, bloomsberry and has also received the best paper award. She has attended and presented many research papers in conferences and completed her Ph.D in labour laws.

Meghna Khurania is a doctoral candidate at the Zakir Hussain Centre for Educational Studies, Jawaharlal Nehru University. Her research focuses on intersections between vocational education, gender and labour market. She approaches these questions through an inter-disciplinary understanding of sociology, development and labour studies. Previously, she completed an honors in Sociology from Lady Shri Ram College for Women, New Delhi. She has pursued a MA in Development and Labour Studies from Centre for Informal Sector and Labour Studies at JNU, New Delhi. Her MPhil was from Zakir Hussain Centre for Educational Studies, JNU. The MPhil research was titled, 'Student's Choice for Vocational Education and their Labour Market Aspirations: A Study of Select ITIs in New Delhi'.

Nandita Mishra is an academician with a demonstrated history of working in the higher education industry for nearly two decades. Ambassador to International Integrated Reporting Council (IIRC) London and Country Director- India -HETL (Higher education teaching and learning). A researcher in the fields of finance & accounting, corporate governance, sustainability and integrated reporting. A Cost and Management Accountant by profession with a doctorate in corporate governance.

Ashok Nimesh is an Assistant Professor at Department of Contemporary and Tribal Customary Law, Central University of Jharkhand, Ranchi, Jharkhand. He has done his Master, MPhil and Doctoral Studies from Jawaharlal Nehru University (JNU), New Delhi. He has many research publications in his account in various National and International Journals including book chapters. He has been invited as a Resource Person in Human Resource Development Centre (HRDC) of various universities across the country. His area of expertise are Human Rights, Gender Studies, Tribal Customary Law and History of International Peace & Conflict.

Pawan Prabhakar is a life science and entrepreneurship professional and pursuing PhD in the specialization of herbal drug development and entrepreneurship at Rajendra Mishra School of Engineering Entrepreneurship, Indian Institute of Technology Kharagpur, Kharagpur, India. He has authored many publications in international journals and presented research papers at various international conferences. His area of research interest is herbal drug, entrepreneurship and innovation in healthcare.

Sonam Prabhakar is a PhD research scholar at Department of contemporary and tribal customary law, Central University of Jharkhand, Ranchi. She has completed her BSc. and MSc. from Dr. Rajendra Prasad Central Agricultural University, Pusa, Samastipur, India with specialization in family resource management. She has many publication in her name in national and international journals. Her area of research interest is entrepreneurship, gender and tribal studies.

Chetan Rathod is a research scholar at Centre for Studies in Social Management and is pursuing his doctoral research in area of Corporate Social Responsibility. In addition, he has rich experience of working as a CSR professional.

Kailash Kumar Sahu is associated with Pandit Sundarlal Sharma (Open) University Chhattisgarh, Department of Management.

Nisha Saini completed her MPhil from University of Madras in domain of South and Southeast Asian Studies. Professionally, she has worked in think tanks and government organisations. She has interested in writing on varied topic of relevance. Her work has been published in journals as articles, book chapters in books and research papers in think tank. Presently, she is working as Research Assistant in Arun Jaitley National Institute of Financial Management.

Albina Sibirskaya graduated from the University with a degree in world economy, in 2013 - postgraduate study in the same specialty. She also received a second degree in "law". Currently she is working as a senior researcher at the Institute of Economics of the National Academy of Sciences. Her area of interests are International integration processes in the economic and social spheres.

Index

www.ingramcontent.com/pod-product-compliance
Lightning Source LLC
LaVergne TN
LVHW081327300926
849161LV00008B/1897
* 9 7 8 1 6 6 8 4 6 8 7 8 4 *